CALIFORNIA WRITERS

By the same author

WAGNER TO 'THE WASTE LAND': A Study of the Relationship of Wagner to English Literature

CALIFORNIA WRITERS

Jack London   John Steinbeck   The Tough Guys

Stoddard Martin

St. Martin's Press   New York

ISBN 0-312-11420-6

Library of Congress Cataloging in Publication Data

Martin, Stoddard, 1948–
  California writers.

  Includes bibliographical references and index.
  1. American fiction – California – History and
criticism.   2. American fiction – 20th century – History
and criticism.   3. California in literature.   I. Title.
PS283.C2M35   1983 813'.54'099794   82-20451
ISBN 0-312-11420-6

---

*In memory of my father
and for my wife*

Contents

Acknowledgements

I am particularly indebted to James Jameson, who encouraged the writing of this book, contributed to it financially, and read it in proof. I should also like to thank Martha Stevens, Geoffrey Layton, Felifity Buirski; the officers and crews of the U.S.S. *Worden* and *Downes*; my editor Julia Steward, and Valery Brooks of the Macmillan Press; the staff of the British Library; the Rodney Beard family of Stanford University; and Hensley C. Woodbridge of Southern Illinois University, who published two sections of Chapter 2 in his *Jack London Newsletter*.

S. M.

1   Introduction

This book was conceived originally as a survey of California literature. The idea was to study what has come to stand as classic in an essentially romantic body of work, and to define what has never been defined adequately: a California tradition. The undertaking proved as vast as the state itself, and some principle of limitation had to be found. Would the book be a survey *per se* or a critical appraisal along 'great tradition' lines? The primary need seemed to be for the latter. Surveys, particularly of the early period, have been churned out with regularity by anthologisers and collectors of 'Californiana'. They are still appearing. Lawrence Ferlinghetti's recently published *Literary San Francisco* is typical of the common approach and has the typical shortcomings.[1] It is a coffee-table book full of glossy photographs and gossipy vignettes; it devotes as much space to Joaquin Miller and William Saroyan as to Jack London and John Steinbeck; it studiously avoids any taint of the 'academic' or 'critical'. This kind of book, whatever its charms, ends by being dilettantish. The tendency to all-inclusiveness and resistance to singling out individuals as 'great' inhibit serious discussion. Essential discrimination is lacking. How can a literature, or a culture for that matter, begin to be understood unless there is some consensus as to what is most unique and representative in it? In asking this question, I began to realise that what was needed was a book about the few: the handful of outstanding writers who have emerged in California's brief history. Working from this principle, I set about limiting the field. Poets, playwrights and journalists were passed over in favour of novelists. Among novelists I avoided those either too early and obscure to have earned continued attention, or too recent to have settled into their proper places as major or minor voices.

Among the many omitted on this basis were the twin literary gods of the Gold Rush, whose names have been given to an El Doradan town, and whose memory is hallowed by all who attend

1

leaping-frog contests or pan for nuggets in the Sonoran hills. Mark Twain, claimed by San Franciscans as a laureate to this day,[2] was not in fact a Californian in any important sense. He was born on the Mississippi and spent only a few years of his thirties in the 'Golden State'. His humorous and admiring treatment of the Forty-niners was almost entirely journalistic. He never wrote a novel set in California or about Californians. He left San Francisco after having gained notoriety and went to the East, never to return. His literary reputation rests on novels thoroughly American as opposed to Californian; and many informed Twain readers will not even have read the Californian sections of *Roughing It* (1872). Twain's fellow humorist of San Francisco days is dismissable on similar grounds, though perhaps less readily.[3] Born in New York, Bret Harte came to California as an adolescent and grew up in the heyday of the boom. Like Twain, he was primarily a journalist; but Harte's writings about the Forty-niners eventually appeared in three other genres – poetry, drama and fiction. He wrote several novellas and one full-length novel, *Gabriel Conroy* (1875), on Californian subjects. Now, however, he is best remembered as a story-writer. 'The Luck of Roaring Camp' and 'The Outcasts of Poker Flat', his most celebrated pieces in his own time, are among the few works to have survived. In later life, Harte 'escaped' to New York, then London. Sporting a gold-knobbed walking-stick and frequenting the same drawing-rooms as Whistler and Wilde, he became a cosmopolitan stage-Californian. Still panning Forty-niner tales for literary gold twenty years after he left California, Harte ended by being a parodist rather than a sincere voice of the emerging culture.

Harte was careless of his subject-matter. He entitled a story 'The Judgement of Bolinas Plain' forgetting that Bolinas is not a plain at all but a marsh-bound coastal hamlet. Reality became ephemeral to him. The later tales might as well have been set in some Celtic dreamscape, Shakespeare's 'Italy of the imagination', or the macabre venue of a story by Ambrose Bierce. Bierce was another who hailed from the East, spent some years in San Francisco as a journalist, then pursued literary fortune to London armed with frontier notoriety. Like Twain and Harte, Bierce was an eccentric. All three belonged to an era before California truly existed. Though it left a legacy of the big gamble which has enlivened and plagued the culture ever since, the Gold Rush was an illusory beginning. A culture grows out of a sustained relationship of a people with an environment, not out of a flash-in-the-pan succession of mining-camps and boom-towns. Only when women began to appear as other than whores-with-hearts-of-gold, and families began to form and communities take root, did California as a culture begin to exist. With this the virtuosities of Twain, Harte and Bierce had little connection. Their small comedic adventurers danced their dances of blithe self-expression on the furthest edge of the Western World, and the significance was probably greater for the Old World with its repressions and projected fantasies than for what was growing on the new soil. The works of these early writers bear a relationship to the mainstream of California writing analogous to that which *Robinson Crusoe* bears to the mainstream of English literature. As Richardson and Fielding, coming three decades after Defoe, mark the beginning of the 'great tradition', so Jack London, coming three decades after the first leaping-frog leapt, represents the beginning of serious California literature.[4]

As Austen and Eliot and James flow in the same bed as these English precursors of the eighteenth century, so Steinbeck and the Tough Guys – Hammett, Cain and Chandler – flow in the bed that London's works wore at the outset of the twentieth century. This is the position I determined to start from: California to date has produced two great novelists, London and Steinbeck, and one great school, that of the so-called 'Tough Guys'. Important antecedents may be found in the work of the writers mentioned above and of others of the late nineteenth century: the Californian writings of Robert Louis Stevenson; the poetry of Miller, Charles Warren Stoddard and Ina Coolbrith; the romantic novels of Gertrude Atherton and Helen Hunt Jackson; most of all, the socialist–Naturalistic novels of Frank Norris, who might have overshadowed London had he not died at age thirty-two and thus deserves special attention. Important successors may also be found: Ken Kesey and Joan Didion among traditional novelists, Ross MacDonald among the tough guys still working the 'mean streets' of Los Angeles. Some concluding paragraphs about what has happened to California writers in contemporary times may be in order. Meanwhile, given the thesis that no 'tradition' can be defined without studying its outstanding figures, I have written three largely self-contained monographs. In each I treat the works and motifs of the figure(s) in question that seem most revealing of the California mind as a whole. Extensive reference is made to the already large body of secondary materials. There is also some attempt to point out valuable aspects of the *oeuvres* that have been overlooked previously, neglected, or even suppressed.

It is reasonable to argue that a culture as eclectic as California's, made up almost entirely of newcomers and with virtually no tradition in English before 1840, has had little chance to produce a distinctive literature. From the outset it should be understood that these California writers exist within the larger body of American literature, and in a more intimate relation than, say, English or Russian novelists of the late nineteenth century existed within the larger body of European literature. At the same time, American literature is not a monolith: the writers of the South are customarily regarded as reflecting the history and climate peculiar to that region, and there are still some who regard the literature of New England as the only true American 'literature'. Leslie Fiedler has characterised the disparate strains in American letters by reference to the compass:[5] the Eastern, by writers such as Henry James and Scott Fitzgerald, who aspire to the European and mannered; the Northern, by those, such as Robert Frost, who celebrate a modest ascetic rural order; the Southern, by the Poes and Faulkners and Tennessee Williamses, who see imaginative fertility amid material decay; the Western, by Hemingway in some phases and even such an eccentric as Ezra Pound, who pit themselves against Fate and the elements in pursuit of increasingly elusive frontiers. In a like manner, both within and beyond the confines of what Fiedler characterises as the Western, something more precisely typical to California can be found.

Much has been written about the spirit of the place; only a little needs to be mentioned here. As indigenous politicians are fond of pointing out, California on its own would be the eighth richest nation in the world. Its population is one-tenth that of the United States as a whole, which makes it about the size of Canada, about half the size of the major Western European nations, and considerably larger than those nations in the first great era of the novel, the age of Balzac and Dickens. California has become the melting-pot of the melting-pot and with its large population of blacks, Mexicans and Orientals, the first frontier of the racial multilateralism typical of the twentieth century. Land of Hollywood, the aerospace and electronics industries, vast agribusiness, the freeways and suburban sprawl, California since the beginning of its consciousness of itself as a cultural unit has been the testing-place and first home of a preponderance of phenomena distinguishing this century from its predecessors. These things should be taken into account when considering California's writers. Geographically, California occupies a unique position in the West ('This is the last place/There is nowhere left to go'),[6] a position remotely analogous to that which the Celtic fringes of Europe held through the Dark Ages. Temporally, California stands in a 'symbolic relation' to the twentieth century, a relation perhaps similar to that which the 'new' nations of Germany and Italy came to hold in Europe in the late nineteenth century.

As opera provided those new nations with a unique synaesthetic art by which to proclaim themselves to the world, so Hollywood has provided California. A popular provincial prejudice, most typical of the 'older' culture of San Francisco, is that Hollywood is not part of California as such, but an independent city-state of a sort, as distinct from California culturally as the Vatican from Italy politically. This view has not survived without some justification. Hollywood has been run and populated until recently by 'outsiders': New Yorkers, Jews, German exiles, Viennese homosexuals, British expatriates, and so forth. These have brought with them an older-world sophistication: that mix of cynical scepticism and excessive enthusiasm toward the land of orange-groves and Rose Bowls which has characterised much of the literature about Hollywood. West's *Day of the Locust*, Fitzgerald's *The Last Tycoon*, Schulberg's *What Makes Sammy Run?*, Huxley's *After Many a Summer Dies the Swan*, Isherwood's *Down There on a Visit* and Waugh's *The Loved One* are the seminal works in this important sub-genre of California writing. The last three fall into the equally distinctive and even longer-lived sub-genre of works by the British who have lived in the state. Unfortunately there is not space here to consider these enriching external strains. But Raymond Chandler, who started his literary life as an English aesthete and spent his most productive years as a Hollywood scriptwriter, is the great figure in whom they merge with the indigenous experience.

Hollywood has in fact played an important role in California writing through most of the period under discussion. About half of London's novels resulted in movies, about the same proportion of Steinbeck's. Hammett's *The Maltese Falcon* was transformed into one of the classics of the art. Cain's somewhat neglected opus produced eleven movies, including the classic *Double Indemnity*, which Chandler scripted. Chandler's novels, all but one, found their way to the screen; and several have been remade recently. By the end of the period the phenomenon of writers writing with an eye to screen adaptation had set in. Cain was criticised on this basis. Steinbeck was criticised for it, in relation to *The Wayward Bus* notably; and in fact Steinbeck was preoccupied throughout his middle years by writing screenplays – *The Forgotten Village*, *Lifeboat*, *Viva Zapata!*, and so on. This interplay of screen and novel stretches back as far as London, who sold the film rights of *The Sea Wolf* before anyone had ever heard of Hollywood and whose last effort, in proof when he died, was the novel version of a screenplay commissioned out of Hollywood, the unmemorable romance *Hearts of Three*. Here then is another element which marks these writers for special consideration. Theirs was the work which grew up most contemporaneously and closest to the revolutionary art-form of modern times. As such, it has particular qualities in both form and content which relate it intimately to the film genre. The analogy is to the European works of the turn-of-the-century, the novels of D'Annunzio or Mann for instance, which partook of techniques and configurations of music drama.

In a sense California writing of the period aspires toward the condition of film. The point has often been suggested. Edmund Wilson implies it in the ironical poem with which he begins his study *The Boys in the Back Room*:

> To see the principles of truth and right
>   Embodied in Paul Muni with a beard;
> The toiling masses and their touching plight,
>   Paul Muni with his chin and cheekbones smeared![7]

Wilson goes on to remark on two motifs which will probably prove the most important to be found in the following chapters. In the first place,

The only theme, when all is said and done, that keeps its seriousness for these California novelists is the theme of the class war. . . . The labor cause has been dramatized with more impact by these writers than it has been on the whole in the East. . . . This tradition [of radical writing] dates from Henry George, who saw the swallowing of the whole state by capital accomplished in record time during the sixties and seventies of the last century.

In the second place, 'California, since we took it away from the Mexicans, has always presented itself to Americans as one of the strangest and most exotic of our adventures; and it is the duty of the literary artist, precisely, to struggle with new phases of experience, and to give them beauty and sense.' Here are Scylla and Charybdis through which these writers, like the Hollywood of the period, had to steer: a struggle between labour, landowners and the dispossessed more intense than anywhere else in America and perhaps more comparable to that within contemporary Germany, with equal tendencies toward socialism and fascism; an exoticism induced by a remarkably varied and beautiful environment, proximate to a primitive foreign culture, filled with the ghosts of Indians and missionaries and rancheros, and giving birth to fantasies as blithe as tales from the *Arabian Nights* or as dark as visions of the Decadents of the *fin-de-siècle*.

In spite of the strong tug toward fantasy, these writers were all firmly based in the Naturalistic mode which Frank Norris had pioneered in before them. Tall, blond and hearty, Norris had a dynamic personality, yet a friendliness and style 'like a great wet dog'.[8] His father had moved to San Francisco after making a small fortune in jewellery in Chicago. His mother was a member of the Browning Society and read Scott and Dickens to her children. Young Frank travelled to Europe as an adolescent and, like a latter-day George Moore, developed a taste for Wagnerian opera and Impressionist painting. For a time he aspired to be a painter himself, the most naturalistic artistic vocation. Later he turned his efforts to poetry and published, with money his mother advanced, a three-canto epic on a medieval subject, *Yvernelle*. Norris went to university at Berkeley, joined a fraternity, and wrote for the campus humour magazine, as Steinbeck would do at Stanford three decades later. Going east to Harvard in the early 1890s, he immersed himself in George Eliot and Zola and drafted his first two novels. After taking his degree, he travelled to South Africa as a journalist. He returned to New York to become the 'boy wonder' of the new Naturalist literati. Personally responsible for the publication of Dreiser's classic of the genre, *Sister Carrie*, Norris tragically did not live to complete his own great Naturalistic project, *The Epic of Wheat*. He died unexpectedly in San Francisco in 1902. He had been searching the northern California foothills for a piece of land on which to settle with his young wife.

The concerns on which Norris built the two published novels of his trilogy were already present in his juvenilia. *Yvernelle* compares villainous feudal barons with the crooked nabobs of the post-Gold Rush age. (It also uses the image 'iron heel' which London was to put to effect in his most radical novel.) *Vandover and the Brute*, written at Harvard but only discovered and published twenty years later, dramatises in a more personal and psychological light Norris's suspicion of the system which had produced him. Vandover is the son of a wealthy owner of San Francisco slum property. He has some artistic talent and a carefree charm but is given to idleness and susceptible to drink and gambling. Exposed to temptation in the city, Vandover degenerates until he finds himself padding around the floor on all-fours, naked and howling like a wolf. This startling denouement foreshadows motifs in London – *The Sea Wolf* and *Call of the Wild,* for instance; in Steinbeck – *Of Mice and Men* notably; and in the Tough Guys, with their preoccupation with outbreaks of criminal–primitive instincts. The last image of the book, in which the hero gazes hungrily into the eyes of a little boy eating his last mouthful of bread, underlies the bias of Naturalism which these successors would share in varying degrees with Norris: urban life is unnatural and potentially brutalising; in the modern city the innocent suffer, the weak-willed go astray, the corrupt flourish; one needs to be ever strong and wary to survive.

A similar message is conveyed by *McTeague* (1900), the other novel Norris wrote at Harvard. The title character of this book is big, lovable, sluggish, unambitious, easily pleased and easily duped. A dentist by trade, McTeague lives and works in the commercial district of Polk Street, San Francisco, an environment Warren French aptly describes as 'a sort of run-down Eden'. Here

McTeague confronts Eve in the form of Trina, an adorable girl who unfortunately has miserly instincts. The 'serpent' is represented by an old Jewish junk-dealer, whose greed for gold is Balzacian. Where *Vandover* was an autodidactic tract against self-indulgence, *McTeague* is an attack against greed. *Greed* is the title of the silent *film noir* Erich von Stroheim made of the novel in the 1920s, and *McTeague*'s metaphysics have much in common with those current in Germany in the inter-war period. The action is linked by the symbol of gold, varying from the 'heart of gold' of McTeague's pet canary to the bits of metal the junk-dealer hoards. This is reminiscent of Wagner's *Ring*, where gold begins as a symbol of natural innocence but becomes a force for inhuman power; and, like Wagner before him, Norris is 'fighting a rear-guard action' against the new order of what S. I. Hayakawa describes as 'symbol-handlers':[9] men-of-barter, whether junk-dealers or international financiers, who create no concrete product by their own labour. McTeague remains ethically and sentimentally tied to an older order, that of 'thing-handlers': agricultural and industrial workers who create concrete products by their labour and are rewarded in direct relation to them.

Between these early essays in city corruption and his trilogy, Norris wrote three novellas focused on young women.[10] *Moran of the Lady Letty* (1898) presents a heroine who believes in the doctrines of strength current at the time. She is a Social Darwinist: 'The strongest of us are going to live and the weakest are going to die.' She is an Anglo-Saxon supremacist: 'Somewhere deep down in the heart of every Anglo-Saxon lies the predatory instinct of his Viking ancestors.' She is a proponent of action rather than reflection: 'It is what you do that counts, rather than what you think or read about.' *Blix* (1899) presents a somewhat sweeter embodiment of related impulses. The heroine rebels against the elegant but hypocritical society of her parents and, like a child of the Haight–Ashbury in the 1960s, declares herself in favour of 'the simple things of the world, the great, broad, primal emotions'. With sincerity as her beacon virtue, she induces a young poet to 'drop out' with her. Together they learn to live for immediate sensation: 'They did not think, they felt.' They become like 'two fine, clean animals'; and, in the northern California pastoral to which they retreat, 'everything was young with them'. *A Woman's Man* (1900) rounds off Norris's youthful attempt to create an ideal woman by praising the virtues of masculine superiority and utter sincerity. Describing an expedition to the North Pole which Norris himself never took, the book anticipates the atmosphere of London's early tales without having their grisly veracity. It also lacks, unfortunately, London's more mature perception of what balance between the sexes might achieve.

While these books were being published, Norris returned to California to research the first volume of his magnum opus. *The Octopus* (1901) would be acclaimed as a pioneering work in the genre of muck-raking, standing beside Upton Sinclair's *The Jungle,* published five years later. But, beyond being one of the seminal novels of 'The Cause', *The Octopus* deserves attention as the first important novel about California. The setting is the great central valley. The dramatis personae are the men and women who grow and transport food. The protagonists are not poor pickers as in Steinbeck's derivative *Grapes of Wrath,* but a group of growers threatened by that new and all-powerful capitalist institution, the great corporation, in this case the railroad. The railroad stands for the new order of 'symbol-handlers' while the growers remain 'thing-handlers', living directly by the product of their farms. Shelgrim, the god who sits atop the power structure of the railroad, embodies the unsentimental code of the age of automatism and mass-man: 'You are dealing with forces . . . when you speak of wheat and the railroads, not with men.'[11] Shelgrim rules through a ruthless lieutenant, S. Behrman, whose genius is for the sort of city corruption Norris constitutionally detests: 'If the freight rates are to be "adjusted" . . . if there's a judge to be bought . . . if there's an election to be jobbed, it is S. Behrman who manipulates it' (109). In the end the growers fail to escape the stranglehold 'the octopus' has on their fortunes. But, among the many killed, S. Behrman, in a stroke of poetic justice reminiscent of Hagen being inundated at the end of Wagner's *Ring*, is drowned by a torrent of grain whooshing down an unused chute.

The Octopus begins with the poet Presley coming into the central valley and longing to turn its beauty into a work of literature. Like Byron before him and Hemingway after, he is in search of a theme: 'something magnificent . . . heroic, terrible, to be unrolled in all the thundering progression of hexameters' (9). His version of the romantic aspiration is peculiar to the place: 'Whatever he wrote, and in whatever fashion, Presley was determined that his poem should be of the West, the world's frontier of Romance.' Against Presley's aspiration, however, as against the peaceful agricultural order of the valley, the octopus looms up as antagonist: 'The Railroad [was a] stubborn barrier against which his romance shattered itself to froth and disintegrated, flying spume' (13). The symbol of corporate capitalism is not the only thing which threatens Presley's poetic intentions. A force more subtle and typical of the place is applied by the shepherd Vanamee, who has wandered the West from Winnipeg to Guadalajara and appears as the ideal individual. 'To Presley's morbidly keen observation, the face was that of an ascetic, of a recluse, almost that of a young seer' (32). Vanamee is a precursor of what Allen Ginsberg in the 1960s would describe as the native Californian shaman. 'So must have appeared the half-inspired shepherds of the Hebraic legends, the younger prophets of Israel, dwellers in the wilderness, beholders of visions, having their existence in a continual dream, talkers with God, gifted with strange powers' (33).

Unlike Presley, Vanamee needs no worldly avocation to lend meaning to his existence. He lives in isolation, sustained by the vision of a lost girl, Angelé Varian, who loved him with 'one of those legendary passions ... untouched by civilisation, spontaneous as the growth of the trees' (36). A more mature male version of Blix, Vanamee encourages his poet to drop out into the pastoral: 'Why write? Why not *live* in it? Sleep oneself in the heat of the desert, the glory of the sunset, the blue haze of the mesa and cañon' (41). Presley is attracted by this siren-song. That Norris is sympathetic to it is indicated by the fact that Vanamee survives the chaos wreaked on the valley, while Presley, embroiled, fails to salvage his epic. Presley's artistic ambition is after all another intrusion of alien civilisation, less destructive than the railroad but also wrong. The native of Eden, left to his own devices, has no need to leave off idling, even for art. Subsistence requires only minimum activity. Stress and drive are the result of pressures applied by forces threatening to exploit the natural peace. Great industry, capital from the East, immigrants who themselves have not heard the internal Eden-calling, the values of civilisation – against these, *The Octopus* suggests, the Californian will have to defend himself lest he be ploughed under like the Spanish and Indians before him. This anxiety – that the goodness of life is about to be confiscated by some ruthless conspiratorial 'unseen' – is the seed from which native radicalism has grown, both of the left and of the right.

Behind the depiction of the class war for which Wilson commends Californians stands in almost every case an ideal vision of the individual in a state of nature. Vanamee finds his way into Jack London in various guises. In *The Game* he is the boxer concerned about losing his 'silk'. In *Burning Daylight* he is the capitalist who gives up city corruption to return to the pastoral. In *The Valley of the Moon* he is the young sailor who dreams of distant seas; also Mark Hall, who lives for 'body-culture'; also Billy Roberts, who begins like the boxer of *The Game* fearing for his 'silk' and ends like Burning Daylight as a farmer. London's most succinct portrait of the type comes in the 'nature man' chapter of *Cruise of the Snark*: a young man contracts tuberculosis while working in a factory in Portland and is given six months to live; after bumming around the California foothills for three months, however, he returns to health; and after two decades of clearing jungle in Tahiti, he has become the most inspiring physical specimen London has ever seen. This type recalls Vanamee; but the cult of the young man in harmony with nature is in fact ubiquitous. In *Roughing It* Twain describes sleeping under the stars around Lake Tahoe and his reluctance ever to rouse himself and stray from the spot. In 'The Judgment of Bolinas Plain' Harte shows his penchant for a related ideal through the young wife's admiration for the fugitive stranger. In 'Chrysanthemums', which Gide praised,[12] Steinbeck presents an almost identical situation. In 'Flight' Steinbeck offers an indelible image of this romantic tendency in the final tableau of the fugitive atop the coastal mountains silhouetted against the horizon.

The Grapes of Wrath, a book about the necessity of working co-operatively to create a decent civilisation, contains notwithstanding another remarkable glorification of the perfect individual in harmony with nature yet threatened by man: the Indian brave described in the Okie campfire tale as standing naked and arms spread before the oncoming settlers, a symbol of freedom and defiance that for a moment freezes the trigger-fingers of those who must kill in order to gain the land.[13] Invested in the Indian, the image suggests a larger American significance. In fact, by the time of *Grapes* Steinbeck was rebelling against his reputation as a provincial and identifying his point of view with the tradition of Emerson, Whitman and Thoreau.[14] But belief in an 'oversoul', cults of the road and of secular *caritas*, and renunciation of material civilisation are motifs that had found particular emphasis in California writing from the first and would only come up against serious refutation with the advent of the Tough Guys. Outlanders from older cultures and chillier climes, the Tough Guys were not prepared to view Vanamee or his Eden-dream with special sympathy. The relative laws of natural life may have been beautiful to contemplate, but they had little value in melting-pots where relativity was all-too-present and some absolute code had to rule. The perfect individual in tune with nature had to make way for the practical citizen a beat ahead of the urban fury. Yet no one who has read Chandler's description of his hero in 'The Simple Art of Murder' can doubt that this supposedly ultra-realistic detective is any less an expression of the ideal.

A critic of Chandler, reading his mysteries against his unpublished writings, suggests that in Marlowe he is 'chasing' a glorified vision of himself. The charge, in a word, is narcissism; and narcissism is clearly an important factor in California writing, as in the culture as a whole. All the figures this book will discuss shared with Norris the preference for autobiographical personae. They all also valued subjective passion. This may be part of the reason why Jack London, one of the most self-dramatising of writers, achieved such immense popularity. It may also contribute to the fact that Steinbeck, many of whose biases will not stand scrutiny, remains a best-seller. Cain made no pretence of appealing to other than the passions. Hammett and Chandler were not ratiocinators; in fact, as with Gutman in *The Maltese Falcon*, they often associated great thinking with crime. To some degree the whole body of writing discussed here, while not unintelligent, ends by being anti-intellectual. As such, it is also, ironically, anti-artistic. Vanamee is the ideal figure, not Presley. Martin Eden, London's writer hero, ends in failure as a human being and suicide. Joe Elegant of *Sweet Thursday*, one of Steinbeck's few artists, is thoroughly mocked. Hammett's evil genius in *The Dain Curse* is a writer. Philip Marlowe is a philistine who describes a valuable piece of modern sculpture as 'two warts on a fanny'.[15] Cain's opera-singer in *Serenade* ends like most Cain heroes by overreaching and burning himself out.

The overall progression this study deals with is from the immanent Eden where perfection seems given to the corrupt city where it can only be approached through smartness and untiring will. The strains of the transition are enormous. The desire to run away from the city permeates Norris and London; yet in each there remains a recognition that problems of urban organisation cannot finally be avoided. This desire to turn and run has vanished substantially by the time of the Tough Guys; and in Chandler there are passages which laud city life, however corrupt, over the smug and unengaged new counterfeit Edens, the 'idle valleys' of suburbia. Some equilibrium might for a moment be found in the work of Steinbeck, who hailed from a small agricultural town but ultimately chose to live in Hollywood and New York. Slim in *Of Mice and Men* is a compromise between the ideal man-of-nature of Norris and London and the practical man-of-the-mean-streets of the Tough Guys.

> He moved with a majesty only achieved by royalty and master-craftsmen. He was a jerkline skinner, the prince of the ranch, capable of driving ten, sixteen, even twenty mules in a single line. . . . There was a gravity in his manner and a quiet so profound that all talk stopped when he spoke. His authority was so great that his word was taken on any subject. . . . His hatchet face was ageless. He might have been thirty-five or fifty. His ear heard more than was said to him, and his slow speech had overtones not of thought, but of understanding beyond thought. His hands, large and lean, were as delicate in their action as those of a temple dancer.[16]

Craft, capability, majesty, quiet, profundity, agelessness, sureness, gentleness, understanding, strength yet delicacy – these qualities represent the standard by which in Steinbeck's lifetime Californian culture measured its men. The John Wayne or Ronald Reagan figure superseded, while absorbing aspects of, both the simple man of nature and the hard man of the cities. But Joan Didion in her *Slouching toward Bethlehem*, published the year Steinbeck died, complains that 'the centre cannot hold';[17] and in her second essay in that book she hints at what she means by admiring John Wayne and the code he represents and implicitly lamenting its passing. In a second book of essays about the same period of the late 1960s, *The White Album*, Didion describes with barely concealed distaste the new man ascending: Jim Morrison, rock-singer in skin-tight leather trousers, prophet of the corrupt urban gospel of sex and drugs, seducer of the new suburban youth.[18] In fact, the change Didion identifies with these images was already lurking in *Of Mice and Men*, where the simple Edenic order still preserved in part by Slim is under threat by an Eve-figure, herself an early victim of the lurid attractions of city-life. Curly's wife has 'full-rouged lips'. Her eyes are 'heavily made-up'.[19] Her fingernails are red, her hair carefully curled and teased. She is bored with her life as a kept wife on a farm and longs for the abandon she reads about in movie-magazines. Were she not so pathetic, she might be a kind of Salomé. In her fatal ennui she wanders into the bunkhouse and, half against her will, teases men into making plays for her.

Curly's wife is a new and disturbing type, one in whom yearning has become unnatural and fantasy is a danger rather than a release. Clare Booth Luce, who created the role in the Broadway adaptation of *Mice*, complained to Steinbeck's agent and Steinbeck was obliged to deflect a charge of misogyny in order to prevent the actress from quitting.[20] Curly's wife, however, was neither the first nor the last such *femme fatale* in Steinbeck: Cathy Trask of *East of Eden* is, by his own description, a 'monster' on similar lines. The male type may have changed as Didion suggests, but so too has the female; for Curly's wife and Cathy Trask are seen repeatedly in other guises in the work of the Tough Guys. Back in Norris's and London's times, this type hardly existed. Woman, however strong, was not threatening to man; characteristically, she was an inspiration for her fortitude, a help by her industry, and a joy in her feminine 'otherness'. She was the earth-spirit who would reach her titanic apotheosis in Steinbeck's Ma Joad. As Hilda Tree, beloved of one of the growers in *The Octopus*, she radiates the same Eden-dream which inspires Presley and Vanamee:

> There was a certain generous amplitude to the full, round curves of her hips and shoulders that suggested the precocious maturity of healthy, vigorous animal-life. . . . Her hair seemed to have a life of its own. . . . Her greatest charm of all was her simplicity. . . . Yet there were about her small contradictory suggestions of feminine daintiness. . . . Not the refinement of education, nor culture, but the natural, intuitive refinement of the woman, not as yet defiled and crushed out by the sordid, strenuous life-struggle of overpopulated districts.[21]

Embodied here is an ethic which partakes, as I have said, of the transcendental and essentially anti-urban idealism of Emerson, Whitman and Thoreau. This will dominate in London and the Californian works of Steinbeck. But, as they struggle with the problems of city life, these authors begin to deal in motifs more reminiscent of Poe, say, or even Wilde and the European Decadents. The attraction–repulsion of degeneracy, crime, sexual licence; the giving-way to passions, the polemicising, the fear of atavism – these spectres loom up as the native psyche confronts the new cities burgeoning against the backdrop of Eden: San Francisco of *The Iron Heel*, Oakland of *The Valley of the Moon*, Hollywood of the obsessions of Steinbeck's little people, Los Angeles of Chandler's almost surreal vision. The socialisation of the provincial into the cosmopolitan is perhaps the common theme of all great literature. In these California writers it can be found both overall and in specific works repeatedly. Nor is it surprising that two gentlemen hailing from the city of Poe and Mencken and one transplant from London should have found more facile means to cope with the new Californian cities than their native precursors. But the development does not end on the 'mean streets'. California even within the period of Hammett, Cain and Chandler was fast becoming a suburban society. To the urban-wise as much as to the Eden-dreaming this posed new problems; and Chandler's distaste for suburbia in *The Long Goodbye* and *Playback* is no doubt symptomatic of a 'rearguard action' against the new cultural transformation as much as Norris's and London's attacks on city life were of the previous one.

2 Jack London

I THE UNDERMAN AND THE CAUSE

London's first great novel was *The Sea Wolf* (1903). Its hero, Wolf Larsen, captain of the sealing-ship *Ghost*, is the classic literary embodiment of the Nietzschean *Übermensch*. Its narrator, the poet and critic Humphrey Van Weyden, whom Larsen has shanghaied from his pleasant dilettantish life in the San Francisco Bay Area, seems Larsen's natural opposite in his over-civilisation and timidity. Only temporarily, however, can Larsen reduce Van Weyden to the status of an Underman. In the perfect 'X' the novel forms, Van Weyden grows to physical as well as moral strength at the same time as Larsen's physical dominance is sapped by his moral brutality. Education and culture preserve Van Weyden from the abyss. The true Underman in London's Dantesque scheme must issue from some hideous and blighted background. He must be a villain totally lacking knowledge of his villainy; a man so consistently wronged by the ways of the world, so consistently remote from access to decent civilisation, as to defy the existence of morality altogether. This type will be the true brute, not the Nietzschean like Larsen, who is conscious of his brutality as much as of the morality it is designed to supersede. He will exist through the pragmatism of satisfying immediate needs. He will not shrink from crime if it serves his interests – he will not recognise crime as crime if it serves his interests – and he will be condemned by his fellows perpetually, scapegoated whenever there is any provocation, because of his evident ignorance of, and transparent carelessness for, the minimum fellow-feeling. He represents the lowest order of man in that scale of moral evolution that London, himself a bastard from Bay Area slums, spent his life trying to ascend: 'I look forward to a time when man shall progress upon something worthier and higher than his stomach, where there will be a finer incentive to impel men to action than the incentive of

17

today. . . . I believe that spiritual sweetness and unselfishness will conquer the gross gluttony of today.'[1]

Spiritual sweetness and unselfishness may lie somewhere in the remote racial-existential past of Thomas Mugridge, the cook of the *Ghost* and Underman of *The Sea Wolf*, but they are eclipsed by a more immediate legacy of oppression in the slums of the greatest city of the capitalist world: '[He was] a Cockney, with the clean lines and weakly pretty, almost effeminate face of the man who has absorbed the sound of Bow Bells with his mother's milk. . . . [He had] the subservient smirk which comes only of generations of tip-seeking ancestors.'[2] Though in its way potentially as noble as that of Wolf Larsen, Mugridge's physiognomy has taken on a twist of the grotesque. An ear is bruised and swollen, 'cauliflower' in the parlance of the sailors, one of whom has caused the deformity by hurling a boot at its owner's skull. Why is the wretch so detested? His subservience is merely a cover for unbearable arrogance, we discover. As soon as Larsen relegates Van Weyden to the scullery, for instance, Mugridge's attitude toward the newcomer changes: 'Servile and fawning as he had been before, he was now as domineering and bellicose. . . . I was no longer the fine gentleman with a skin soft as a "lydy's"' (36). Van Weyden on the spot becomes an abysmal creature in Mugridge's crude hierarchy of power, deserving to be ordered about 'much in the fashion that Bill Sykes would have routed his dog' (44). Hypocrisy masking the desire of the oppressed to oppress is the leitmotif of the Cockney's character. The effect on Van Weyden is stunning. Almost instantly he begins to descend into brutishness himself: 'My manhood [had] in unaccountable ways been smirched and sullied. . . . His chitter-chatter drove me to distraction. . . . His oily, insinuating tones, his greasy smile, and his monstrous self-conceit . . . he was the most disgusting and loathsome person I have ever met' (60). 'Life assumed the same sordid values to me . . . nothing pretty about it, nothing divine – only two cowardly moving things' (92).

The Bill Sykes allusion alerts us to Dickens; and Mugridge is not only a thief like Sykes, but also a manipulator of the masks of humility and arrogance in the tradition of Uriah Heep. On one occasion he steals money from Van Weyden, which Wolf Larsen in turn wins back by getting him drunk and then beating (or cheating) him at cards. The Cockney's pathetic hubris is nowhere as apparent as in this episode. As he grows increasingly tipsy, his motions take on more exaggerated swagger, his hobnobbing with the captain grows more presumptuous, his confidences become maudlin and familiar until he goes entirely over the top: 'He hooked Wolf Larsen's buttonhole with a greasy forefinger and vacuously proclaimed and reiterated . . . "I got money, I tell yer, an' I'm a gentleman's son!"' (77). Mugridge would be monstrous; yet his pretensions are so crude, and his dog-eat-doggism is so base and alienating, that they lead in almost every encounter to his further impoverishment and humiliation. Back in the scullery he tries to bully Van Weyden with a knife. Though 'under all his cowardice there was a courage of cowardice', Mugridge's bullying turns to subservience once more as soon as Van Weyden starts whetting a knife himself. Mugridge accepts it as his lot to be foiled by superiors. Still, relentlessly, eternally, he remains watchful, pressing for the weak spot in his opponents–oppressors, waiting in defiance and with the sarcastic humour of the embittered. This last is particularly galling to his shipmates. In moments of tension between them and the captain, they are apt to turn on this mocking embodiment of city slime – not a Jew, but much the same as the stereotype of the little Jew of the time. The crew's torment of Mugridge oscillates between farce and terror. The crowning incident is when Wolf Larsen uses him as a scapegoat for his own failure to appeal to Maud Brewster, a blue-stocking the *Ghost* has taken aboard following a shipwreck. Ostensibly to impress upon his cook the necessity of cleanliness, Larsen throws Mugridge overboard and drags him in the ship's wake. The crew find this uproarious. Their glee turns into horror, however, when a shark appears and devours one of the Cockney's legs.

Mugridge is not wholly defenceless. He is no Christian martyr, or passive little Jew ready to go to slaughter. His background has schooled him in a pertinacious will to survive. When he senses malevolent intent against him, he becomes so nimble that the crew has difficulty catching him. He is 'nine-lived', Van Weyden tells us. Moreover, like the brutalised Buck in *The Call of the Wild* (1902), he has developed a capacity for cur-like revenge. Once dragged back on deck after losing his leg, he 'flounders' over to Larsen and buries his teeth into the man's ankle. Within his maimed soul the flame of defiance burns white-hot, animating his will-to-live: 'I'll never rest 'appy till I see that 'ell-'ound bloody well dead. . . . 'E's got no right to live, an' as the Good Word puts it, '"E shall shorely die", an' I say, "Amen, an' damn soon at that"' (228). In Mugridge's mouth the reference to Christianity degenerates into sheer self-interest. Still, the evidence builds that Mugridge is more sinned against than sinning, and he himself is far from ignorant that from the moment of birth he has been a victim of the world's injustice: 'I never 'ad no chance. . . . 'Oo was there to send me to school, or put tommy in my 'ungry belly, or wipe my bloody nose?' (123). Van Weyden, who has become 'oppressed by the enormity of the sin' of applauding the Cockney's torment, now seeks to extend liberal sympathy: 'You've long years before you, and you can make anything you please of yourself.' But Mugridge's experience is of a different order, and he is by no means ready to accept this naive bourgeois optimism native to the Land of Opportunity: 'It's a lie! . . . It's all right for you . . . You was born a gentleman. . . . If I was President of the United States tomorrer, 'ow would it fill my belly for one time when I was a kiddy?' The horror eventually registers in Van Weyden: 'I had come to see a malignant devil in him which impelled him to hate all the world . . . he even hated himself, so grotesquely had life dealt with him . . . a great sympathy welled up in me. . . . How God must have hated [him] that [he] should be tortured so.'

Here might be detected an anticipation of the response of another American to other maimed creatures produced by the greatest and oldest city of Anglo-Saxon capitalist civilisation: 'I had not thought that death had undone so many!', T. S. Eliot laments in *The Waste Land*; and London's view of the Underman of the East End of England's capital is at least as inferno-like as Eliot's panorama of the metropolis. Mugridge of *The Sea Wolf* rises out of London's major opus of the previous year, the sociological study of the East End entitled *The People of the Abyss*. There is indeed a character in that book named Thomas Mugridge, an old seaman of seventy living in retirement and penury with his dogged and carping wife, by whom he has produced a brood of children, all gone now, either 'rotting in the cities' or escaped to the colonies and the New World.[3] Such are the only alternatives for the children of what London sees as this slowly dying race of proletarians; and Thomas Mugridge of *The Sea Wolf* is a more composite picture of that race than his actual namesake. Perhaps he was once a happy child dancing along the narrow streets as the organ-grinder went by (238). As such he would have been doomed to a swift fall from the Blakean 'age of innocence' into *la misère*. As a young man he may have been a Cockney Adonis, a 'young god' gracefully built and strongly featured but nevertheless inevitably 'doomed to rack and ruin in four or five short years', and already demonstrating the 'unconscious hedonism, utterly unmoral and materialistic' that comes from the sure knowledge that there is no real possibility for betterment (33–4). Confronted in his own environment with either a low-paying and soul-destroying industrial job or the stupefying existence of street-wandering and the doss-house, he would have sought what happiness could be found in 'dull, animal' pleasures, gravitating towards 'the deadly inertia which precedes dissolution', and finally taking the chance if offered of escape to the ships. There he might at least escape what he sees as the predatory demands of the even more oppressed women – mothers, sisters, and wives of his kind – and end in anonymity without heirs.

This typical tragic development London exposed and deplored. At the same time, with his characteristic doctrinal insistence on the necessity of the evolutionary betterment of the race, he came to the conclusion: 'It is criminal for the People of the Abyss to marry' (35). Life is not worth reproducing if this is all it can offer. Middle and old age become a curse of physical deformity, disease and neglect. A young woman who will look with pity on the strapping young sailor who finds himself in the doss-house door will hardly recognise the existence of the emaciated old men that hover beside him in the queue. The old men's minds are stunted. With a little food in their bellies they become capable of a few mean curses against the Eastern European immigrants whom they see as responsible for having pushed them out of their jobs. Some few are capable of revolutionary outbursts against the oppressor classes in the West End. Intelligent radical activity, however, is stunted by malnutrition, depression, and lack of leadership. The self-taught and ardent burn themselves up in a few short years. Attempts to return to the countryside as hop-pickers result in an even more destitute gypsy-like existence. Unlike in the United States, hostile climate and overpopulation take all romanticism out of the life of the tramp. Suicide is epidemic, but the young girl who fails at drowning herself in a canal is punished rather than rehabilitated. The 'ginny laugh' of the harlot echoes up from Leman Street; and, in another anticipation of *The Waste Land*, the only pleasure to be found is in the snatches of old songs drifting occasionally from the river. The spectacle in the end moved London to this indictment: 'If this is the best civilization can do for the human, then give us howling and naked savagery' (251). In a bleak anticipation of

Lawrentian primitivism he went on, 'Far better to be a people of
the wilderness and desert, of the cave and the squatting-place,
than to be a people of the machine and the Abyss.'

London spent only six weeks in the East End. He had come directly
from the balmy plentitude of California, where he had only
recently begun to draw himself out of an existence as a 'work-beast'
and extreme, degrading poverty. His first stories had sold well and
were gaining him a reputation. Still, the 'Kipling of the Klondike'
was no Bret Harte coming to the bright ambience of Henry James's
city after two decades of lionisation as the witty chronicler of the
'49 Gold Rush. Where Harte came to England looking for the
sophistication he had bearded the first Californians for lacking,
London came on a prearrangement with his publisher to write a
study illuminating the socialist doctrines he and his comrades had
been propounding in the relative comfort of the Oakland Ruskin
Club. From this point of view Andrew Sinclair's criticism seems
just: 'London's conclusions were prejudiced. . . . *The People of the
Abyss* has all the merit of the urgent first impression, none of the
saving grace of the judicious survey.'⁴ The reader familiar with the
traditions of the working-class in England, and the community
cultures of the old East End, may object with reason that London,
the outsider, failed to perceive the underlying strength of a people
whose apparent weakness moved him to slightly patronising
partisanship. Some may note a puritan and typically American
over-fastidiousness in his reaction to habits of bathing, and his
revulsion at 'grease' in the food; also a tendency to let the
experience of the 'wide-open spaces' of California colour his
response to the size of the living-quarters. At the same time, one
should remember that London was sufficiently schooled in
hardship to be some judge of its relative horrors. Even the most
sceptical reader must find it impressive when he remarks on the
condition of the wandering homeless: 'I have travelled all day with
the spirit thermometer down to seventy-four degrees below zero;
and though I suffered, it was a mere nothing compared to carrying
the banner for a night, ill fed, ill clad, and soaking wet' (102).

    In the last year of his life London singled out *The People* as his
favourite book. Clearly the experience in the East End was
formative. Philip Foner suggests that it may have precipitated
London's turn from the youthful position that atavism could be

beneficial to the mature position that atavism was destructive.[5] Before *The People*, London had written *Call of the Wild* with its romantic finale of transcendence 'into the primitive'; afterwards, he would write *White Fang* (1906), which reverses the process with its happy ending of domesticisation into the civilised pastoral. *The People* reflects London's shift of attention from the issue of man's struggle with the forces of nature to that of man's struggle to live decently with other men. The process is mirrored in *The Sea Wolf*, which on one level is a dialogue between the principle of the Superman that London had celebrated in his Klondike tales and the less attractive fact of the Underman that had forced its way into his consciousness in the East End. Van Weyden's admiration for Wolf Larsen and repulsion at Mugridge belie the fear of the author that he himself might be forced back into the abyss from which he had so recently extricated himself. But London the artist was too tough-minded and balanced to allow his characters simply to reflect emotional admiration or repulsion. In his tenaciously defiant way, with his utter lack of world-weariness or moral paralysis, Mugridge is paradoxically a more compelling figure than the brooding Wolf Larsen (on whom, incidentally, the Cockney wreaks revenge in the end by cutting all the *Ghost*'s ropes). The fact that London was painting from life in this case gives Mugridge a grisly reality that Larsen sometimes lacks. The terror of Mugridge's situation is arguably the most dramatic element in *The Sea Wolf*. Considering as much, it seems a shame that London did not cultivate his love–hate for England or create quite such a fascinating composite of odium again. But what he had uncovered in Mugridge and *The People* was to animate one of the enduring theoretical problems of his life and art.

At the end of *The People* London suggests that the English should get rid of the Empire, get rid of 'the gentlemen of no profession', take over the management of industry, maximise the rules of efficiency, and assure that every increase in productivity resulted in immediate increase in standards of living *not* in gradual degeneration of the producing class into blighted 'work-beastism' (277–8). This socialist cry is followed by a quotation from Long-fellow which links the struggle against class oppression to the martyrdom of Christ; and such a doctrine became the driving force of London's second great novel. *The Iron Heel* (1908) moved Trotsky to remark that London was a better social prophet than Lenin or Rosa Luxemburg.[6] Many have noted the accuracy, down to small details, with which London predicted the rise of fascism. American critics since the 1950s have tended to see the prediction of class warfare in the United States as a fantasy disproved by the preservation – indeed, the growth in strength – of the middle class. Time will tell whether these critics have been over-hasty to judge. Certainly, as the world shrinks into opposition between a few rich nations and the vast lumpen-proletariat of the Third World, London's overall pattern has credibility (the fate of the Allende government has been put forward as an example of the 'iron heel' still at work).[7] It is not the purpose here to rehash the saga of London's socialism, which has been told many times and with varying degress of objectivity. *The Iron Heel*, however, is built upon it. The *Übermensch*–Underman–mediating middle-man configuration of *The Sea Wolf* is now reproduced in characterisa-tions of class. Larsen's tyranny becomes that of the 'oligarchy' or 'iron heel'; Mugridge's defiant baseness becomes that of the lowest rung of society, fittingly labelled the 'people of the abyss'; the Van Weyden–Maud Brewster civilised position is taken up by another pair of lovers, Ernest Everhard and Avis Cunningham, a professor's daughter and the book's narrator.

The oligarchs inhabit mansions in the cities and estates in the suburban countryside. Superficially they exercise democratic principles and are willing to allow exceptional and admiring members of lower classes into their circle, though only to 'prattle sweet little ideals and dear little moralities'.[8] In fact the oligarchs at base are shockingly anti-intellectual and 'materialistic'; and, when pressed about the inefficiencies and inequities of their system, they have only one answer: 'When you reach your strong hands for our palaces and purpled ease, we will ... grind you revolutionists down under our heel' (105–6). On the individual level the oligarchs respond to those of the middle class who would consort with preachers of revolution by admonition first, then dispossession, finally incarceration – the social exclusion of Avis Cunningham, the cancelling of the stock-certificates held by her father, the committing of Bishop Morehouse to a 'rest-home'. On the public level the oligarchs respond to general strikes and socialist victories at the polls by organising the farmers into a conservative 'Grange' party, the religious into an Anglo-Catholic revival, and the patriotic into a war against the most unco-operative of fellow capitalist powers (with historical foresight London identifies this as Germany). The media is transformed into a propaganda machine; independent publishers such as Hearst are dishonoured; the socialist press is sabotaged and suppressed. The cream of the industrial working class is formed into favoured unions, membership in which is passed on by heredity. The proceeds of surplus production are devoted to the building of magnificent roads, great achievements in science, and construction of 'wonder cities' whose glittering towers rise not to the groans of serfs but to 'the sounds of singing'. Sons and daughters of the oligarch order become artists; art becomes exclusively for entertainment and 'the worship of beauty'; artists are rewarded in proportion to their inattention to 'the slime-dripping maw' of the abyss. In fear that if they ever weakened 'the great beast would engulf them and everything of beauty and wonder', the oligarchs put great stress on 'high ethical righteousness' (319). Though apparently effete, they become supremely strong – and supremely able to smash any threat to their omnipotence.

The middle class is ploughed under by this process. Few are willing to suffer the consequences of defiance. As Everhard says, they are 'tied by their heartstrings' to protect their families and children: 'My father! He lied, he stole, he did all sorts of dishonorable things to put bread into my mouth. . . . He was a slave' (62). The middle class is seduced by the rewards the oligarchs provide for the docile and intimidated by the example of the fall that comes for those who dare open opposition. A few such as Ernest and Avis are able to carry on a struggle for social justice, though only by operating as double-agents, using disguises and secret hiding-places, and other highly calculated forms of deception. Everhard claims that this struggle is working-class in origin. In fact it is grounded on the quasi-Christian principles traditionally espoused by the middle-class elite. Bishop Morehouse's speech about 'the pale Galilean' is lifted from an article by Frank Harris and inspired by 'The Soul of Man under Socialism' by Oscar Wilde, 'one of the lords of the language of the nineteenth century of the Christian era' (124). Everhard himself is compared by Avis to Christ: 'He too had taken over the part of the lowly and the oppressed' (68). Everhard refers to Christianity as 'a mere poulticing of the ulcer', sees the Bishop's fate as proof of the outdatedness of Christian solutions, and finds his own remedy in removing 'the ulcer' itself – 'Give the worker his product!' When confronting a collection of oligarchs in a private club, however, he argues that the superior morality of socialism derives from its pursuit of 'the Holy Grail, Christ's own Grail' (87). One foot is in the realm of nineteenth-century 'soft' socialist millennarians such as Ruskin and Morris and the aforementioned Wilde, the other in that of twentieth-century 'hard' socialist men-of-action – contemporaries such as Shaw, or successors in this genre of radical fiction such as B. Traven. Everhard is also another version of London's blond Superman. Avis describes him as a 'god'; and it may be that the novel breaks off abruptly before we learn whether Everhard has escaped from Alcatraz to a secret hideaway in Sonoma County so that we may imagine that the spirit of revolution, like a god, transcends.

The hideaway in Sonoma constitutes the first appearance in London's writing of the 'valley of the moon'. It is here, while waiting for Ernest, that Avis writes her narrative. From the first the horrors she relates are juxtaposed against 'the soft summer wind [that] stirs the redwoods', the 'sweet cadences [of the] wild water rippling over its mossy stones', the 'butterflies in the sunshine', the 'drowsy hum of the bees' – all the quiet and peace which, in the light of events, 'seems unreal' (7). The contrast is nowhere more brutally apparent than in the apocalyptic finale of the novel. Avis tells the tale of the Chicago Commune, in which the Iron Heel precipitates a revolt of the masses in order to discourage revolts the socialists are planning in Canada and Mexico. A chapter entitled 'The People of the Abyss' chronicles the worst of Iron Heel atrocities, 'warfare in that modern jungle, a great city' (341). As city and jungle are contrasted to semi-rural Sonoma, so their denizens are contrasted to the best in civilised man. These people of the abyss are the atavistic mass: 'It surged past my vision in concrete waves of wrath, snarling and growling, carnivorous, drunk with whisky from pillaged warehouses, drunk with hatred, drunk with lust for blood.' Like the denizens of the East End these people have 'nothing to lose but the misery and pain of living'. Hiding under dead bodies, Avis escapes the death that awaits most. When she finally issues forth, it is to discover the futility of the struggle: 'Never once did they succeed in reaching the city of the oligarchs over on the west side. . . . No matter what destruction was wreaked in the heart of the city, [the oligarchs], and their womankind and children, were to escape unhurt.' For the scapegoats, however, it is tragically otherwise. Grotesque images confront Avis. It is the lowest circle of the urban inferno. Survivors drag their maimed bodies around with 'the dumb pathos of the

wounded and hunted animal'. Avis comes upon a quiet street of
the dead 'as a wanderer in the country would come upon a flowing
stream. Only this stream I gazed upon did not flow. It was
congealed in death.' Carrying on the allusion to the pastoral, she
concludes, 'Poor driven people of the abyss, hunted helots – they
lay there as the rabbits of California after a drive.'

The Iron Heel dates from the period when London was crossing
the country lecturing university audiences about the socialist
'Cause'. Earle Labor has criticised Everhard as a doe-eyed glorification of Jack as projected through his new wife, Charmian,
who in turn was the model for Avis.[9] That Avis derives from
Charmian raises some question: Anna Strunsky, herself a socialist
from a university background, would seem a more logical
inspiration. As to the objection against Everhard: Sinclair has
pointed out that such glorifications seem excusable when one
considers that London was actually living an existence of heroic
action at this stage.[10] The risk of such an existence, Sinclair goes
on, was to precipitate a public *auto-da-fé*; and many have argued
that after *The Iron Heel* that is exactly what occurred. The novel
gratified some socialists, but it hurt London's sales and did not
please his publisher or his new Bohemian friends.[11] Caught
between committing himself yet further to an ideal which had the
potential to drag him back into 'the slime' or committing himself
to formulae for a vapid but entertaining art that would assure sales
and acceptability, London chose to escape into 'adventure': sailing
his custom-made schooner, the *Snark*, around the world. Sinclair
and others make much of the fact that the cruise had to be
abandoned in the South Seas owing to bad boat-design and
London's bad health. They see London's subsequent return to
ranching in the Valley of the Moon as a retreat from life that
involved on one level dropping his socialism in favour of
landed-gentryism, and on another subverting his art to the
necessity of accruing capital. They see *Martin Eden* (1909) as the
watershed work: summation of the early phase of ascent,
expression of the individual's disillusion with socialism, and
prelude to pessimism and moral decline. This view, especially in
relation to *Martin Eden*, has been argued so well elsewhere that it
need not be repeated here. It depends, I think, on exaggeration of
tendencies that London may have demonstrated at times but never
allowed to become dominant.

Above all the attack on his social conscience inflamed him. As late as 1912 he would write, 'I was a socialist before I was writer. . . . I am not an individualist. . . . *Martin Eden* was written as an indictment of individualism.'[12] When he finally resigned from the Socialist Party shortly before his death, it was to protest at the Party's unwillingness to be sufficiently revolutionary, and its reluctance to take a position on a war which he saw as a conflict between the values of civilisation and barbarism.[13] His instinctive ideal was a pastoral free of the oppressors and maimed victims of the industrial jungle; but the political significance of this ultimately was either neo-feudalist or, as Sinclair suggests, pre-Maoist.[14] London never did become a ruthless capitalist. In *The Iron Heel* the outgrowth of the crushed socialist dream is outlawry, guerrilla warfare, and urban terrorism giving birth to such gangs as 'the Danites, the Valkyries (the most terrible of all), the Widows of War, the Berzerkers, the Bedlamites, the Helldamites, the Wrath of God, the Bleeding Hearts, Sons of Morning, the Morning Stars, the Flamingoes, the Triple Thinkers, the Three Bars, the Rubonics, the Vindicators, the Comanches, the Erebusties' (373). This clearly was no alternative for a man who aspired to the decencies of civilisation; and the fact is that in his later years London the socialist gave way more and more to London the artist. Through his craft he had developed a wide range of understanding, foreshadowed in his stunning perception of all classes in *The Iron Heel*. No longer the middle-class saviour determined to lead the oppressed to the light by revealing and destroying the dark motives of the oppressors, he could project himself on one hand into the oppressor who becomes human in *Burning Daylight* (1910), on another into the middle-class aesthete who becomes an oppressor in *The Mutiny of the Elsinore* (1914), and on a third into the proletarian who escapes to the pastoral – Billy Roberts in *The Valley of the Moon* (1913). He could even project himself into the position of a man as oppressed as – *more* oppressed than – Thomas Mugridge and, in spite of his lifelong fear of the abyss, write an entire novel from the point of view of being trapped in it.

The Iron Heel comes from the brightest phase of London's career, *The Star Rover* (1915) from the bleakest. In the first case he was experiencing the high tide of success: his strength of invention was producing some of his finest and favourite books; he had just married the love of his life; he had discovered the piece of land where he wanted to make his home; he had national notoriety behind him and the open skies and seas of the world ahead. In the second he was experiencing a precipitous drop in his sales, critical opprobrium, troubles with his publishers; his cherished 'Wolf House' had been burnt to the ground by some envious employee; his wife had miscarried for the second time; and he himself was wracked by physical disabilities and fears, which had already destroyed his magnificent body and were threatening to cut short his life. Sinclair tells of London's dependence on opiates, belladonna and salvarsan in this period and goes on to imply that the novel is marred by an excessive influence of drug visions: '*The Star Rover* prais[es] the triumph of the spirit over the torments of the body, and . . . signal[s] Jack's escape from his physical pain through drugs. . . . The White Logic of alcohol [is] replaced by the beatitudes of morphine.'[15] A new, perhaps drug-induced, fluidity is apparent in passages near the beginning and end of the book, and the entire fantastic theme has an hallucinogenic quality. But, far from marring the product, these qualities might be seen as refreshing in an opus which so often demonstrates a tight, almost puritanical control and Hemingway-like concision. As a break-through of the inner cry of the spirit, *The Star Rover* is perhaps the most moving of all London's books. At times bracing, at times chilling, it is a novel which requires, I think, a degree of physical courage from the reader. Its strength lies predominantly in this. Its weakness lies in the prodigality by which, as Joan London remarks, her father tossed off in the 'star-rovings' several tales' which might have made successful novels on their own.[16]

As in *The Iron Heel* and *The Sea Wolf*, the narration is first-person; only here the narrator is neither a woman nor an aesthete, and the hero is himself not some observed 'other' of Nietzschean grandeur. Sinclair says that London identified more with Nietzsche's miserable end in madness than with his philosophy;[17] and, whether or not this is the case, Darrell Standing, like Nietzsche, is a professor who, through giving way to a mad paroxysm of 'red wrath', has fallen into the abyss. From his chair in agronomy at the University of California, where he promoted new farming-methods like his creator and championed efficiency like Ernest Everhard, Standing has moved to death-row at San Quentin, where he is confined in solitary owing to a false assumption that he has concealed dynamite preparatory to a mass outbreak. The first level on which the novel operates then is an

attack on prison conditions – this is the level on which it achieved
what contemporary acclaim it did, satisfying that audience which
looked to London as a partisan of social justice. As in *The Iron
Heel*, the masters are ruthless creatures of no heart: the warden
and prison doctor conspire, in violation of California law, to
torture Standing with up to one hundred hours straight in 'the
jacket' in order to get him to tell the location of the suspected
dynamite. Also as in *The Iron Heel*, the hero relentlessly beards
the oppressor – 'You've the heart of a rabbit', he sneers at the
warden[18] – and keeps up his struggle to the bitter end with
unwavering defiance. Unlike in *The Iron Heel*, however, he
identifies directly, on a comrade basis, with his fellow 'people of
the abyss'. Ed Morrell and Jake Oppenheimer, both denizens of
San Quentin's death-row in actuality, are Standing's companions
in crucifixion; and in the course of their weird acquaintance
Standing comes to regard these who are 'deemed by the world as
the very bottom-most of the human cess-pool' to be 'great spirits'
marked by 'all cardinal traits of right humanness', 'faithful and
loyal', 'brave', 'capable of self-sacrifice', and possessed of 'splendid
minds' (36–7).

'Strong minds,' Standing avers, 'are never docile'; and, when
their fellow is subjected to the strait-jacket, Morrell and
Oppenheimer risk further punishment themselves by undertaking
to communicate with him through a sort of Morse code of tapping
on their cell-walls. Using this method, Morrell is able to impart the
secret of how to survive the jacket by the mental trick of making the
body seem to die. Here enters the second level on which the novel
operates, as a fantasy on the power of mind over matter. Slowly,
starting with the extremities and working toward the centre,
Standing is able to put his body to sleep. Time and space undergo
'an enormous extension'; the walls of the cell recede until it
becomes 'like a vast audience chamber'; the heart beats seem to
cease; and, suddenly,

> with flashings of light, I was off and away . . . I had vaulted
> prison roof and California sky, and was among the stars . . . clad
> in frail, fleece-like, delicate-colored robes that shimmered in
> the cool starlight . . . bound on vast adventure, where, at the
> end, I would find all the cosmic formulae and have made clear
> to me the ultimate secret of the universe . . . the ineffable goal of
> infinite wisdom.   (78–9).

Here enters the third and major theme of the novel: the Faustian pursuit of knowledge. Like Goethe's hero, Standing is seeking in defiance of his mortal limitations amoral–immortal life beyond space and time. The novel now becomes a dream-book, relating sequentially a history of man, with Standing projected into personae from before Christ to the present. Here there are anticipations of Joyce's intention in *Finnegans Wake* to explore dream-space and recapitulate history via the fantasies of Earwicker. There are also suggestions, yet more prominent, of Jung's theories of archetypes and of the racial unconscious. Indeed, toward the end of his experience Standing prefaces a sweeping recollection of his most primitive incarnations with this Jungian quote from Pascal: 'In viewing the march of human evolution, the philosophic mind should look upon humanity as one man, and not as a conglomeration of individuals' (284).

Like a character in the ideal realms of Symbolist fantasy, Villiers's Axël or Huysmans's Des Esseintes, Standing finds reality painful: 'My aeons of star-wandering were aeons of dread', he says of the experience of returning to consciousness (80). Paradoxically he begins to long for the jacket; and he becomes irate when a San Francisco newspaper '(seeking, as every newspaper and as every commercial enterprise seeks, a market that will enable it to realise a profit)' promotes an investigation of prison conditions which results in abandoning its use (274). Eventually, however, he discovers that the tricks he learned through torture he can now perform virtually at will. And so, liberalism having proved meddlesome where oppression has ironically proved instructive in self-liberation, he is free once again to 'roam throughout time'. Where does he roam? First he becomes a French swordsman of the late Middle Ages, given to spouting such Nietzscheanisms as 'God is dead', raging with 'the red wrath' when calumniated by an Italian opponent, and playing in general the heroic cynic whose regard for the mass is as scornful as that of Coriolanus. Next, in a swift incarnation that anticipates a future one, he is a cave-dwelling child in a Middle Eastern desert, surrounded by imagery suggesting the Book of Revelation. For a time he is a young Mormon going west with wagon-trains, surrounded by patriarchal figures of authority, risking his life to deliver messages in a battle with the Indians. Then he is a blond-haired blue-eyed 'splendid figure' of an English seacunny who, stranded in the Orient, wins a king's daughter through feats of strength, lives for some years as a violent autocrat, then loses his kingdom through hubris and chicanery and spends the last forty years of his life in a 'red wrath', plotting revenge. Next he becomes a Viking superman who is a centurion in the Roman army of Judaea, falls in love with a female exponent of Jewish rationalism, and witnesses the crucifixion of Christ. Finally he is a Yankee sailor who alone survives shipwreck in the Antipodes and lives for seven years on a lonely storm-wracked rock through a combination of his own resources and what he interprets as the will of the terrible yet unpredictably benevolent God of his puritan background.

On first reading, one may suspect that London-as-Standing is merely projecting the London hero into various historical situations that he may have wished to live; in which case the novel ends by seeming somewhat self-indulgent. I suspect, however, that London is attempting to show Standing's psychological trans-formation through dreams from self-destructive wrath to control and self-reliance. The emphasis of all the tales, as befits the mind of Standing, is on defiance against great odds and strength of will; but gradually an undercurrent of fellow-feeling seems to grow; and the appearance of the Christ-story and Puritan faith in the last two tales seems a signal development. London was personally proud of this element in the novel and upset that readers seemed to miss it: 'I have read and enjoyed every bit of your book', he wrote to Mary Austin in praise of her neglected *Jesus Christ*; 'I have again and again written books that failed to get across. ... It is a very bone-head world. ... Heavens, have you read my "Christ" story? ... [*The Star Rover*] has been praised for its red-bloodedness and no mention has been made of my handling of the Christ situation. ... Those who sit alone must sit alone.'[19] Are we to suppose from this that the creator of Wolf Larsen and Ernest Everhard was gravitating, like some of his European contemporaries, toward 'the foot of the cross'? A letter to his daughter Joan from this period indicates tendencies in this direction: 'Christ was a big man ... not a little person in a little place in a little portion of the world. ... If in studying out these simple problems I gave you, you come to the wrong conclusion and elect for yourself to become a little person in a little portion of the world it will be a great misfortune.'[20] The high moral tone, tinted with shades of resignation, became more characteristic of London in later years; and an ascent of Christianity in his values would not have been inharmonious with his public movement toward pastoralism and universality, nor with his physical pain and his growing conviction that as an artist he was being misunderstood. Though he does not intervene to rescue Christ from crucifixion, the Viking persona of that tale in *The Star Rover* is spiritually touched by the 'regal' stoicism of His suffering: 'The serenity of Jesus in the heart of the tumult and pain became my serenity' (231).

The Star Rover ends, more characteristically for London, on these three notes: the oneness of the individual with all his evolutionary incarnations, and of all mankind, including the oppressors, whom in other lives he has numbered himself among; the anagogical power of woman through all time – Corn Goddess, Ishtar, Sheba, Cleopatra, Esther, Hérodias, Mary the Madonna, Mary the Magdalene, Mary the sister of Martha, Martha, Brünnhilde, Guinevere, Iseult, Juliet, Héloise, Nicolete, Eve, Lillith, Astarte, *et al.* (304); the indestructibility of 'THE SPIRIT TRIUMPHANT': 'Here I close. . . . There is no death. . . . The flesh dies and passes. . . . Spirit alone endures and continues to build upon itself through successive and endless incarnations as it works upward toward the light' (314–15). The passionate final pages of Standing's testament are composed, anticipating the device Cain was to use in *The Postman Always Rings Twice*, in the last hours before the narrator is taken to the electric chair; they break off suddenly, in the manner of *The Iron Heel*. To the end the tone is defiant: 'Morality is a social fund, and accretion through the painful ages . . . "Thou shalt not kill" – piffle! They are going to kill me tomorrow morning. "Thou shalt not kill" – piffle! In the shipyards of all civilized countries they are laying today the keels of dreadnaughts and superdreadnaughts . Dear friends, I who am about to die, salute you with – "Piffle!" ' (311). Readers familiar with the work of B. Traven will notice in this last line the persistent refrain of the Underman hero of *The Death Ship*. He, like Standing, is another of the millions who in the early twentieth century felt themselves to be thrown by the will of some invisible malevolent Kafkaesque 'iron heel' into the abyss, there to live a hopeless cur-like existence, surviving on deceit, defiance, and an unquenchable thirst for revenge, like Thomas Mugridge. Fearing it though he did, London defined this type, the process by which it suffered and survived, and the process – social and individual – by which it might one day hope to transcend. For his socialism London's books were banned in Germany in the 1930s. For his supposed lapse into individualism his books were discounted by

American Marxist critics. For his lifelong devotion to the
Underman and 'THE SPIRIT TRIUMPHANT' London deserves better
recognition.

II   WOMAN, RACE AND THE LAND

London is Wagnerian in his romanticism. Women stand at the end,
as the destiny of his heroes, in nearly all his major novels, just as the
Sentas and Isoldes and Brünnhildes stand at the end of Wagner's
great works, providing their codas: their maternal benedictions of
peace, goodness and rest. Like Sieglinde to Siegmund, London's
women provide the spark to his heroes' heroism. Woman's
devotion allows man to become woman's saviour–redeemer, and
woman in this way functions as the saviour–redeemer of man. The
'other' is the mirror in which the self can perceive the perfectibility
of its spirit. Marriage is looked toward as a state of joy, equality
and partnership in which both man and woman gain reason to
dedicate themselves more wholly to realisation of individual, dual,
familial, collective and racial strength. In *The Sea Wolf* Van
Weyden comes to life and opposes Wolf Larsen only after Maud
Brewster appears on the *Ghost*. Like Siegfried upon wakening
Brünnhilde, he discovers a fear greater than he has ever imagined
– he is on the threshold of pledging his energy to the well-being of
another, of taking on external responsibility for the first time. His
philosophy has prepared him for this experience, he tell us: '[I] had
always recognised the inevitableness of the love-call. . . . love [is]
the greatest thing in the world, the aim and summit of being, the
most exquisite pitch of joy and happiness to which life could thrill'
(215). Van Weyden remains constant to this idealistic principle;
Maud fulfils his expectations; at the end of the book they sail off
'happily ever after'. London himself remained likewise dedicated
to the principle; and toward the end of his career, through Darrell
Standing as noted, he expressed it with a passion as extreme as that
of Wagner's Tristan:

> I see myself, the one man, the lover, always the lover. . . . There
> is no escaping her, that eternal, splendid, ever-resplendent
> figure of woman. . . . I am no callow ardent youth . . . [but] an
> elderly man, broken in health and body, and soon to die. . . .
> But – and the everlasting, irrefragable fact remains: *her feet*

are beautiful, her eyes are beautiful, her arms and breasts are
paradise, her charm is potent beyond all charm that has ever
dazzled man; and as the pole willy nilly draws the needle, just
so, willy nilly, does she draw man. (289)

The modernist in reaction against romanticism will be quick to
point out that the beloved, thus defined, can become Nemesis as
well as inspiration. Van Weyden's fear in the presence of Maud
Brewster suggests a subconscious wariness of this fact, as does
Standing's curiously left-handed phrase 'there is no *escaping* her'
(italics mine). Many critics, especially the socialists, have seen
London's dedication to Charmian, his personal repository for a
romanticism equally extreme, as the destructive element in his
career. Richard O'Connor cites Charmian's physical competitive-
ness, superior health, and latent professional jealousy as factors
that may have sapped London's confidence.[21] Sinclair sees the
abandonment of the cruise of the *Snark* as the point when London,
having to acknowledge Charmian's superior capacity for 'adventure', began his decline.[22] Sinclair, delving further, tells of a
recurrent nightmare of Nemesis in London's later life: 'He saw in
this dream an imperial figure, inexorable as destiny and yet
strangely human, descending a cascade of staircases, while he
looked up at it and waited to be vanquished.'[23] And O'Connor
makes much of the fact that London once stated that he would like
to write a memoir entitled *Jane Barleycorn*, which would do for the
deceits and perfidies of woman what *John Barleycorn* (1913) had
done for the evils of alcohol.[24] With his obsessive antipathy for
Charmian, O'Connor may well have missed a minor strain of
misogynist humour here, a strain perhaps emphasised in London's
later years by his association with the all-male Bohemian Club; nor
has O'Connor managed to take into account the natural presence
of some querulous strain in most men who have loved women
ardently all their lives. What of James Joyce? of Wagner? of D. H.
Lawrence? Compared to this last, for example, London seems
remarkably constant in his romantic dedication to women. Nor
does he anywhere in his works suggest the hysterical fear and
contempt that sometimes overpowers Lawrence – the attack on
Lady Ottoline Morrell in *Women in Love*, to wit. The closest
London ever comes to an actual fear of woman overpowering man
is in the extended trepidation of Elam Harnish in the first half of
Burning Daylight; but this is in fact a set-up for Harnish's

redemption from ruthlessness by Dede Mason, one of the most pro-woman developments in the opus.

London was not so starry-eyed that he could not depict romanticism going sour; but in the novels where this occurs the fault is arguably predominantly the man's. The heroes of *Martin Eden* and *The Mutiny of the Elsinore* are both aesthetes. As such, they are extreme in their attachment to the romantic ideal, dedicated to Love rather than a real beloved. The women they fix on are embodiments of the bourgeois culture they aspire to master in their art. Ruth Morse in *Martin Eden* fails to live up to her lover's expectations when she proves more dedicated to the bourgeois than the art. Margaret West in *The Mutiny* manages through force of events to sustain an association, but it is clear that this is fated to break down as soon as the events change. 'Sad it is to end love with lies', the aesthete hero, Pathurst, opines; 'sadder still is it to begin love with lies.'[25] Wrongly condemned as his worst novel, *The Mutiny* is certainly London's most ironic, and Pathurst and Margaret his one really odious couple. The point, which careless readers have missed, is how the effete children of an oligarch order can grow into oppressors even more ruthless than their forbears. Students of the epoch of Huysmans to Proust will recognise Pathurst as a decadent who feeds off capitalist excess and lives life as an exercise in aesthetic sensation. He claims to be weary and wary of women, who hunt men 'with quite the same blind tropism that marks the pursuit of the sun by the sunflower' (57). At the same time, he is infatuated with an image of those beautiful women who are ignorant that there could be anything on earth more important or desireable than themselves. Believing that Love is the one great achievement, Pathurst decides to relieve the boredom of the long sea-journey by cultivating Margaret. Like Dorian Gray with Sybil Vane, he is disappointed by her shortcomings as an artist – she is a poor pianist rather than a bad actress. But he reads her Arthur Symons's 'Daughters of Herodias'. And, when the crew finally mutinies, he finds her a help in working up to a high pitch of '*iron-heeled*' brutality. As Pathurst takes on the role of the oppressor, Margaret assumes that of Lady Macbeth. She 'gurgles low laughter in [his] ear' as they triumph (395). The final tableau shows them laughing 'shamelessly and loudly' on the forecastle as the crew returns to its 'work-beast' existence below.

The Mutiny's particular interest in the opus derives from the way it echoes and undercuts several of London's most characteristic formulae. One of these is the progression of the overcivilised aesthete through tests of violence to potent, active, full-blooded manhood. The pattern was set out with Van Weyden in *The Sea Wolf*; and, as in that novel, the progression typically involves association with a brave woman. Sinclair has suggested that when feeling strong London wrote novels about individuals and supermen, and when feeling weak about socialism and the necessity for collective action.[26] *The Iron Heel*, by all odds a work of strength, demonstrates the error of this contention; there may be something, however, in Sinclair's characterisation of a strong versus a weak London. More accurately, we might point to an active versus passive London – a 'yang' versus 'yin' London, if you will – and go on to suggest that the first was dominant in the great manly novels – *The Sea Wolf, Martin Eden, Burning Daylight, The Star Rover* – and the second in the more female-oriented outings – *A Daughter of the Snows* (1902), *Adventure* (1911), *The Valley of the Moon,* and *The Little Lady of the Big House* (1916) – though this last, as I shall discuss, is a complex and unique case. Characteristically, these 'yin' books find London in his most idealistic 'happily-ever-after' vein, and they follow directly upon works which by contrast find him at his most autobiographical and realistic: *Adventure* was written immediately after *Martin Eden*, for instance; *The Valley* after what one critic has called the 'sequel' to *Martin Eden*,[27] the self-revelatory *John Barleycorn*. It is almost as if, with his most fully integrated male persona having just been expressed, London were able to relax, let his masculine ego drift, and focus his imagination on the muse, the anima, the feminine stirring in his nature – that vision of the heroic young woman which had compelled him since his initial, imperfect novelistic outing.

A Daughter of the Snows follows this pattern in that it comes after the realistic, manly tales of the Klondike. Its heroine, Frona Welse, embodies the principle that would be common to all London's heroines: 'I stand, not for the new woman, but for the new womanhood.'[28] No suffragette nor sister of the nascent career-woman, no society-queen of Europe or the American East, Frona is a creature unique to the frontier ethic from which she springs: a rugged and dauntless daughter of the wilderness. 'In the young Northland, frosty and grim and menacing, men stripped off the sloth of the south and gave battle greatly. ... And so it is not well for women, born south of the fifty-three and reared gently, to knock loosely about the Northland, unless they be of great heart' (202). Unlike her city-bred rival, Lucile, who recalls the vaudeville queens and whores-with-hearts-of-gold of the popular Gold Rush tradition, Frona can hike the trails, run the rapids, and brave the winters as cheerfully and resourcefully as the best of men. She is identified with the good earth (having no mother, she 'nursed at the breast of nature'), and with a father on whom she dotes, in this case a well-known and respected fur-trader. Hearty as she is, she is nevertheless feminine and attractive to men. Ultimately, she finds herself torn between a ruthless man's man and an overcivilised Yale graduate struggling to progress to full manhood; and, characteristically for this type of London woman, she chooses the civilised idealist, suspecting that the amoral brutality of the other would eventually 'cheapen' her (333). In the pattern of the novel Frona's choice suggests marriage, but all along she has eschewed this institution in favour of 'comradeship' (297). Like Wagner's Brünnhilde, she is fearful of being possessed and restrained by any mortal master; for, like that favourite of Wotan's Valkyrie daughters, she sees herself above all as heiress to the heroism of her ancient Germanic forbears: 'We are . . . Vikings, and the earth is our heritage. Let us arise and go forth!' (84).

Frona Welse was criticised by contemporaries as being offensively and unbelievably rugged; she is scorned by later critics as being a receptacle for London's youthful dreams of woman and his racist doctrines. Perhaps because *A Daughter of the Snows* owed a good deal to Bret Harte and other models, London concurred that it was not a completely successful work. Still, its themes remained dear to him, and eight years later he attempted them again in the more menacing setting of Melanesia. Joan Lackland, whose Christian name curiously is that of London's own daughter, is shipwrecked on an island where David Sheldon, 'a very sick white man' of English extraction, is trying to master his 'two hundred niggers' and turn the jungle into a successful coconut plantation.[29] Joan wears a Baden-Powell hat and a Colt .45, both *de rigueur* for London himself in later life. Like her creator, Joan has a hot temper and grey eyes. Ardent seeker for 'romance' and 'adventure', she was born in Hawaii and brought up by a restless frontier-seeking father, whom she doted on but lost in the shipwreck. As a young girl, Joan was a tomboy and learned to ride and shoot before being sent for her education at Mills College in California, where she spurned her overcivilised classmates.

Though capable of nursing and cooking for Sheldon, and described as 'hopelessly and deliciously feminine', Joan is prejudiced against Englishmen, wants only to be a planter, and despises the idea of marriage. 'Some spot where I shall escape the indignity of being patronised and bossed by the superior sex' is what she is seeking (117); but, because Sheldon is 'enervated' by the climate and 'a muddler' by nature, she offers her 'good American hustle' to his enterprise. We have here a confrontation between the female embodiment of the most Far Western ethic and the male representation of the most Eastern (in the Anglo-Saxon context) social values. Sheldon proposes that, if Joan is to stay, she must either marry him or find a chaperone. 'Mine was a business proposition', Joan indignantly retorts; 'I wonder if somewhere in this world there is one man who could accept me for a comrade' (159).

For Sheldon Joan has a long way to go before she will become a proper woman. He describes her as 'more a boy than a girl', a 'female Shelley', guilty of the 'logic of youth' which 'always runs up smash against the facts of life' (164). Joan, with her 'soul that doesn't yearn for a man for a master', avers that Sheldon would have to be 'trained' before she could conceive of him as an acceptable husband, i. e. 'one who considered his wife was just as much an individual as himself and just as much as a free agent' (288). This confrontation takes on an almost Lawrentian dimension when complicated by the appearance of an 'adventurer' named Tudor, who is an embodiment of the swash-buckling, world-wandering London hero and, as such, superficially the man to meet Joan's zest for romance. 'Two men and a woman', the young London had written in *A Daughter*; 'the most potent trinity of factors in the creating of human pathos and tragedy!'[30] In *The Little Lady* he was to explore this 'trinity' to its tragic conclusion, and *Adventure* anticipates the development. By the fact Sheldon has warned her about – that she stays on the island unchaperoned and unwed – Joan leaves herself open to rough advances by Tudor, who turns out to be a blackguard. Joan is dumbstruck. Sheldon is forced to confront her assailant. The latter, with his zest for the violent and anachronistic, proposes that Sheldon and he fight a duel by stalking each other through the jungle. For Sheldon this is the fearful yet unavoidable moment of initiation into full manhood. Tudor tries hunting-tricks to snare his prey and proves that he would kill if given the chance. Sheldon, however, through superior instinct for survival, wins this 'most dangerous game'.

Bringing the wounded Tudor back to camp, he 'sneers' to Joan: 'Romantic, isn't it?' (367). Joan is chastened. She forswears her immature lust for 'adventure' and agrees to marry Sheldon – though not because he has 'won' her, she clarifies, but because she has loved him in secret ever since their 'man-to-man' talks, and because he has always exhibited a 'coolness' which reminds her of her father.

It may be contended that this development is more patriarchal than feminist, and that *Adventure* anticipates a tendency that was to become more apparent in London's later years. This might be considered further in the light of *The Little Lady*. Meanwhile, I would submit that London was not, like Lawrence, a proponent of women's liberation through sexual initiation into the primitive; rather he sought to show that the spirit, strength and zest for masculine adventure which he admired in women had to be bound by certain limitations if the values of civilisation were to be maintained. As with Maud Brewster and Van Weyden, all is ultimately a question of survival; and paradoxically, when it comes to the sub-theme of *Adventure*, race, it is primitive brutality on the part of Sheldon rather than the instinctive liberalism of Joan which becomes the saving factor. Brought up in the racial harmony of Polynesia, Joan believes that habits of trust and kindness will obviate racial tension. Sheldon, however, warns that these Melanesians are 'niggers . . . lower than in Africa' (97), and events are again to prove him correct. With the same blithe courage that provokes her to commandeer a ship and procure needful provisions for the plantation, Joan rides out unarmed to a remote spot of jungle the Melanesians are clearing and finds herself confronted by the murderous plot of a worker whom she has punished previously. Through luck and daring, she escapes with her life. Later, when a party goes deep in the jungle to find the culprit, she discovers with a horror what Sheldon already knows: the people of this island are among the most primitive of mankind, decorating their huts with the shrunken heads of white men, torturing their own for obscure petty reasons, feasting off human entrails with cannibalistic zest. These things disgust Joan and contribute to her disillusionment with unrestrained 'adventure'. They confirm the motif of 'the inevitable white man' which marks all London's South Sea tales: '[We have] to rule, I suppose. . . .

Blind destiny of race ... land robbers and sea robbers from remotest time. It's in our blood, I guess, and we can't get away from it' (104).

Joan Lackland's lesson on race is not a happy one, nor has the question of race been the happiest element in her creator's reputation. Critics have dismissed entire novels for what they regard as this alternately sentimental and savage aberration in London's thinking. The prejudice may have contributed to the fact that, apart from the dog stories, London's works have not been reprinted widely or considered seriously in America for most of this century. London belongs to that school which, following the theories of Darwin and Spencer, believed in an evolutionary hierarchy of races: the northern Europeans had conquered the world not merely because they were the strongest but also because they were the most adept at science, the most advanced in law and institutions, the most cultured artistically and civilised. Considered from this point of view, it is ironic that London's books were burnt in Nazi Germany. Even his most left-wing book, *The Iron Heel*, with its emphasis on the world-dominating intentions of a WASP Establishment ready to scapegoat the Germans, suggests affinities with National Socialism. His affection for the Jews alone among non-Nordic races is of course out of line with the racism which swept Europe; but many other more prominent tendencies do in fact anticipate Hitler: his Nietzschean attraction to the blond Superman; his obsession with the wolf as a personal symbol; his early celebrations of primitive strength and comradeship; his later emphasis on Aryan oneness, as in the long chromatic speeches at the end of *The Star Rover*; his personal myth of struggle from lower-class degradation and bohemianism in the cities to quasi-lordship amidst admiring guests and retainers at a beauty-spot in the country; his brand of paternalistic maleness laced with a curiously feminine and homoerotic nostalgia and with yearning for *Das Ewig Weibliche* of the German Romantic dream. It is intriguing to speculate whether the immense popularity of London's books may not have been one of the factors which deceived the Nazi *Führer* into thinking that the American people would never wage war against his millennarian regime.

This is another matter that might be considered further in the light of *The Little Lady*. Meanwhile, as to race theory in the novels, especially as it is expressed through the women, we turn to Saxon Brown, heroine of *The Valley of the Moon* and perhaps

London's most fully realised heroine. Saxon alone among London's heroines is motivated by exemplary women: an old Hispano-Californian named Mercedes Higgins schools her in the lore of wifeliness and sex; a widowed farmer named Mrs Mortimer later schools her in how to make a livelihood out of the land. These associations with surrogate-mother guides are foreshadowed by the motif of Saxon's love for her real mother, now dead. Mrs Brown was a pioneer who came to the 'promised land' in a covered wagon. No mere rude settler, she was well-educated and penned a book of poetry which gained some renown. She also apparently shared in the romantic yearnings for a grander past which characterised the waning nineteenth century. She gave her daughter a name invested with an heroic lore of which the young woman is exceedingly proud: 'The Saxons were a race of people . . . wild, like Indians, only they were white', Saxon tells Billy Roberts when she first meets him.[31] 'They had blue eyes, and yellow hair, and they were awful fighters', she goes on to this blue-eyed blond young god of Scandanavian stock, who also happens to be a prize-fighter. 'They were the first English, and you know the Americans came from the English . . . all the Americans that are real Americans, you know, not Dagoes and Japs and such.' From the innocent poetic romanticism of her mother to the trumpet-call for racial regeneration is the movement of Saxon's sentiment. The 'promised land' for which her mother suffered the hardships of the pioneer journey is now being slowly taken away from her race by the coercion of absentee capitalists in the cities, the industry of immigrant ethnics on the land, and the hubris of the race itself. 'It's a great country', says one of the few successful WASP farmers Saxon and Billy encounter; 'But we're not a great people . . . crowded out and sitting on the stoop . . . [while] the immigrant, who has learned in a hard school, beats [us] out' (365).

By rekindling the ancient impulse that made the race great, Saxon dreams that she and Billy may succeed against the weight of factors grinding their kind down. Saxon's dream takes imagistic form from an engraving she finds in the chest of drawers her mother brought over the plains: 'Between bold headlands of rock and under a gray cloud-blown sky, a dozen boats, long and lean and dark, beaked like monstrous birds, were landing on a foam-whitened beach. . . . The men in the boats, half-naked, huge-muscled and fair-haired, wore winged helmets . . . and they were leaping, waist-deep, into the sea-wash. . . . Opposed to them

... were skin-clad savages' (102–3). Saxon sees Billy among these heroes 'leaping past ... sword in hand'. Her attraction to him is intimately tied to this secret, mother-begotten, racial vision. 'The striking blondness, the face, the eyes ... somewhere out in the ruck of those warring races had emerged Billy's ancestors.' Billy himself, unlike Corliss or Sheldon or Pathurst, is not an overcivilised aesthete representing the result of a history of racial success but a strong and simple working-man of honest values, who finds himself chained to a life of dog-eat-dog work-beastism by factors beyond his ken and control. His manhood needs not be established so much as saved. Again, it is the strong woman who provides the spark; and in her intuition of the land as the means of salvation, Saxon again draws her strength from the racial vision:

> Again she identified Billy as one of the Vikings, and pondered ... on the strange wanderings of the seed. ... Always had her race been land-hungry, and she took delight in believing she had bred true; for had not she, despite her life passed in a city, found same land-hunger in her? ... Was she not going forth to satisfy that hunger, just as her people of old? ... She remembered her mother's tale of how the promised land looked to them through the early winter snows of the Sierras to the vast and flowering sun-land of California. (297)

Recent critics have deplored the way Saxon and Billy draw strength from their prejudice against the 'Porchugeeze' and 'Japs' who have supplanted white farmers in the San Joaquin Valley; also the way they applaud their eventual success in terms of race-competition: 'Them San Leandro Porchugeeze ain't got nothin' on us when it comes to intensive farmin'' (517). But by the laws of realism which govern this most Naturalistic of London's novels, the emotions are neither surprising nor out of line. London himself had little time for critics; and it is not hard to imagine how he might have responded to disparagers observing from their ivory towers of the East, secure in the patronage of capitalist masters and committed to almost propagandistic tenets of liberal orthodoxy. The facts of the matter as London saw them were that America was increasingly filling up with immigrants of a variety of races and becoming a land of competition. That this competition should be expressed on a racial as well as individual basis seemed not only natural but good; for collective identification, on racial as much as

on class grounds, gave the individual a strength he was fatally
lacking on his own. Nowhere was this more apparent than among
the proletariat; and it is entirely credible that Saxon and Billy
should find their way from the urban *inferno* to a congenial version
of the pastoral through the guidance of those few of their kind who
either had not lost it in the first place or had found their way back
previously by a similar process. In terms of the multi-racial
superego America went on to develop in the twentieth century, this
form of expressionism would come to seem inadmissible. But
celebration of race and the triumph of one's own in the
competition among many has been a leitmotiv of European
literature since well before Shakespeare. And from this point of
view Saxon's desire to blend racial coherence and glory with the
sense of place might seem no less moving, nor noble even, than
John of Gaunt's paean to the soil of England.

   The pathos in Saxon's desire and the error in London's
sentimental attachment to Anglo-Saxon *virtù* derive from the
inexorable fact that, in a quickly shrinking world, such impulses
were 'beating back against the current'. Grounded in dreams of
the past, they were ultimately insupportable, impractical, and
romantic. When held *in extremis*, they could only lead to
holocaust and self-immolation. Devotion to racial tradition might
give strength, but it could also close the devotee off from the world.
In this sense, Saxon's and Billy's retreat to 'the valley of the moon'
is, as much as London's own, an expression of the quest for an
'ivory tower'.[32] The reader familiar with Henry James might
consider in this connection that Master's recoiling from the new
immigrant America chronicled in *The American Scene*, which is
roughly contemporaneous. James's response was to turn back to
England, where the race was still largely homogeneous and issues
of competition could be avoided substantially. London, coming
from an opposite background and class, was not able to 'beat out
his exile' in the mother country, where his dream of past glories
might have been tolerated better; nor, apart from the interlude of
The People of the Abyss, did he ever make the attempt. London
was a Californian born and bred. He loved his homeland with as
much ardency as his romantic nationalist precursors and
contemporaries in the new nations of continental Europe. The
difference was that London did not have a coherent nation to
dedicate this feeling toward. America seemed too big, run by the
alien entrenched oligarchy of the East, and flooding with others to

whom he could feel little racial or historical affinity. California, alas, was only one part of that nation – half pioneer homestead, half imperialist outpost; nascent haven, it seemed, for every would-be capitalist held out of money and power in the East; land where the natives, lulled by a temperate climate into visions of an orderly healthy pastoral, were prevented by land-grabbing and competition from establishing an indigenous identity and ploughed under by the energetic, malcontent waves driven west upon their shores.

London's racism should be seen in this light. It is the fear of the native of being swamped; of being bereft of a pastoral dream he has glimpsed but cannot hold. The analogy is to the plight of the most original native American, and Saxon also perceives this:

> Looking at [Billy's] moody face, [she] was suddenly reminded of a lithograph . . . of a Plains Indian, in paint and feathers, astride his horse and gazing with a wondering eye at a railroad train rushing along. . . . The Indian had passed, she remembered, before the tide of new life. . . . And were Billy and his kind doomed to pass, she pondered, before this new tide of life, amazingly industrious, that was flooding in from Asia and Europe? (438)

There is an echo here of the fear of Avis Everhard, who also retreats to 'the valley of the moon', of being drowned by the 'people of the abyss' who flood the streets of Chicago in the finale of *The Iron Heel*. As Avis's case shows, this fear was held in balance with a conscientious partisanship for the Underman. Reading this fear back against London's racism, one begins to realise that it is not so much a matter of specific racism as a general human repugnance for the unleashing of the primitivism of the horde. *Adventure*, branded specifically racist, does not in fact turn doctrinaire until Joan Lackland, the defender of trust and kindness, is attacked by a mob-minded group of blacks; nor are these blacks seen to be without reason for their resentment, nor is the racial conflict that ensues seen in a glorious or romantic light. *The Mutiny of the Elsinore* does not become overtly racist until the crew revolts, and again there is ample good reason for their revolt; nor is the 'iron-heeled' contempt of Pathurst seen in anything like a sympathetic light. *The Mutiny*, it might be noted, was written about a voyage London took following a three-month stay in New

York, his longest ever in that city; and the theme of a multiracial 'gangster' class overpowering Yankee oligarchs may reflect a neurosis which he, like James, perceived in the immigrant-cramm-ed metropolis. *The Valley of the Moon* was finished during the same voyage, and the racial fear it expresses may also have been influenced by the months spent in New York.

London was by no means so racially motivated that he would always portray his Anglo-Saxons as heroes and others as inferior villains. Sinclair has pointed out how in the South Sea tale 'Mauki' an Aryan trader is cast as an inhuman brute, while the native boy is seen to have superior instincts for reality, beauty and survival.[33] Numerous examples from the Klondike and Hawaiian tales show London casting Indians or islanders in sympathetic roles, and the hero of *Burning Daylight* is referred to so frequently in terms of his likeness to an Indian that there is some confusion as to whether he is actually a full-blooded white man. Jews, as I have mentioned, were dear to London, though he recognised always their differences in culture and values, as can be seen in *The Wace–Kempton Letters* (1902), written with Anna Strunsky, and in the Jewish versus Nordic dialectic of the Christ-tale of *The Star Rover*, in which Strunsky is romanticised as Miriam. The Jewish surrogate parents of the heroine of *The Game* (1905), though not free of the small-mindedness of petty merchants, are warm and humane. So too is the hero's Portuguese landlady in *Martin Eden*; so too, as noted, the Hispano-Californian gypsy woman in *The Valley*. To no minority under-race was London ever so hostile as to the lean, pale, tight-lipped exemplars of the Eastern WASP ruling-class. These are detested by their fellow-capitalists even, the Californians Harnish and Forrest. Still, they can win the grudging admiration of London: Pathurst reveres what he ironically dubs the 'Samurai' quality in the Yankee captain, Nathaniel West, of the *Elsinore*. In sum, London's 'prejudice' is mitigated by his integrity as an artist. As he wrote to a Jewish publication soliciting a sympathetic statement on the place of Jews in English literature,

> I have made villains, scoundrels, weaklings, and degenerates of Cockneys, Scotchmen, Englishmen, Americans, Frenchmen, Irishmen, and I don't know what others. . . . I have no recollec-tion of having made a Jew serve a mean fictional function. . . .

But it is as unfair for a writer to make villains of all races except the Jews, as it is to make villains only of Jews. . . . Being a socialist, I subscribe to the Brotherhood of Man.[34]

But turning from race back to London's women, let us refocus on that primary association: of woman to the land. We have seen this with Avis Everhard, whose love of her Sonoma sanctuary is contrasted with her horror at urban conflict. We have seen it, if less dramatically, in Frona Welse and Joan Lackland, whose identities are linked with the far outposts where they were born. We can see it above all with Saxon Brown, whose conversion to the idea of return to the land is presented in terms of a religious experience. Oppressed by the class-struggle of the city, which threatens Billy's job and their ability to survive, Saxon wanders along the Oakland Estuary and questions the universe:

> She could not understand . . . a world in which some men possessed so much food that they threw it away, paying men for their labor of spoiling it before they threw it away. . . . She was one of the stupid. She must be. . . . Yet the sun was good; the wind was good, as was the keen salt air in her nostrils. . . . All the natural world was right. . . . It was the man-made world that was wrong. (253–4)

As the natural world is right, then God must be good, for He created it. The idea that He might also be responsible for the botch of the man-made world threatens to throw Saxon into 'the morass of pessimism' or the belief that God does not exist. But faith is essential. 'As long as God was, there was always a chance for a miracle. . . . With God missing, the world was a trap.' God must exist, then, but He is remote. As for the Christian, there must be a flesh-and-blood intercessor. 'Christ was a socialist', one of Billy's union cohorts remarks (257). In the light of the industrial conflict which has thrown Billy in jail, this can hardly satisfy Saxon. A different 'Christ' is needed. Finally, again as she walks along the Estuary, Saxon discovers him: a version of Jack London as a very young man, 'slender . . . frail . . . with sunburned freckled face, and large gray eyes that were clear and wistful . . . a child of the people' (261–2).

This intercessor takes Saxon out in a little boat which he, like the young London, has bought for himself and learned to sail, earning his livelihood both within and beyond the law, fishing the oyster-shoals. In the course of conversation he fills Saxon with a sense of peace, possibility, and inspiration.

> Turning his head slowly, he followed the skyline, pausing especially when his eyes rested landward on the brown Contra Costa hills. ... The wistfulness in his eyes was overwhelming and went to her heart. ... 'Don't you sometimes feel you'd die if you didn't know what's beyond them hills an' what's beyond the other hills behind them hills?' ... I've lived in Oakland all my life, but I'm not going to live in Oakland the rest of my life, not by a long shot.'   (263-4)

The lesson for Saxon is clear: the city is 'just a place to start from'. By unearthing the ideal vision buried under layers of city frustration, she and Billy *will* find a better life somewhere. When Billy returns from jail, the 'silk' of his young body bruised and the quick of his spirit dulled by brutal treatment, Saxon sets out to restore the sense of possibility in him. She takes him to a picture-show one evening. A rural drama situated somewhere in America's heartland follows a cowboy-film and a French comedy. A farmyard scene, domestic tranquillity, the sun blazing down through the clear air – these things charm Billy as much as Saxon. Preparing to find the rural dream themselves, he sings the old song on which the movie ended – an expression, as country music so often is, of the lost soul of the American peasantry:

> O treat my daughter kind-i-ly
> An' say you'll do no harm,
> An' when I die I'll will to you
> My little house an' farm ....
>
> We'll have a little farm
> A pig, a horse, a cow,
> And you will drive the wagon,
> And I will drive the plow.   (287-8)

The land is redemptive, to both body and soul – this is the message as well of the novel which preceded *The Valley*, *Burning Daylight*, arguably London's most virtuoso performance and best portrait of his completely mature man and woman. Elam Harnish is a fully-tested hero. He has triumphed over the elements in the Klondike and torn a great fortune from the earth. He has lost the fortune to crooked Eastern financiers and won it back by superior daring. Through ruthless capitalist competition and city life, he has come to lose his health, physical and moral. He is paunchy and weak. His features have taken on signs of 'indulgence, harshness, and brutality' in place of their former 'Indian sharpness'. Life seems to him 'a vast bunco game'; an affair of 'battle, courage, and cocktails' ruled only by Luck, Death, and the zest for Revenge.[35] God is dead; human affairs are ruled by self-interest; the only type who can succeed is the Napoleonic Superman. Like his superman forbear, Wolf Larsen, Harnish is a sick man, diseased with his own ambition. He realises the extent of his disease one day when riding the Sonoma hills to inspect a quarry he has been hoodwinked into buying. Amid 'the air, the scene, the distant sound of larks', he feels 'like a poker player rising from a night-long table and coming forth from the pent atmosphere to taste the freshness of morn' (183). The vaultings of manzanita, madrone and redwood seem to him 'like a church'. Like Saxon Brown, he experiences a religious revelation. A white-bearded man of eighty-four comes down the sunny road with a pail of milk. '[I had] never seen so contented a being', Harnish reflects. Recalling his boyhood in eastern Oregon, he addresses the old one as 'Daddy'. Isn't Daddy lonely in the country? No, the old one replies, he only ever feels lonely in the city. Harnish rides on. He comes on a widow he addresses as 'Mother'. Mother farms Riesling grapes. These she sells for a modest price, only to have them marked up enormously by the middle-men in San Francisco. 'There's a sucker born every minute', Harnish might have thought at any other time. Now the philosophy has a sour taste (196).

Back in the city, he becomes re-embroiled in the speculative rat-race and forgets his revelation. Like Saxon, he needs not only intercession, but also a helpmate; and in his case this must be a woman. Dede Mason works in his office as a stenographer. Well educated, she attracts his attention by correcting his grammar. Curiosity leads him to investigate what she does at the weekends. Finding that she rides in the Berkeley hills, he buys a spirited stallion. Breaking the stallion is his first step to regeneration. Dede Mason, however, proves less than delighted to have her solitary rides intruded upon. She objects to his presence; Harnish counters with a proposal of marriage. Though astounded by his directness

and flattered in her 'sex-vanity', Dede rejects Harnish. 'Birdlike in
her love of individual freedom', she sees life with his type as 'a
future of inevitable stress and storm' (242). Fearing she may lose a
job which is well paid and not disagreeable, she nevertheless ceases
to ride where Harnish might find her. Harnish, however, proves
undaunted. For the first time in his life he has come upon a thing
he wants but cannot easily win, and he persists until Dede is forced
to reveal the moral underpinnings of her rejection:

> You have too much money. . . . It makes you less and less nice
> . . . when you first came down from Alaska . . . you were my
> hero. . . . Now you, a man of the open, have been cooping
> yourself up in the cities. . . . Cruelty is not only in your heart
> and thoughts, but it is there in your face. . . . It would be easier
> to share you equitably with another woman than to share you
> with this business.   (292–3)

Jolted, Harnish remembers the old man in Sonoma. Realising that
the only way to restore himself and win Dede is that pastoral
dream, he declares, 'You are my Lord God, and I'm sure going to
serve you' (319). In an operatic outburst he claims that his old self
is dead and that his old self's brother is proposing marriage. Dede,
perceiving that his will-to-life can be renewed, gives way to this
passion ('You are such a hurricane!'). After the wedding, the
couple retires to a ranch in Sonoma. The lyrical, religious note
sounds again in the landscape. They live happily and simply as
farmers, Harnish's one regret being that he doesn't have Dede to
win over again.

Woman is intimately and inevitably connected with the
regenerative power of the land – this is a dominant motif. Dede
Mason also embodies another motif strong in London's women:
the uplifting power of education, good manners, and what for lack
of a better term might be described as Christian optimism. 'The
surest remedy for the male disease of self-contempt', Nietzsche
wrote, 'is to be loved by a sensible woman.'[36] So much Harnish's
case proves; so much was London's lifelong faith. Also applicable
is Nietzsche's observation: 'When a man is in the midst of *his*
hubbub, in the midst of the breakers of his plots and plans, he sees
there perhaps calm, enchanting beings glide past him, for whose
happiness and retirement he longs – *they are women*.'[37] The love of
peace and beauty, allied to a tenacious will-to-survive and 'Dr

Jordan's precept' of making things work, first seen in Maud
Brewster and later in Joan and Dede and Saxon,[38] make London's
women the ideal complements to the brave, energetic, full-blooded men who might run otherwise to Nietzschean excess. The
civilising, domesticating role of the American pioneer woman
which Lawrence identified in *Studies in Classic American
Literature* as often driving the white male into a sort of
blood-brotherhood with a more primitive and usually dark-skinn-
ed male, has in London, the poet of the closing of the frontier,
become almost wholly a force for the good. Only in Ruth Morse of
Martin Eden is this domesticating principle seen as down-pulling,
anti-courageous; but the turn of the hero of that book toward a
sort of blood-brotherhood with the decadent poet Brissenden, far
from being a solution, only serves to hasten his disillusionment
with life, self-contempt, and suicide. The cult of the male body
offered by Brissenden's successor, Mark Hall of *The Valley*,
attracts Billy Roberts for a time. But Hall's Nietzschean word-
mongering does not lead to happiness; *Blutbruderschaft* is
ultimately infertile; and Billy decides, 'One kiss of [Saxon's] lips is
worth more 'n all the libraries in the world' (411). The love of
women, then, in London's ideal vision, triumphs over the cult of
strength, whether of body or of mind.[39] Woman alone can restore
man's faith in life and in his own soul; lead him from the depths of
dog-eat-dog corruption to the uplands of human fertility.

III *THE LITTLE LADY* AND THE TRADITION

London's first great hero carried his power within himself: the
strong mind and will within the superior body are all Larsen
possesses, and by them he must live and die. London's last great
hero carries his power around and about him. Dick Forrest does
not have the young hero's indestructible body: his legs are scarred
and need to be massaged before he can get out of bed in the
morning. Dick Forrest, however, has the immense advantage of
material mastery: 250,000 acres of the finest farmland in the
world. He has accumulated this neo-feudal empire through
puritan efficiency and the gambler's luck. But he has something
else as well which has given him advantage over capitalist
predecessors such as Elam Harnish: Dick Forrest has birth; he is
heir to a fortune which his father, Lucky Richard Forrest, accrued

in a silver-mining deal in the 1870s. An orphan, young Dick has been brought up by conservative WASP-prototype guardians whose intentions are to train him in the ways of the Iron Heel. But with an adolescent version of the daring that allows Harnish to triumph over the machinations of Eastern financiers, young Dick rebels, goes 'on the road' with a working-class companion, learns 'the mischance of life and faith', the harshness of reality, and the values of comradeship, self-reliance and pluck. Instead of attending university in the normal fashion, the maturing Dick, already 'a man in a hurry', buys his education, cramming three years of learning into one by wining and dining the foremost minds of northern California in his schooner on San Francisco Bay. Purchase of knowledge and draining of other people's minds become leitmotivs of his style in adult life. To reverse the process of land-exhaustion begun by the old 'Bonanza farmers' is his mission. He buys the best land hand-over-fist. He becomes the first in the state to pay $10,000 for a single bull. Proponent of efficiency in use of the land and eugenics in the breeding of livestock, he intends to bring on an era of fertility unmatched since the passing of the Indians. His creed is their 'Song of the Acorn Planter':

> The acorns come down from heaven!
> I plant the short acorns in the valley!
> I plant the long acorns in the valley!
> I sprout, I, the black-oak acorn, sprout, I sprout![40]

The reader will recognise from the initial chapters that *The Little Lady* constitutes a major shift for London. The first signal is the style, which is laconic and tight in a manner contrasting the fluid finale of *The Star Rover*, which preceded. The sentences are short. Attention is to concrete detail. The tone is matter-of-fact and realistic rather than romantic – a modernist style which breaks more completely than London ever had before with the niceties and mannerisms of the nineteenth century, anticipating the 'hard and clear' precepts of Hemingway after Pound and the emphasis on the external and visual which Raymond Chandler would hone to a fine art. We might recall in the progression of London's novels that the realistic breakthrough of the third-person *Martin Eden* succeeded the subjective psychological study of *The Sea Wolf* and the doctrinal fantasy of *The Iron Heel*; that the straight autobiographical memoir of *John Barleycorn* succeeded the celebration of glorified personality in *Burning Daylight* and the intensely personal vision of the pastoral in *The Valley*. Here, following what reveals itself to be a characteristic pattern, a breakthrough to a new form of third-person realism succeeds the ironic first-person fantasy of *The Mutiny* and the even more intensely subjective *Star Rover*. *The Little Lady* belongs to London in that phase where he turns to his own life and considers its facts with the objective cool of 'the vivisectionist'. Critics and contemporaries who recoiled from the book as an embarassing revelation of personal fetishes and fears missed the point entirely, I think. For all his superficial similarities to Jack London the patriarch of the 'Beauty Ranch', Dick Forrest represents a new type belonging to a new culture. He is the Californian who, unlike London, comes from a dynamic and privileged past; who, in spite of his tragic temporal situation, remains the survivor and inheritor of the future. His huge 'Hispano-Moresque' country house, 'planted for a thousand years', is no mere fantasy of a lumpen-proletarian contemporary of Hitler's; nor is his business-empire a mere glorification of London's own ambitions as a rancher. Forrest is the fictional anticipation of William Randolph Hearst with his San Simeon; of Howard Hughes, who turned capitalism into a Napoleonic game of conquest.

As admirers of *Citizen Kane* will remember, Hearst's nemesis was his romantic obsession with Marion Davies. Hughes's 'tragedy' involved an inability to harmonise obsessive adventurism in business with romantic attachment to a female ideal; thus, frustrated affairs with a series of actresses was followed by retreat into solitary eccentricity. London plants Forrest in a dramatic situation involving similar motifs. Dick's wife may be the most overt representation of Charmian ever produced;[41] the fact is irrelevant. Paula Forrest satisfies perfectly the requirements of the fiction: princess in the tower, consort in Dick's neo-feudal majesty, she is the consummate hostess and mistress of a vast pleasure-domain who appears to have all a man could give a woman and yet lacks the thing most necessary to her inner well-being. Her relationship with Dick is not superficial; her love is real, yet forever frustrated by the constraint that Dede Mason fears in a relationship with the capitalist Harnish: the man is wed first and above all to his business. That in innumerable ways, big and small, intervenes between the Forrests. Dick realises the danger. Breakdown of the tenuous personal–professional balance is never far from his mind. To please Paula he performs manifold material obeisances, including constructing a secret garden where life-sized babies carved in pink marble cavort among rare blooms and over an ersatz-Italian fountain. The babies are a symbol – too crude perhaps, as critics complain, but essential to the overall scheme. If only she had a child, Dick thinks, Paula would be fulfilled. Dick, however, the great breeder of livestock and inventor of new fertilisers, has failed in this ultimate task of creation. Paula, as a result, is not impervious to the eventual attraction of other possibilities. Evan Graham, a version of Dick who still has full health and strength and has kept the youth of his romantic spirit alive through travel, adventure, and writing, comes to the ranch. Enter a situation as simple and concrete as any in literature: 'Two men and one woman', the young London had written; 'the most potent of factors in the creating of human pathos and tragedy!'

London, in short, after two imperfect attempts at a similar subject, *A Daughter* and *Adventure* as we have seen, set out, like Lawrence after two failed attempts at *Lady Chatterley*, to write his own definitive version of the conventional adultery-tale. 'It is all sex, from start to finish – in which no sexual adventure is actually achieved or comes within a million miles of being achieved, and in which, nevertheless, is all the guts of sex, coupled with the strength.'[42] The reader will note the sense of propriety character-istic of the author who makes Maud Brewster and Van Weyden treat each other with such incongruous decorum during their escape from the *Ghost*. This sense reigns over the actions of Forrest, Paula and Graham as well – London again is as unlike as like Lawrence, for he would never dream of descending to the truly embarrassing discussions between 'John Thomas' and 'Lady Jane' in the intruded-upon privacy of the gamekeeper's cottage. Still, London was condemned for his direct attention to a sexual subject; also for the substantial baggage of Freudian imagery – Dick's love for his stallion, and his neighing and stomping and singing of 'The Song of the Mountain Lad' being the most remarked-upon instances. 'Erotomania', 'sensualism', 'continence', 'voluptuous', 'desire', 'ingrowing concupiescence' and 'perverted' are words one reviewer used in condemning the book.[43] A personal admirer was more stinging: 'I didn't object to *The Little Lady*', he wrote; 'It's her surroundings and the 300 bulls that gets my goat.'[44] London reacted angrily to the first, contending, 'I am proud, damn proud, of *The Little Lady of the Big House*.' In reply to the second he sent a copy of the more typically ideological and partisan *Star Rover*, by which, in the admirer's eyes, he was 'redeemed'. To the end of his life London maintained that *The Little Lady* was a better book than anyone recognised. But he was not, like Lawrence, so certain of its rightness, or his righteousness, to mount a counter-attack like 'À Propos of *Lady Chatterley*'. Without the notoriety of censorship to provoke extra-literary celebrity, *The Little Lady* quickly became forgotten. Its accomplishment has never been properly vindicated.

In *Martin Eden* London recalls for a moment his early wish to be a musician or poet. In *The Sea Wolf* he shows Wolf Larsen in a rare moment of lyrical appreciation singing a song to the trade-winds. In *The Valley*, as noted, he makes a simple country refrain attend and motivate the pastoral quest of the protagonists. In *The Little Lady*, against the impressive realism of Dick Forrest's empire, London uses music for the first time as a major symbolic and psychological force. Dick, as I have said, has his favourite songs – of the Acorn Planter and the Mountain Lad – which he sings at significant junctures. Evan Graham, an erstwhile troubadour, introduces a song of a gypsy to his beloved, which underlines his freedom as opposed to Dick's land-boundness. Paula above all is associated with music. She is introduced waking 'like a bird, with song' (69); and customarily after dinner she leads her guests out around the piano where, like a heroine in an early novel by Thomas Mann, she plays Schumann or Rachmaninov while some young man turns the pages. Paula has acquired her skill through the best teachers, one of whom comes on designated mornings to join her in cello–piano duets. But, on these evenings performing for the collected, she informs the pieces with a spirit all her own. She doesn't 'play like a woman', Evan Graham reflects; she 'commands the composer' with the same restraint and aplomb with which she presides at her husband's dinner table (104). Dick for his part customarily circumnavigates the room while his wife plays, turning the lights low until there is only a glow around her. The lofty room seems 'to grow loftier', like a 'feast hall in some medieval castle'. It is the classical setting for a tale of love and adultery, a realm redolent of Wagner's *Tristan*. 'Music is the refuge from blood and iron and pounding the table', Dick observes with a Nietzsche-like recognition that the grandeur wants deflating; 'weak souls, and sensitive souls, and high-pitched souls flee from the crassness and rawness of the world to drug-dreams of the over-world of rhythm and vibration.'

Music stimulates Dick and the 'philosophers' he gathers around him to remark with varying degrees of seriousness on the theories of Pater and Wagner and the Greeks, and the musical aesthetics of English poets from Milton to Shelley and Swinburne. Critics have found these passages gratuitous or pretentious; but Forrest's tastes are catholic. He has equal zest for the lofty and the lively, and his musical wife shares it. Her piano playing can change without warning from Beethoven's 'Pathetique' to ragtime to Hawaiian hulas, then give way to recital of a German love-song. The first time Evan Graham hears Paula sing one of these, he discovers 'a sweet voice, a rich voice, with the same warm-fibred thrill of her laugh; but the volume so essential to the great voice was not there' (142). The lack gives a check to Graham's growing ardour. He wonders for a time if Paula may not be more likely to have an affair with one of the young men who turns her pages than with a seasoned lover like himself. He is on the verge of suspecting that her attentions have merely been hostessly coquetry when, half by accident, he finds himself in the music room with her and prevailed upon to sing:

> Back to the road again, again,
> Out of the clear sea track;
> Follow the cross of the Gipsy Trail
> Over the world and back . . . .

Paula, her voice suddenly taking on a bewitching tone, joins in the finale:

> The heart of a man to the heart of a maid
> Light of my tents be fleet –
> Morning waits at the end of the world
> And the world is at our feet.   (180–1)

As in so many novels of the *fin-de-siècle*, music becomes the essential link for the lovers. In a way that anticipates the device James M. Cain was to use to such effect in *Serenade*, it becomes the outward and audible sign of an inward and spiritual transformation. A few days after, Paula and Graham accidentally meet in the

woods. There is a fatal brush, then a kiss. That evening when
Paula is called upon to sing there is 'a new note in her voice', so
Graham reflects; 'fuller, rounder, with a generousness of volume
that had vindicated that singing throat' (216).

The Little Lady anticipates important developments in
twentieth-century fiction, as I shall show presently; but in this use
of music, as in the adultery theme, London is looking over his
shoulder as well. Stepping back across the boundaries of the
adventure–*machismo* genre he had been associated with, he is
attaching himself to the more genteel 'great tradition' of Europe
and the American East.[45] The critics were surprised. It seems
entirely logical, however, considering his career and where he
came from, that London should have wanted to portray the mores
of the nascent post-frontier aristocracy. Late Romantic music and
poetry constituted a soma which this society equated with
civilisation. In terms of the novel this soma becomes a screen
against which psychological transformations are projected, thus
avoiding a need for direct dramatic confrontations of a kind which
might seem evidence of civilisation coming unstuck. Dick hears the
new note in Paula's voice almost before Paula recognises it. While
his philosophers prattle in quasi-Celtic terms about it being thick
and round as 'a great golden rope for the mooring of argosies in the
harbors of the Happy Isles' (231), he drops into the pool of his mind
and, glimpsing from past to future, recognises the potential for
tragedy. 'Once before he had heard her sing like that – in Paris,
during their swift courtship, and directly afterwards, during their
honeymoon' (232). Too gentlemanly and stoical to voice his
suspicion, Dick watches and tests until finally he discovers that the
suspicion must be correct. Paula can sing with new beauty with
Graham in the evening, but the following afternoon she cannot
even read poetry with him. 'In trouble she was', Dick concludes;
'but would she keep this trouble to herself? It had never been her
way. Always, soon or late, she had brought her troubles to him.
But then, he reflected, she had never had trouble of this nature
before. ... On the other hand, he reasoned, there was her
everlasting frankness' (251).

Suddenly, like Athena from the head of Zeus, a new mode
springs from London's art, fully matured; and here is where the
modernism of *The Little Lady* becomes pronounced, for the new
mode is interior monologue. One might think of Eugene O'Neill,
who greatly admired London, and of such a play as *Strange*

Interlude; and more than any other novel of London's *The Little Lady* has dramatic irony. Dick agonises inwardly over the faintest signs dropped between Graham and Paula, while outwardly he continues to laugh and pour cocktails and organise practical jokes for his guests. Graham castigates himself for remaining under Dick's roof; he tries to get away, yet accedes through his deep ambivalence to Dick's hostly protests that he stay. 'Dick had certain rights', Graham rationalises; 'but Paula had her rights. . . . Surely it was the lesser evil to be perfidious to the man than to the woman. . . . Some one would be hurt', he concludes characteristically; 'life was hurt . . . it was nothing new . . . the countless triangles of countless generations had all somehow been solved' (214–15). Paula is caught between the two men, both of whom she loves and both of whom insist she must choose one or the other. As she falls further into quandary, she radiates an ominous new energy: 'She was in a flushed awakening, burgeoning like the full spring all about them, a happier tone in her happy laugh, a richer song in her throat, a warmness of excitement and a continuous energy of action animating her' (261). But this is the quick-burning flame of the impossible secret, the inner fire that consumes the person who harbours it, trying futilely to avoid admitting its existence. 'She persisted in her ardent recklessness, trying not to feel the conscience pricks of her divided allegiance, refusing to think too deeply, riding the top of the wave of her life – as she assured herself, living, living, living.' Living in a constant state of tension between the exposed and the concealed, these characters suddenly become as much embodiments of the 'inward romantic principle' as the creations of Henry James or Marcel Proust.

The greatness of an author depends on the depth of his characters and the complexity of their relationships – so Edmund Wilson contends in *Axël's Castle*: Dostoyevsky is great as his characters are informed from within, Dickens is less great as his characters remain essentially types.[46] Up to *The Little Lady* London's principals are generally ideological types driven toward some predestined transformation and set against a cast of less significant characters sketched largely externally – Martin Eden, the embodiment of existential pessimism and individulism gone bad, set against a petty and deceitful world. *The Sea Wolf* previewed the three types that London would substantially inform from within: the decaying Superman, the strengthening aesthete, and the 'boy–woman'. Apart from the villainous Mugridge, these are all London ever really offered in terms of character; and from this point of view his opus might be fairly criticised. A greater Jack London might have attempted to 'get under the skin' with Ruth Morse in *Martin Eden*, say, or the Eastern financiers in *Burning Daylight*, and thus have expanded his psychological range to more Shakespearean dimensions. The decision to substitute social class for character in *The Iron Heel*, or type for character in *The Mutiny*, is symptomatic of London's overuse of the novel ideologically, analogous to Lawrence's tendency between *Women in Love* and *Lady Chatterley*, and equally damaging to his critical reputation. A defence, behind which London never hid, might be looked for in considerations of century, class and nation: how could London, any more than Lawrence, write psychologically perfected social drama when most of his life he felt threatened by repulsion back into the pit of his origins? The 'great tradition' novel was hardly expected from the new man of the new class of the new country of the new century. When it came, the critics were less willing to applaud the renovation that had brought it forth than to disparage the author for presuming that he had the wit and facility to portray the class, deal with the sort of problem, and use the genre he was supposed to stand against.

F. R. Leavis in *The Great Tradition* numbers the works of Jane Austen, 'Gwendolen Harleth', *The Portrait of a Lady, Hard Times, Nostromo*, and certain works of Lawrence as the finest examples of the novelist's art because, among other things, they present a number of characters at once, all psychologically informed, in a state of balance between conflicting interests, playing out the dialectic between the internal and the external with degrees of civilised grace, pride and humility, self-detection. *The Little Lady* is the first novel in which London consciously attempted something of the kind. There is a new largeness of authorial spirit, a mature consideration, a questing objectivity rather than commitment to imposed directions. There is no villain. Not since *The Sea Wolf* has the male persona been split and questioned so thoroughly. The pursuit of the romantic ego has given way to what now seem more important than individual yearnings: the requirements of social well-being. Forrest and Graham parallel Larsen and Van Weyden; but Forrest as superior man also recognises his shortcomings, and Graham as aesthete recognises that his strengths may come to threaten his friend fatally. Here for the first time are characters who embrace inner contradictions they are trying conscientiously to balance; who perceive and sympathise with the interests of others; who attempt to compromise their own interests and establish limitations when necessary for the general good. 'Anyone can run to excesses', Ezra Pound would quote from Confucius; 'it is hard to stand firm in the middle.'[47] Dick Forrest is above all dedicated to the principle of *making things work*, of finding solutions. Even Graham and Paula Forrest, inflamed as they are by romantic passion, remain committed even more to averting disaster. Their consideration for Dick matches his patience with them. 'When the tale is ended, the reader will take off his hat to each of the three of the trio: "By God! he was some man!" or "By God! she was some woman!"'[48] So London hoped. For, as he went over the novel himself, he believed, 'This is what I've been working toward all my writing life.'

One day some enterprising scholar will discover whether and when F. Scott Fitzgerald read London's last novel, and now much it influenced his works from *The Great Gatsby* to *The Last Tycoon*. Above all one is struck by the similarity between Dick Forrest and Dick Diver, both of whom are trying to cope with a wife devoted alternately to his guidance and to her own freedom; a wife who brings on disaster not so much through adulterous infidelity as through subconscious rebellion against being the captive princess. Paula Destern Forrest is a precursor of the American girl whom Zelda came to typify, both in life and through her husband's glorifications. Daughter of a father whose gambler's pluck won a fortune, Paula was a tomboy who 'was continually guilty of the wildest and most chivalrous things'. Paula was never timid of animals; she was game for any adventure; her 'heart and soul were full of beauty'. As an adolescent she, like Zelda, developed a taste for dancing; but later she turned from dancing to other arts, and finally to music. 'She was not flighty', an aunt explains to Evan Graham; 'her trouble was that she was too talented.' She was the child of promise for whom no activity was barred, for whom any achievement was possible. 'But talent to genius is a far cry', the aunt concludes (183–8); and in adult life we find Paula's talents spread thin between riding, piano-playing, hostessing, embroidering, and raising goldfish. In all her actions there is a touch of the

dilettante's narcissism – even her affairs. She is an insomniac.
Why?

> It is the excitement from immediate events that holds me back
> from the City of Sleep . . . I invite my soul to live over again,
> from the same and different angles, the things that keep me
> from unconsciousness. . . . Take the swimming of Mountain
> Lad [the occasion when Graham first lays eyes on Paula] . . . I
> lived it in reality . . . I lived it as a spectator – as the girls saw it,
> as you saw it . . . I put it to music . . . I chanted it, I sang it –
> epic, lyric, comic. (128–9)

This is delightful, yet ominous; for the narcissistic invention
which may lead to controlled creation on the part of the artist may
lead to the verge of existential abandon on the part of the person
whose creative talents are dispersed and limited to life. Dick
Forrest like Dick Diver like Scott Fitzgerald is in love with the
vitality of such a woman – 'the boy–girl, the child that never grew
up, the grittiest puff of rose-dust that was ever woman' (89). Semi-
consciously he is aware of the danger of excess inherent; still, he
lets this vitality determine his own social code: 'Paula and I have
one magic formula: *Damn the expense when fun is selling*.' With
hubris he adds: 'D'ye know, we've never been gouged on the price
yet.' As with the legendary Gerald and Sarah Murphy, there are
the stream of guests, flow of cocktails, and splash of horseplay.
Graham's first private tryst with Paula takes place in an under-
ground grotto that Dick has built into his swimming-tank in order
to hoodwink newcomers into thinking that some reveller has
drowned. Additional games and pranks read like a list that Fitzgerald might have concocted when a fraternity-boy at Princeton:
the game of strip 'Bean Porridge' that scandalises Graham for a
moment into thinking that Dick would reduce his wife to complete
undress in front of guests; the 'kiss of welcome' which results in the
unsuspecting newcomer getting a glass of water in the face; the
trick camera which is supposed to take snapshots as the guests
dance to pre-jazz on the veranda, but shoots a stuffed snake at
them instead. These all provide low counterpoint to the high
abandon of philosophical repartee over the dinner-table and the
classical recitals of Paula afterwards. All are designed to fulfil the
precept of 'living!' that Dick and Paula embody; to sustain their
semi-mythical reputation among a crowd of *bon vivants*; to render

their domain into a kind of apotheosis of the little cabaret on the Left Bank in Paris which Dick was amusing himself by running when he and Paula first met, two renegades from the responsibilities and privileges of their backgrounds.

The Paris note again previews Fitzgerald. But Dick and Paula left Paris after a brief fling (the cabaret degenerated into an anarchist's club), took a honeymoon around the world in their yacht, and returned to their fixed place in homeland and class to take up those responsibilities. For all their abandon, Dick and Paula are mature enough to have discovered that there is a time and place for work as well as madness. Fun on the ranch is limited by a sacrosanct schedule to the proper times of the day. In this the Forrests' antics contrast with those of the Fitzgeralds. The drinking never runs to excess; the thrill-seeking never takes complete control; the aimlessness that afflicts the Divers and Buchanans does not make its ugly appearance. Where Fitzgerald's characters can become selfish and trivial when driven to excesses of *ennui*, where their *joie de vivre* can teeter on the edge of the psychological abyss, Dick and Paula take genuine pleasure in their pranksterism and perform out of pure exuberance. No longer the whimsical jokesters of the Harte–Twain era, they by no means have become the potentially vicious eat-drink-and-be-merry-for-tomorrow-we-die types who would grow up in the anomie following the First World War. Their author is still the man who, when living under the most inhospitable conditions in the Klondike, determined to put on the genial mask of the 'Malemute Kid', engage all comers in eager conversation, and challenge the endless winter with a stoical code of cheerfulness.[49] The disillusionment of Martin Eden is not here. The American optimist rather than worldly pessimist is the London behind these scenes. This is one element that gives the dénouement of *The Little Lady* tragic stature. As with Wolf Larsen, we are witnessing the defiance of the strong against inevitable suppressions by Fate. London's characters are bigger than their antics. Paula in particular never descends to the spoiled bitchiness that Gloria Patch, Daisy Buchanan, and Nicole Diver would share with their prototype; and, if it is a portrait of Charmian that London paints in Paula, her critics might note that she seems a woman of real feeling and grace.

The Fitzgerald comparison applies in other important ways, with regard to male personae in particular. We have noted the parallel between Dick Forrest and Dick Diver. A further parallel exists between Forrest and Gatsby, who is also a grand host of great parties paid for by big business deals, his shady associations with Meyer Wolfsheim being analogous to Forrest's cynical manipulations of the revolution in Mexico. At the same time, Forrest plays Tom Buchanan to Evan Graham's Gatsby, for he is the unfulfilling husband and Graham the interloper who harbours the precious romantic flame. In Graham's case the flame is perhaps more like Monroe Stahr's than Gatsby's, for Graham has never laid eyes on Paula before; he merely sees in her aspects of the wife he loved and lost as a young man adventuring on the South Seas. Ford Madox Ford, who met London in the period of *The Little Lady,* found the Californian to be 'Celtic';[50] and, though London was only partly Celtic through his mother, he does share with Fitzgerald certain characteristics associated with the race: the romanticism; the love of drinking, parties and talk; the myth-making and self-dramatisation. In *The Little Lady* London puts a heavy dose of the Celtic into one of Forrest's 'philosophers', the poet, Terrance McFane; and generally he puts a Wildean–Shavian–Fitzgeraldish social irony above ideological commitment for the first time. Though we are treated to a whole range of opinion on subjects that had always preoccupied London, there is now enough balance in the oppositions of the novel, enough down-playing of association between author and spokesman, and enough primacy of emphasis on the personal and situational that ideology can become irrelevant. Forrest's attitudes on race, for instance, though far more intelligent than Buchanan's regurgitations in *Gatsby*, become, like Buchanan's, one more factor contributing to his wife's alienation: 'I suppose Dick is right', Paula sighs to Graham after one of Dick's dinner-table disquisitions; 'but I confess . . . I don't know what bearing sporting dominants and race-paces have on my life' (219).

Those concerned with London's changing ideas on race would do well to consider this passage in which Forrest argues that, apart from a handful of thinkers and men-of-action, whites are no more civilised or less 'bestial' than others; and the divorce of the heroine from the romantic doctrine of Anglo-Saxon adventurism is certainly a signal development. But keeping to the matter of *The Little Lady* as an anticipation of subsequent literature: beyond the work of Lawrence, whose *Trespasser* London seems to have read while conceiving the novel and whose *Sons and Lovers* he praised generously,[51] and that of Fitzgerald, whose similarities have been suggested, the opus which most springs to mind is Hemingway's. The stylistic connection has already been remarked on. Beyond this stand deep sympathies in disposition and content. Forrest's relations with women exhibit on their crudest level the combination of patriarchal protectiveness and idealisation that would lead Hemingway to create incredible characters such as Maria in *For Whom the Bell Tolls*. Forrest's fatherly–big-brotherly treatement of both Paula and her Jordan Baker-like younger sister, Ernestine, partakes of the psychological syndrome that would lead the aging Hemingway to refer to female friends as 'daughter'. Colonel Cantwell in *Across the River and into the Trees* is the most comparable essay on the middle-aged man-of-the-code. That code is strength ultimately; for, in spite of Forrest's willingness to compromise, he feels compelled in the end to remain guardian of male authority and values. The competitive drinking, sporting and prankstering are exterior sings of this; the stoical retention of calm, the fatalism, and the commitment to suicide as the proper response to failure are the inner imperatives. 'By God, he was no coward to run away with his wife in fear of any man', Dick reflects in deciding to fight Graham for Paula (240). It is with the resolve of the just lawgiver that he finally confronts his wife. He only avoids self-sacrificial suicide by the fact that she, with an equally Hemingway-like commitment to the code in the end, 'beats [him] to it'.

The suggestions by some of London's more heartless contemporaries that *The Little Lady* signalled his semi-conscious wish to get rid of Charmian is neither provable nor finally relevant.[52] The novel explores a fictional situation which, whatever its connections with London's personal situation and probable suicide, is self-contained, suspenseful, deep, logical, and tragic in its conclusions. Critical disdain for the Freudian symbolism of the last sentences is part of a stubborn reluctance to accept London's new ironical style, and a question of taste.[53] The book's conclusion is surely no less logical or satisfying than that of such an acknowledged classic as *Portrait of a Lady*; and, as always with James, the critical verdict must rest on the entire development. The accomplishment here is so substantial that I submit that London's critics must have either not read the book or been blinded by considerations external to it. So much is surely true of the one whose criticism hurt London the most, his great male friend as an adult, the poet George Sterling.[54] Having been in covert competition with Charmian for years, Sterling may have in part been reacting against the fact that, in addressing male–female relations with more directness than ever before, *The Little Lady* was finally confirming London's superior devotion to his wife. Sterling may further have been annoyed by the amusing but trivial McFane, last in a series of characters inspired by himself – Brissenden, Larry Hegan of *Burning Daylight*, Mark Hall – all of whom show a debilitating streak of decadence under their sympathetic cultured veneers. Though he loved 'the Greek', London was clearly sceptical about the values implicit in a life-style of body-culture on the Carmel beach, patrician poeticising in finely pressed self-published slim volumes, and *macho* high and low 'jinks' among the wealthy 'Bohemians' of California's most exclusive businessmen's club. Sterling in turn could privately dismiss as naive the attempt by a working-class 'Superman' but a decade away from 'the abyss' to portray the behaviour of the nascent Californian ruling-class.

The trajectory of London's career ordained that he should have attempted to get under the skin of the oligarchs in the end. The socialists decried this, seeing in it his demise; and one can only consider with sadness the spectacle of the greatest writer California had produced virtually begging to be allowed to write the play for the 1916 Bohemian Hing Jinks, and in the event having that play rejected. *The Acorn Planter*, source for Dick Forrest's song, was a glorification and call for revitalisation of the divine California land. The patrician Bohemians, some of them inheritors of bonanza-farming fortunes, found London's ardency insufficiently amusing and his poetry, by their dilettantish standards, artless. They preferred the *macho* 'dancing dog' London who would awaken Bohemian Grove at 2 a.m. with a challenge to open the bars and drink Ambrose Bierce under the table in a two-day bout that became legend. At that 1916 Jinks where his play was not performed, the already diseased and physically disintegrating London danced to the tune for sixty liquor-sodden hours and returned home in a state that made Charmian fear for his life. The fact that he was dead within two months may or may not be connected with these Bohemian escapades. But the horseplay of Dick Forrest, and the character altogether, certainly is. At the end of his life, London, whose love for his native land had become, of all his passions ideological and otherwise, the supreme motivation, came to attempt, semi-consciously perhaps, to be court-poet to the forces which ruled the land and to provide them, in a tradition of the artist which includes Shakespeare and Wagner, not only entertainment but also a mirror and an indication of ways in which to generally enrich the realm. But 'a prophet is not without honor save in his own country', he was forced to discover.[55] While his books were read and admired in foreign nations, his fellow-Californians, still only a few steps from the frontier, were content to use his name for commercial purposes[56] and construct a great inegalitarian civilisation that had little in common in spirit with the utopian pastoral society of the strong of which he had most consistently dreamed.

3 John Steinbeck

I RADICALISM

The Grapes of Wrath (1939) may not be Steinbeck's best novel, but it is his grandest and most celebrated, and on it his reputation will rise and fall. The book presents the classic tale of the Depression in the Sun-belt. The animating myth is that of the Garden and man's struggle to get back to it. The small farmers of Oklahoma and adjacent states have been dispossessed of their land by drought and the recalling of mortgages. The first is a cosmic antagonist: the wind and dust evoked so remarkably in the opening chapter, reminiscent of the disembodied antagonist of Eliot's *Waste Land* and answered in the end, as in that poem, by rain; a rain which in this case is not benevolent but causative of another natural antagonist, flood. The second antagonist is the banks. The system they typify is the chief object of Steinbeck's ire. No more than London is Steinbeck willing to rail for long at the cosmic order; but, where man has intruded on the ability of other men to make a living from the land, his wrath is like that of an Old Testament prophet. He vilifies the machines that plough under the barren old farms: 'The tractors came over the roads and into the fields, great crawlers moving like insects, having the incredible strength of insects.'[1] He vilifies the men that work the machines: 'The man sitting in the iron seat did not look like a man. . . . He loved the land no more than the bank. . . . He could admire the tractor . . . twelve curved iron penes erected in the foundry, orgasms set by gears, raping methodically . . . without passion' (48–9). he vilifies not only the banks but those who stand behind them: 'Fellow was telling me the bank gets orders from the East . . . "Make the land show profit or we'll close you down" ' (52). He stops short of accusing Wall Street directly, as contemporary radicals would do: 'Maybe there's nobody to shoot. Maybe the thing isn't men at all.' But he does not hesitate to satirise petty capitalists who, struggling themselves to survive, exploit the dispossessed: 'If

67

the woman likes it,' the used-car salesman says, 'we can screw the old man. . . . Get 'em under obligation. . . . Make 'em put you out, then sock it to 'em. . . . Squirt a couple quarts of sawdust in. . . . We sell 'em, but we don't push 'em home. . . . This is the machine age' (83–9).

Steinbeck's position is like London's in *The Valley of the Moon*, or Norris's for which French accuses Norris of fighting 'a rearguard action' and taking up 'a cause as lost as that of the old Confederacy'. The ideal is Jeffersonian democracy: that every family should have a small plot of land on which to achieve self-sufficiency. Take away his land and man begins to descend to the status of animal, to become the rural counterpart of London's people of the abyss. 'What's come over you, Muley?' Tom Joad asks an old friend whom he finds cowering in the brush; 'You wasn't never no run-an'-hide fella. You was mean.' Muley replies, 'I was mean like a wolf. Now I'm mean like a weasel' (78). Human dignity is threatened. The descent is laden with pathos. The dispossessed, like latter-day Israelites, must make an exodus. Nostalgia laces the atmosphere: 'They saw Muley standing in the door looking after them. . . . Then the hill cut them off' (156). A conflict commences between the disintegrative effect of flight and the residual power of the people's culture. 'Two days the families were in flight, but on the third the land was too huge for them and they settled into a new technique of living; the highway became their home movement, their medium of expression' (222). Sustenance is found in food – Steinbeck's people, as Edmund Wilson points out, are marvels of appetite[2] – in sacraments such as burials or weddings, in revivalism in both its solemn and joyous guises – preaching, singing, dancing country reels. Above all what is necessary is togetherness: 'Without any signal the family gathered by the truck, and the congress, the family government, went into session. . . . The people were changed. . . . They seemed to be part of an organisation of the unconscious' (135). The people, as often noted, are the protagonist of the novel.[3] While petty capitalists and other agents of dispossession are predominantly unsympathetic, so the people – cavilling of such critics as French and Wilson notwithstanding – are predominantly sympathetic. It is a Manichean universe, in spite of the liberalism Steinbeck is thought to espouse. Understanding of the victimisers is no more apparent than of the criminal in a TV cop drama.

Nowhere is this more apparent than in California, the promised land to which the neo-Israelites proceed. 'Jus' let me get out to California where I can pick me an orange when I want', Granpa Joad proclaims; 'Or grapes. There's a thing I ain't never had enough of. Gonna get me a whole bunch a grapes off a bush, or whatever, an' I'm gonna squash 'em on my face an' let 'em run off my chin' (112). Hope is inversely proportional to the despair of dispossession. The migrant vision of California carries the classic Steinbeck hubris: 'The best laid plans of mice and men go a-glee'.[4] The migrants do not heed the warning of the ragged man they meet coming back down the road: 'I tell you men you're gonna get fooled. . . . Took me a year to find out . . . two kids dead, my wife dead. . . . But nobody could tell me, neither' (260). The dual nature of this promised land is hinted at for Tom Joad in his first glimpse across the river at Needles: 'Never seen such tough mountains. . . . This here's the bones of a country. . . . I seen pitchers of a country flat an' green with little houses like Ma says, white' (278). The green country with white houses exists, but not for the taking. 'She's a nice country,' a man in Needles explains, 'but she was stole long ago.' The native gas-station attendants marvel at the migrants' jalopies and conclude brutally, 'Them goddamn Okies got no sense and no feeling. . . . A human being wouldn't live like they do' (301). The cops harass rather than help, trying to prevent the newcomers from settling or, optimally, to drive them back out of the state. At last Steinbeck breaks in with a grand general chapter echoing *The Valley of the Moon* in its panorama of the fate of the Californian and his land:

Once California belonged to Mexico and its land to the Mexicans. . . . Americans poured in. . . . Hunger for land. . . . Possession and ownership. . . . Squatters were no longer squatters. . . . Children grew up and had children. . . . Those farmers who were not good shopkeepers lost their land. . . . The farms grew larger and there were fewer of them. . . . Farming became an industry. . . . They imported slaves. . . . Chinese, Japanese, Mexicans, Filipinos. . . . If they get funny – deport them. . . . And the farms grew larger and the owners fewer. (315–16).

Steinbeck's racism is implicit, unlike London's. This new wave of land-seekers, he points out, is 'seven generations back American'. Still, the small tradesmen hate them because 'there is nothing to gain from them'. The labouring people hate them because they are willing to work for cheap wages. Only the great landowners benefit from the influx of so many. The threat to the landowners is the New Deal, which offers welfare assistance and decent campsites, things which·might allow the vicitimised people to organise. Attention is not long concentrated on this classic Californian conflict between agribusiness and government, however. From the point of view of the migrants the striking first impression is of the difference between the bigness and wastefulness of the system they are confronting and the tidy personalised methods they knew back home. The Jeffersonian ideal does not exist in the new land. The family does not articulate the problem in quite this way, of course. The Joads are 'thoughtless, impetuous, suspicious, ignorant' according to Warren French. They are not only unintellectual but anti-intellectual, he contends, and this overshadows the 'loveableness' and 'long suffering' qualities for which they are usually noted.[5] French's opinion is overstated. Were it accurate, *The Grapes of Wrath* would have become unread long ago. Steinbeck does show 'a fascination with twisted mental and emotional types';[6] but the Joads' crudeness is in the purely human tradition and gives them the wide appeal that similarly sentimental types have in, say, Dickens. Granpa is an old crank who spends his days eating, sleeping, and childishly whining that he can't button his fly: 'Fella's come to a nice – to a nice . . . I want to button up my own pants!' (125). Granma is Granpa's doting nursemaid; she dies shortly after he dies in what amounts to an act of will at not wanting to leave Oklahoma; her utterances are limited to revivalist outbursts – 'A-men!', 'Hallelujah!' and the like. Pa Joad is Steinbeck's stock weak male. His brother John, preoccupied with vague guilt, is an early essay in the Cain persona. Little Ruthie and Winfield function as a chorus of childish comments and antics. Their adolescent brother Al combines Steinbeck's incorrigible 'tom-cat' instinct with a proud practical sense of how to run a car.

Along with more anonymous people of the road, these minor characters carry the entertainment value of the novel. Three major characters provide the substantive response to the thematic problem: displacement from the old land and adaptation to the new. The first of these three is least in narrative concreteness and perhaps greatest in significance. Jim Casy is an ex-preacher. He has fallen in part because of his inability, now deepened to a non-desire, to free himself from sexual urges. Christopher

Isherwood found in Casy 'a new-Tolstoy figure, agnostic and perplexed, whose provisional creed is: "You gotta do what you gotta do." '[7] In fact, Casy's position is more carefully conceived than the patois in which it is delivered makes it appear.[8] In sexual morality, Casy is a novitiate in the philosophy of Whitman: 'Maybe it ain't sin. Maybe it's just the way folks is. Maybe we been whippin' the hell out of ourselves for nothin'' (31). In metaphysics, Casy is an exponent of the Emersonian oversoul: 'Why do we got to hang it on God or Jesus? . . . Maybe it's all men an' all women we love; maybe that's the Holy Sperit – the human sperit – the whole shebang. Maybe all men got one great big soul ever' body's a part of' (32–3). In deed, Casy is a pragmatist as well as an idealist. When Granpa dies, he accedes to Granma's demands – 'Pray, damn you!' – and recites the Lord's Prayer. When Tom hits a deputy to prevent women and children from being shot, Casy takes the rap: 'Somebody's got to. . . . I got no kids' (363). There is a streak of Sidney Carton in Casy. After being incarcerated and released, he becomes a labour-organiser. His motive is simple: to improve the lot of the people. He allows himself to be taken for a leader, 'cause I talk so much' (521). When the vigilantes beat him to death with pickhandles, he sounds the note of the Christian martyr: 'You fellas don' know what you're doin'. You're helpin' to starve kids. . . . You don' know what you're a-doin'' (527). The identification with Christ (JC) is apt. Tom echoes it in his moving farewell to Ma: 'Casy! . . . Says one time he went out in the wilderness to find his own soul, an' he foun' he didn' have no soul that was his'n . . . jus' got a little piece of a great big soul' (570).

Tom has been taken to be a Christ-figure himself. 'Tom "heals" the blind man with one eye', Charles Doughtery says; 'Tom teaches in parables. . . . Tom hidden in the cave and being ministered to by his mother is Christ in the tomb. . . . It is from there that Tom promises to be with us always. He disappears, but he does not die.'[9] Doughtery goes on to suggest that Casy is a John-the-Baptist figure, operating as a precursor to Tom. But Kelly Crockett likens Tom to St Peter, the rock on which Christ built his Church; and Gerald Cannon contends that 'Tom is unmistakably to Casy as St Paul is to Christ'. Thomas Dunn, on the other hand, thinks that, consistent with the overall Old Testament allusions, Casy is Aaron and Tom himself Moses.[10] Clearly some critics have let Steinbeck's biblical indications lead them to the outskirts of baffled imbecility. Steinbeck does present a belief as the goal of Tom's development, but this belief is primarily secular, socialist as well as transcend-entalist, and to the end pragmatic. 'I'm still laying down my dogs one at a time', Tom begins by stating (13). On the road he is forever wrestling with his own impatient nature, as well as the innards of the family jalopy. Though trying to get along 'without shovin' nobody around', he repeatedly asserts his opinion – to gas-station attendants, to his little brother, to deputies. In the end he finds himself doing exactly what sent him to prison in Oklahoma a few years before: killing a man out of passion. Starting as a parolee, Tom ends as a fugitive. Materially he has been reduced to the condition of an animal; ideologically, however, he has learned through suffering – his own, Casy's, that of his family, that of their kind at large. He too must live now for something like the Emersonian oversoul. This is the creed he describes to Ma in their last moment in the twilight and light rain under the willow by the stream: 'I'll be aroun' in the dark. I'll be ever' where – wherever you look. Wherever they's a fight so hungry people can eat, I'll be there. Wherever they's a cop beatin' up a guy. . . . See? God, I'm talkin' like Casy. Comes of thinkin' about him so much. Seems like I can see him sometimes' (572).

Ma Joad is the last major character to experience the conversion. This is fitting. As Crockett says: 'Tom was apparently meant to be the central figure . . . [but he is] completely dwarfed by Ma . . . a truly great character creation of modern fiction . . . the spirit of her people, their source of ultimate regeneration.'[11] Ma is both earth-mother and Mother of God. Large yet not unattractive, comfortable yet sharp as an axe when necessary, she is the embodiment of the best values of the old life – its stoicism, sympathy, coherence and cleanliness – coming up hard against the new realities. Ma is the one who has to shrive Granpa and supervise the death-watch over Granma. She has to lie with the corpse of the latter to conceal it from the cops as the family crosses the California border. Ma is the comforter of her pregnant daughter, Rose of Sharon, after the girl's husband has abandoned the migrant ordeal. She is the one who has to urge resolution on Pa and Uncle John when they despair. She has to find food and clean clothing and some degree of positive direction for Ruthie and Winfield, who in spite of her efforts seem to be 'growing up into wild creatures' (536). Ma alone stands firm against Tom and Jim leaving the family in order to find spare parts for the jalopy: 'We don't want you to go' way from us. . . . It ain't good for folks to break up.' Ma is the one who must convince Al, the sole dependable male left at the end of the novel, not to elope with the girl he wants to marry but to bring her and her family into a larger communal orbit with the Joads. Ma begins with a quasi-religious belief in 'the fambly'. This makes her 'education of the heart' more difficult.¹² Finally, however, she recognises her overarching responsibility to the family of man: 'Use ta be the fambly was fust . . . ain't so now. It's anybody. Worse off we get, the more we got to do' (606). Ma's acceptance of this new populist doctrine is not achieved fully until the last scene, in which she leads the remains of the family to a barn on high ground above the flood-waters. There in the shadows an old migrant is dying of hunger. Perceiving the necessity of the moment, Ma signals to Rose of Sharon, who has just been delivered of a stillborn child. In a symbolic gesture which has annoyed critics and astonished spellbound readers from the first, Rose of Sharon presents her full breast to the old man's toothless gums.

For such an apparently explicit novel, *Grapes* has produced a remarkable variety of opinions about what it affirms. French is adamant that it is 'reforming' rather than 'revolutionary'. He finds Steinbeck hostile to organised charity in the form of the Salvation Army and organised religion in the form of fundamentalist sects; he qualifies Steinbeck's sympathy to organised government by suggesting that he recognises that in the end it cannot create jobs; he argues that, in spite of his castigations of big business, Steinbeck is not substantially hostile to capitalism. These conclusions are disputable. French sums up his argument by sounding the note of equivocation that has made the novel acceptable for teaching in high school: 'At bottom, Steinbeck believes, like his great predecessor, Hawthorne, that the only lasting and meaningful reforms originate in the individual human heart.'¹³ A less housebroken assessment comes from Frederick Carpenter, who sees the novel as weaving three great 'skiens' of American thought: the transcendental oversoul of Emerson, his faith in the common man and Protestant self-reliance; Whitman's religion of the love of all men and his mass democracy; the realistic philosophy of pragmatism (Carpenter refers to William James) and its emphasis on effective action. These skiens do seem to be woven, but the pattern Carpenter sees them making suggests his theological bias:

'It develops a new kind of Christianity – not other-worldly and passive, but earthly and active.'[14] Both French and Carpenter sidestep the socialistic sympathies that scream out of the novel the first page. One might have expected orthodox critics to have found fault on this basis: the book is too polemical. In fact, perhaps owing to its popularity among all classes, most critics have continued to characterise *Grapes* as other than primarily left-wing. Only a handful, including Maxwell Geismar, have accepted Steinbeck's motive as radical. Their chief complaint is with a style that leads away from the ascetic fierceness of the 1930s toward bourgeois diffusion: 'Lacking the realism of *In Dubious Battle*, [*Grapes* marks] a return to Steinbeck's glamor, theatrics, and simplicity of view.'[15]

Geismar writes admiringly of 'the conflicts of Steinbeck's earlier proletarian novel'. F. W. Watt notes 'a continuity of suspense' in *In Dubious Battle* and 'a mounting excitment' which makes it more compulsive than *Grapes*.[16] Joseph Henry Jackson praised the earlier book as 'the best strike novel ever written'.[17] Harry T. Moore called it Steinbeck's finest book: 'It has the dramatic force lacking in *Grapes*.'[18] The *Sunday Worker* called it 'one of the most impressive proletarian novels'.[19] Edmund Wilson questioned the picture of Communism presented,[20] but the equally distinguished socialist man-of-letters André Gidé welcomed it lavishly:

It is the best painting (psychological) that I know of Communism and has a perfect clarity. ... What Steinbeck exhibits admirably (without however proving anything) is how those to whom all other means of struggle are denied are led, and even forced into, perfidy, injustice, resolute cruelty; and how the most noble and generous characters find themselves corrupted. From this comes the great anguish which from one part to the next, breathes through this beautiful and cruel book.[21]

Convincing arguments favour this small, tight volume, published three years before *Grapes*. *In Dubious Battle* explores in depth the only practical solution to which the larger novel points: the Cause, the Struggle, the action to which Jim Casy and Tom Joad have committed themselves in the end. In plot *In Dubious Battle* has almost Aristotelian unities of time and place: a strike in the Torgas Valley. In development it follows 'a pattern almost as rigid and conventional as that of a Petrarchan sonnet', that of the proletarian novel, which Malcolm Cowley has described: 'The hero was usually a young worker, honest, naïve, and politically undeveloped. Through intolerable mistreatment, he was driven to take part in a strike. Always the strike was ruthlessly suppressed, and usually its leader was killed. But the young worker, conscious now of the mission that unites him to the whole working class, marched on toward new battles.'[22]

The style of *In Dubious Battle* is straight, descriptive, Hemingwayesque – much dialogue cut by cinematic exposition. In the opening scene Jim Nolan applies to join the Communist Party in the City. 'Why do you want to join?' the interviewer asks him.[23] 'My whole family has been ruined by this system', Jim retorts; also, 'I want to work toward something. I feel dead. I thought I might get alive again.' During the interview Jim reveals the Jack London-like learning of his working-class type: his father made him read Plato, More, Bellamy, Herodotus, Gibbon, Macaulay, Carlyle, Prescott, Spinoza, Hegel, Kant, Nietzsche, Schopenhauer and Marx. Jim's learning is the extent of his patrimony, however, he has nothing to lose by joining the Party, he avers. 'Nothing except hatred', the interviewer retorts and sends him to work in the local cell. The cell is run by Mac, who, like Wolf Larsen, is a big Swede. Like Larsen with Van Weyden, Mac's role with Jim is to initiate him into the ways of strength and action. Jim, however, is no timid Van Weyden. Quickly he grows restless of typing letters and cutting stencils and asks Mac to get him out to the field where the real struggle goes on. Mac replies that Jim is of more use in the office. Soon, however, the need for action comes up. There is trouble in the apple-orchards waiting to be harvested. The growers have organised to reduce the piece-rate, and they have the backing of the American Legion and local vigilante squads. The pickers, restive but cowed, need leadership in order to hold their pay-rate. The Party will provide this leadership, Mac explains to Jim as they hop a freight-train south. The goal of the Party, however, is not a successful strike so much as a drawn-out struggle to bind and radicalise the pickers, goad the growers and Legionnaires into overreaction, and attract greater number until the confrontation spills into the cottonfields and beyond.

Mac is the controversial character of the novel. His mix of idealism and ruthlessness is apparent form these early moments. Down to small details he is dedicated to the Cause. Smoking is 'a nice social habit', he tells Jim: 'I don't know any quicker way to soften a stranger down than to offer him a smoke, or even to ask him for one' (35). French, quoting Dakin, the 'softest' of the strike leaders, regards Mac as 'a cold-blooded bastard' with few redeeming qualities.[24] Geismar, however, likens him to Slim of *Mice* and Ma of *Grapes* as 'wise, courageous, indomitable, though in tatters'.[25] Joseph Fontenrose, taking the clue of the title and epigraph from *Paradise Lost*, sees Mac as a version of Milton's Satan: 'To his confederate angels Satan offered freedom, equality, and power; to man he offered the knowledge which the Lord had denied him. . . . The Party is tempter of the workers, offering them a vision of social justice, cooperative democracy, and economic abundance.'[26] This position seems accurate. The *Paradise Lost*–Eden imagery is carried by the location of the strike in an apple-orchard, and the role of Mac as an ambiguously heroic Satan is sustained throughout. A master of deception, Mac uses the sympathy of a lunch-counter owner to get his father's farm as a camp-site. He pretends to have worked in a hospital in order to deliver the baby of the pickers' leader's daughter-in-law and thus in a swift stroke, gain the confidence of the mass. Repeatedly he manipulates accidents to foment rancour, taking the fall of an old picker from a faulty ladder as the excuse to start the strike and the murder of an old comrade come down from the City to help as a rallying example. Mac is practical to the point of being inhumane. When Jim says that he likes the lunch-counter owner, Mac replies, 'Don't go liking people, Jim. We can't waste time liking people' (101). When Jim says, 'Look at the stars', Mac retorts, 'Look at the road.' In such words one may hear echoes of the harsh realism of London's admirer of Milton's Lucifer; and indeed, London, even to the point of giving his name to the pickers' leader, is a presence behind this book – more predominant than anywhere else in Steinbeck's opus.

Like Wolf Larsen, Mac wins admiration by his strength but alienation by his belief in ends justifying means. He is not weak like Larsen in the realm of ideals, however; nor, as the novel progresses, does he collapse. Paradoxically, like Larsen, Mac is a victim; but in him victimisation is a stimulus to practical action rather than existential despair. Mac is not capable of Larsen's cruelty: he could not cause the suffering gratuitously caused Mugridge. He can, however, beat up a young man with passionless efficiency in order to set an example. In the end Mac is redeemed by not only the consistency and doggedness he shares with Larsen but also his burning sense of injustice. To repeated charges that he is heartless, he points out the disadvantages he must operate under: 'They got guns. . . . They got money. . . . We got to be clever and mean and quick. . . . We got to do it with our hands and teeth' (105). For the cops and vigilantes as well as the pickers he promulgates his creed: 'Most of this valley belongs to a few guys. . . . Those cops out in the road are just working-stiffs' (130). Mac eats as poorly as any picker and sleeps hardly at all, yet keeps a cool head. Toward Jim he is touchingly protective, never letting the boy off on sorties too dangerous and reminding him of a secret place in the willows to hide should disaster occur. By contrast, in the 'X' this novel shares with *The Sea Wolf*, Jim grows increasingly hot-headed and beards Mac for resigning himself to failure of the strike: 'You're getting just like an old woman, Mac.' Always a puritan – a version of Galahad, as French suggests, or the 'pure fool', Parsifal[27] – Jim declares deliriously, 'I'm stronger than anything in the world, because I'm going in a straight line. . . . All the rest have to think of women and tobacco and liquor and keeping warm and fed. . . . All I want is to put over the strike' (243). Jim commences giving orders to Mac. Later, recovering from his delirium, he apologises. In the end, however, Jim's enthusiasm causes him to get blasted by a shotgun. Mac swallows his grief and on the instant, in an act which sums up his whole character, projects it into rallying the Cause: 'Comrades!' he declaims over Jim's dead body, 'this guy didn't want nothing for himself! . . .' (304).

What makes Jim rush off to get ambushed is a report that Doc Burton is banged up out in the orchards. Burton occupies the place in this novel that Casy occupied in *Grapes*: least integral to plot, he is the character most significant ideologically. French, who regards *In Dubious Battle* as 'a curse on two houses, capital and labour', finds Burton the embodiment of a 'third force' and 'the first character Steinbeck has presented completely sympathetically'.[28] This takes Steinbeck's respect for Burton's ideas further than the novel takes it. A note of the 'dubious' about Doc is there from his introduction: he looks like 'a pansy'; his role is to 'perfume' the camp-site with carbolic so the authorities can't disperse the strikers on a health pretext. Though he too is working for the Cause in this way, Doc opposes Mac intellectually. His is 'the posture of the contemplative man', Watt writes: 'It would be a mistake, however, to equate too readily Burton's point of view with the author's. . . . His philosophy is presented with no more finality than the ruthless idealism of the Communists. . . . The author's point of view is larger: the picture he draws embraces both the terrible fatalism of Burton and the terrible optimism of Mac.'[29] Watt's position seems more accurate than French's. It is Steinbeck's objective presentation of his materials that allows critics to suppose that the book rejects Mac's passionate partisanship in favour of this Burton philosophy: 'I want to see the whole picture. . . . I don't want to put on the blinders of 'good' and 'bad' and limit my vision. . . . Group-men are always getting some kind of infection. . . . Maybe the group simply wants to move, to fight, and uses these words simply to reassure the brains of individual men. . . . You might be an expression of group-man,' Doc says to Mac, 'a cell endowed with a special function, like an eye cell, drawing your force from group-man, and at the same time directing him, like an eye. . . . You practical men always lead practical men with stomachs. . . . In all history there are no men who have come to such wild-eyed confusion as practical men, leading men with stomachs' (126–7).

In the midst of the battle in which Steinbeck has thrown his personae, such a character as Burton, who is a 'dreamer, mystic, metaphysician' as well as a doctor, cannot provide the complete answer. 'If he wasn't a doctor, we couldn't have 'im around', Mac confides to Jim; 'we need his skill, but his brain just gets us into a mess' (128). Harsh as it may be, Mac's position is not untrue; nor is sympathy wholly on the side of Doc when he observes of Mac's ability on the stump: 'You sure know how to work 'em, Mac' (201). There is a justice in Mac's retort: 'Quit sniping at me . . . I've got a job to do.' There is a spurious quality too, one suspects, in Doc's lofty purpose: 'I don't believe in the cause, but I believe in men' (171). Considering the situation, many of Doc's utterances suggest an inappropriate sensuality of mind: 'It seems to me that man has engaged in a blind and fearful struggle out of a past he can't remember, into a future he can't foresee nor understand.' He attitudinises, in the manner of Wolf Larsen: 'Man has met and defeated every obstacle, every enemy except one. He cannot win over himself. How mankind hates itself' (225). Mac may have the blindness of the man of action: when Doc asks London's daughter-in-law, one of the few females in the book, what she wants, Mac's comment is, 'Doc must need a woman bad' (227).

Equally, however, Doc has the paralysis of the man-of-thought: when London's daughter-in-law replies that she wants a cow to make milk for her baby, Doc is in no better position (in fact, theoretically worse) to produce the cow than Mac is. Steinbeck 'refrains from comment', as Watt maintains. To the end in this novel he is concerned with presentation, not judgment – at least in regard to those characters on the side of the strike. His resistance to fuller commitment to Mac earned him the wrath of a few left-wing dogmatists and the praise of such an aesthete as Peter Quennell.[30] But his resistance to final commitment to Doc is underlined by the fact, too often missed, that Doc's irresponsible wandering in the orchard is what leads Jim Nolan, against Mac's admonitions, to his untimely and personally wasteful death.

The Grapes of Wrath was condemned by growers' associations and chambers of commerce from Oklahoma to California,[31] and Steinbeck was identified with the radicalism that both *Grapes* and *In Dubious Battle* were thought to espouse. But Steinbeck's radicalism from the first raised questions; and in light of his later opinions – his harangues against Soviet Russia, his chauvinist pronouncements about America, his support of Lyndon Johnson's execution of the Vietnam War – it came to be viewed sceptically. *In Dubious Battle* was not written, like *The Iron Heel*, out of a specific urge to promote the Cause. 'I'm not interested in strike as a means of raising men's wages, and I'm not interested in ranting about justice and oppression, mere outcroppings which indicate the condition.'[32] Further on in the same letter he adds, 'I am sick of the noble working man talking very like a junior college professor.' On left-wing ideology Steinbeck took a lofty position: 'There are as many communist systems as there are communists. . . . Ideologies change to fit a situation. . . . If the fools would only change the name from Communist to, say, American Liberty Party, their principles would probably be embraced overnight' (107–8). When editors at Covici–Friede questioned portions of his text, Steinbeck shot back to his agent, 'Between you and me I suspect a strong communist bias in that office, since the reasons given against the book are all those I have heard from communists of the intellectual bent and of the Jewish race' (109–10). Critics of these persuasions came to include Mary McCarthy: 'Mr Steinbeck for all his long and frequently pompous exchanges . . . is certainly no philosopher, sociologist, or strike-technician.' Also her husband, as noted: 'The book is not really based on the formulas of Communist ideology.'[33] The weight of testimony suggests that the novel, which seems so like a novel in favour of the Cause and was claimed as such by no less than Gide, was written out of some other motivation. Again, Steinbeck's statements indicate as much: 'It is a brutal book, more brutal because there's no author's moral point of view' (105). Prime among considerations, in fact, was strategic: 'I want *In Dubious Battle* printed next [he had just experienced first success with *Tortilla Flat* (1935)]. Myths form quickly and I want no tag of humorist on me, nor any other kind' (112).

In Dubious Battle was meant as a work of art above all: the creation of an artist who subscribed to the Joycean dictum that the maker should imitate God, standing above and beyond, 'paring his fingernails'. Fortunately, the book is more committed and alive than this austere position would militate. The blood and courage of Mac, as I have noted, are at least as persuasive as the ponderings of Doc. Steinbeck's desire to make the novel illustrate his 'phalanx theory' was qualified by his talent as an artist. The theory, however, remains central. 'Until you can put your theme in one sentence,' Steinbeck wrote to Dook Sheffield in the letter which most comprehensively describes it, 'you haven't it in hand well enough to write a novel' (74). What might Steinbeck have offered as his one sentence? 'The group is an individual as boundaried, as diagnosable, as dependent on its units and as independent of its units' individual natures, as the human unit, or man, is dependent on his cells and yet is independent of them' (75). Here is the origin of Doc's pronouncements on 'group-man', couched suitably in terms of biology, the science most closely related to medicine. Steinbeck was attempting to explain human behaviour by an objective, deterministic law: the formula that men in conjunction with other men operate as an entity different from man – a 'phalanx', which has a psychology and nature all its own. Steinbeck's role as observer of the phalanx, like Mac's as its leader or 'eyes', was, in some quasi-Jungian sense, predetermined: 'Art then is the property of the phalanx, not of the individual. Art is the phalanx knowledge of the nature of matter and of life' (80). The artist was involved in a disappearing act from the world of engagement and passion, to become a sort of disembodied voice of prophecy, whispering his unacknowledged legislation to the wind: 'Dr Fischer at Hopkins [Marine Station] said one day that you will find any scientific discovery in the poetry of the preceding generation.'

Art aspires to the state of science? to the state of biology evidently. This is the explanation for the apparent objectivity of Steinbeck's point of view, which any reader coming from the novels of London will immediately note. It is also the source for the substantial criticism of Steinbeck's art which Wilson first enunciated and Alfred Kazin later took up:

> What is constant in Mr Steinbeck is his preoccupation with biology. . . . [There is a] tendency in his stories to present life in animal terms. . . . [He deals] with the lower animals or with human beings so rudimentary that they are almost on the animal level. . . . The close relationship of the people with the animals equals even the zoöphilia of D. H. Lawrence. . . . [But] Mr Steinbeck does not have the effect, as Lawrence or Kipling does, of romantically raising the animals to the stature of human beings, but rather of assimilating the human beings to animals. . . . The result is not to dignify the animal, but to reduce human religion to absurdity. . . . The chief subject of Mr Steinbeck's fiction has been thus not those aspects of humanity in which it is most thoughtful, imaginative, constructive, nor even those aspects of animals that seem most attractive to humans, but rather the processes of life itself. . . . This animalizing tendency of Mr Steinbeck's is, I believe, at the bottom of his relative unsuccess at representing human beings.[34]

To the extent that objective–theoretical coldness triumphs in Steinbeck, his great books even cease to speak persuasively. This tendency is linked to his near hero-worship during his most productive years of Ed Ricketts, a marine biologist whose partner Steinbeck became, and with whom he collaborated on a study of the marine life of the Gulf of California in the book which followed *Grapes, The Sea of Cortez* (1941). Fortunately Steinbeck also derived from Ricketts a tendency to observe with acuteness the activities of men – all men, particularly the stunted and deprived, as they provided the most unusual 'cases' – and to avoid excessive deductive or abstract thinking. To be inductive, to reach his conclusions – at least to appear to reach his conclusions – as a biologist does, through what Ricketts called 'non-teleological thinking', became Steinbeck's stated artistic creed.

This creed is the superego of Steinbeck's art. The latent human passions and resentments provide the id. The success of each novel depends on the balance. *In Dubious Battle* achieves equilibrium: Doc's creed threatens to transcend all, but Mac's passion yanks the whole back onto the firm ground of engagement. *Grapes of Wrath*, in which all characters are led by their emotions, all engaged by the end, and even the author's ubiquitous voice eschews objectivity, is far less balanced; and the novel is both more alive and popular and less artistic and true as a result. *Grapes*, however, was written in a different mood from *In Dubious Battle*. Conditions of labour in the central valley had gone from bad to worse, and the austere artist in Steinbeck was no longer able to convince the man to regard them as simply theoretical material. 'I must go over into the interior valleys', he wrote;

> about five thousand families are starving to death over there. ... The government is trying to feed them and get medical attention to them with the fascist group of utilities and banks and huge growers sabotaging the thing. ... They think that if these people are allowed to live in camps with proper sanitary facilities, they will organize and that is the bugbear of the large landowner and the corporation farmer. ... But the crops of any part of this state could not be harvested without these outsiders. (158)

In Dubious Battle is constructed on theory and its characters, like many of Steinbeck's early characters, are projections of himself and friends like Sheffield and Ricketts. *Grapes* by contrast was drawn largely from life and its characters close to types Steinbeck observed in the field. *Grapes* is informed by Steinbeck's association with the Resettlement Administration, which produced the series of articles on the migrants, 'Their Blood is Strong'; also by his friendship with a WPA (Works Progress Administration) worker, Tom Collins, who shared the objective coolness of Ricketts but joined it with social action. Participation made the difference. 'I'm sorry but I simply can't make money on these people', Steinbeck wrote to his agent; 'that applies to your query about an article for a national magazine. ... The suffering is too great for me to cash in on it' (161).

It was too great as well for him to mistreat it in art. A 60,000-word manuscript, *L'Affaire Lettuceberg*, was abandoned as having been written with too much rush and too little coolness: 'This book is an experiment in trickery and trickery in a book is treachery.'[35] A new script was begun forthwith, with promising resolve: 'I could dash it off but I want this one to be a pretty good one. . . . I'm trying to write history while it is happening and I don't want to be wrong' (162). Considerable personal sacrifice appears to have been expended: 'I was in the mud for three days and nights and I have a nice cold to beat, but I haven't time right now for a cold.' Eventually Steinbeck began to hit a stride he had never achieved before: 'The new book is going well. . . . I don't want it to go so fast for fear the tempo will be fast and this is a plodding, crawling book. . . . I hope I can keep the drive all fall. . . . I only feel whole and well when it is this way' (167). Finally there was a draft of which he felt proud: 'It pulls no punches at all and may get us into trouble', he wrote, echoing London on *The Iron Heel*; 'but if so – so' (168). Shortly after the manuscript was completed, Steinbeck collapsed from overwork and had to be confined to bed 'for the first time in twenty years' (174). There he was nursed by his wife Carol, who simultaneously typed the script for the third time. Carol had typed Steinbeck's scripts since before his first book had been published. She had been his most consistent adviser throughout the 1930s, and in the case of *Grapes* she seems to have been particularly influential. The book is dedicated to her as well as to Collins; and a reader so inclined, suspecting Steinbeck's use of friends as models for previous characters, might be tempted to see Collins behind Tom and Carol behind Ma Joad, with whom she shared a sturdy earth-mother persona. Carol deserves credit, in any case, for the title of the book, from 'The Battle Hymn of the Republic'. This credit Steinbeck readily granted: 'I think it is Carol's best title so far' (171).

It does little harm in considering the flow and emotion of *Grapes* to keep in mind Steinbeck's situation of the period. It would be too much to suggest that he was projecting feelings from other areas into the plight of the migrants or that his diatribes against agribusiness, the California cops and petty capitalists were motivated by guilts he was suffering over matters entirely divorced from them. Still, two factors made the period considerably more unruly than that of *In Dubious Battle* and must have contributed to the heightened subjectivity. The first was the enormous success of *Mice* (1937), which propelled Steinbeck onto the national stage, made him exceedingly uneasy (he was superstitious about the corrupting influence of success), and persuaded him further of an idea already latent in his work: that he had some prophetic role to fulfil. The second was the state of his marriage, which had been stormy and incompletely fulfilling from the first but now was beginning to enter, probably unknown to Steinbeck at the time, its final stages. Nelson Valjean reports that Carol was responding to success in a number of ways annoying to her husband: she wanted a new and larger house, thus convinced him to buy a ranch in the mountains above Los Gatos; she wanted to cocoon them there in a semi-conscious *cloitre à deux*, keeping the increasing number of admirers at bay; she disliked the social life of New York, which since the success of *Mice* was beckoning, yet she did not want to produce the family that for Steinbeck might have been an adequate substitute.[36] On Steinbeck's side the evidence was mounting of a dissatisfaction with Carol as object of his desires: the wandering libido, repressed successfully in *In Dubious Battle*, expressed itself ominously in *Mice* in the desire of Curly's wife and lurked in *Grapes* behind the uneasy suppressions of Jim Casy, the adolescent urges of Al, and the strange guilts of Uncle John. Ma Joad in fact may gain her titanic stature from being in part a representation of the ideal qualities in Carol that Steinbeck knew semi-consciously he was going to have to give up to be free to seek the satisfactions his inner nature was craving.

It is no accident that Tom's farewell to Ma by the willows is the most passionate scene in *Grapes* – indeed, in either of Steinbeck's great radical books. But, while recognising that the tensions of his marriage may have contributed to the superior feeling of *Grapes*, one should not suppose that the polemical message or cultural significance of the book may be discounted. This would be to misuse psychological criticism in the most reactionary fashion. Steinbeck himself appears to have fallen into Freudian confusions after his second marriage and may have looked back on his earlier radicalism with a degree of dismissal. But whether the motor that drives the machine is running on pure petrol or some synthetic gasahol compound is not finally relevant. Frank Norris was having marital difficulties when he wrote *The Octopus*; Upton Sinclair was having severe difficulties when he wrote *The Jungle*; London wrote his two greatest novels, *The Sea Wolf* and *The Little Lady*, in periods of marital breakdown. It is quite natural in a sense that such strains should show up in periods of immense creativity; nor is it surprising that in this century one so often finds divorce following tremendous success. To bring it back to *Grapes*, I would suggest that Steinbeck's first marriage, in its death-throes, contributed to an emotion, a music, a soulfulness that was not achieved in any other book. This is what finally distinguishes *Grapes* from *In Dubious Battle*, on which the prime external force was Ricketts. But in neither case should one let such biographical considerations, or the cavilling and rationalising and polemicising of critics of one persuasion or another – nor even of an author who was rarely his best critic – discount or obscure the fact that these novels stand in the first rank of American radical literature and are integral to that tradition, which Wilson calls California's strongest, of *The Octopus* and *The Iron Heel*: the novel of the class war.

II BOURGEOIS CAREER, PROLETARIAN COMEDIES

Steinbeck was not, like Jack London, a product of the proletarian struggle himself. His father was a respected civic leader in Salinas, his mother a former school-teacher. The Steinbeck home, to be depicted in *East of Eden* (1952), was one of the finer structures in town, and the family had a pride that lived up to it. John was the single boy among sisters. Though big-nosed and awkward and afflicted by pimples, he was the doted-on child. As a boy he enjoyed what French calls 'Emerson's three ingredients for the making of a scholar': nature, books and action.[37] The nature was provided by the mountains, valleys and coastline of Monterey County, lovingly described in *The Pastures of Heaven* (1932), *To a God Unknown* (1933), *The Red Pony* (1938), *The Long Valley* (1938), *East of Eden* and now referred to as 'Steinbeck Country'. The books included classics by Milton, Browning, George Eliot, Thackeray, Lewis Carroll, Hardy, Dostoyevsky, Flaubert, Chekhov, and above all Malory, whose *Morte d'Arthur* remained a favourite work throughout Steinbeck's life, one he would spend years trying to render into contemporary English. The action involved Tom Sawyerish activities along the Salinas River and the kind of boyish pranksterism typified by the formation of the Boys' Auxiliary Secret Service for Espionage Against the Japanese, to be described in *Pastures of Heaven*.[38] It was a middle-class childhood, essentially suburban, marked by the privileges and faults characteristic of the bourgeois. Early on Steinbeck developed an antipathy for what he saw as the excessive 'respectability' of domesticating females. This was linked to a curiosity about lower classes and the wandering sexual instinct of the adolescent. Liberal sympathy appeared when he was a schoolboy. One of his teachers has contended, however, that when John expressed indignation over some social injustice he would characteristically stand back and grin at his own remarks, and if caught at this he would drop his eyes and grin more.[39] The element of insincerity here seems worthy of note. As a youth and as an author Steinbeck found social protest an effective way to command attention. Bourgeois as he remained till the end of his career, it seems fair to argue that the attention was at least as important as the protest.

'What a kaleidoscopic life!' Norman Valjean writes in his admiring biography; 'love of hills and valleys, rocks and earth, dogs and ponies and people ... off-and-on Stanford student, farmhand, and sugar mill worker ... seaman, road-gang flunkie, hod carrier, dam builder ... fish-hatchery assistant, amateur biologist, avid reader from childhood and – with gusto aplenty – a now-and-then devotee of feminine curves and the bottle ...'.[40] Here is a classic typological myth. Steinbeck was a young teenager when London was describing the youth of Dick Forrest and, though the aging author would have been embarassed by Valjean's glorification, the young man was no doubt mindful of the character he wanted to cut in the world and narcissistic in his pursuit of it. At Stanford the complete Californian *Wandervögel* oscillated with the aspiring humourist. Lying by Lake Lagunita staring at the sky, he would compose a Shelleyan piece, 'Fingers of Cloud', for the campus *Spectator*. Later, while eschewing dances and other objectionable evidences of 'the Stanford caste system', he would write a satirical allegory, 'Adventures in Arcademy'. When he did attend dances, it was in the self-conscious persona of a teller of off-colour stories with a hip flask and marijuana-pouch. While Scott Fitzgerald was parading his Princeton pranksterism through the speakeasies of New York, Steinbeck and friends were visiting their favourite bootlegger in San Francisco, Madame Torelli, whose name was to be given to the niggardly booze-merchant of *Tortilla Flat*. On vacations Steinbeck would take up residence in the family summer-place at Pacific Grove. Drinking coffee on the wooden stairs bordering the street, he would watch the town characters drift past and listen to the Mexicans' 'crudely-told stories'. These ditties were to him 'often gems'. Back at Stanford he would repeat them to admirers, transforming them into tales of ghosts or leprechauns, whom he insisted – as he imagined befit the Celtic strain in his blood – were very real. Patrons of the English Club contended that few surpassed him 'in sarcasm and irony'. With his friend Dook Sheffield he liked to talk 'in the synthetic dialogue' that was to typify his Mexicans, carefree drunkards and migrant labourers.

This is the middle-class boy slumming: a kind of Prince Hal who revels in the language and antics of lower-class pranksters in a rebellion against his background, always knowing that he will remove himself from this inferior milieu one day to take his natural place as a social leader. The motif persists throughout Steinbeck's development. Dropping out of Stanford, he went to New York to make his way as a writer. Abysmal tales of the struggling young man are qualified by the facts that his uncle got him a job on the New York *American* and his parents sent him money whenever they could. No doubt it disappointed the future man-about-town to lose a 'dazzling show-girl' on account of poverty, but there were plenty of young ladies to amuse him when he returned to California to take up a sinecure as caretaker of a cottage at Tahoe belonging to a wealthy San Franciscan family. A vignette from this period depicts Steinbeck, drunk, holding a girl by her ankles out of a second-storey window, threatening to drop her unless she acquiesced with his carnal demands. The animal instinct, latent sexual brutality, and misogyny apparent here would thread their way through later work. Valjean, with the startling male chauvinism of Steinbeck's generation, treats the incident as humorous; nor is there evidence that Steinbeck himself recognised a problem until years later, if at all. The relation of the sexes was a jovial war in which the woman would inevitably try to domesticate while the man would struggle to keep free. It seemed only natural to Steinbeck that Carol Henning should have wanted to type up his manuscripts out of pure devotion and that he should have resisted her wish to marry before taking up cohabitation. Carol was, after all, the Californian girl who enjoyed wrestling with the boys, drinking, dancing to loud music, playing pranks, basking in the sun nude and tying John's pubic hair up into pink pigtails when he had the indiscretion to pass out. It was perhaps inevitable that such a tomboy would become too much for the mature writer. But, for the diet of beans, red wine and rejection-slips that Steinbeck lived on in the early thirties, Carol was the perfect partner. 'If she and John fought bitterly at times,' Valjean says, 'mutual friends pictured her as the perfect catalyst in the writer's life.'

It was an extraordinarily productive time, nor was it unhappy. The ardency of social protest did not come till the end of this phase. At the outset Steinbeck's major concern was the art, and his first five books constitute experiments in form and content to which he would return later, sometimes with happier results, sometimes not. 'Whenever he appears, he puts on a different kind of show', Wilson complained at the end of this phase, after *Grapes*: 'he is such an accomplished performer that he has been able to hold people's interest by the story he is telling at the moment without inquiring what is behind it.'[41] Wilson's favourite book out of an opus he suspects is *Tortilla Flat*. Behind this book stands the experience of relative poverty that Steinbeck, his wife and friends lived through during the early Depression; but all is projected through the activities of a group of *paisanos* whom a local social worker, Sue Gregory, had been telling Steinbeck about. It was also the early period of association with Ricketts and theorising about 'group-man', and the 'phalanx theory' hovers behind the depiction of Danny and company, though not in such a doctrinaire way as behind Mac and the pickers in *In Dubious Battle*. As noted, *In Dubious Battle* was written directly after *Tortilla*, and Steinbeck intentionally made it serious in order to avoid 'the tag of the humorist' raised by its predecessor. It seems likely that the models for characters in the two books overlap and that in *Tortilla* we are seeing versions of Sheffield, Ricketts and Steinbeck himself dressed up in *paisano* personae. Steinbeck's lumpen-proletarians often give off a curiously sweet middle-class aroma. The 'literary slumming' he complained about when the book proved popular with the New York establishment[42] was a phenomenon that he – however much he covered it up with boasts of poverty – was guilty of himself from the first.

In *Tortilla* a WASP author is writing exclusively about Mexicans. What are his intentions? All his life Steinbeck espoused liberal ideals. In later years in New York he was concerned to allay the faint whiff of anti-Semitism that had attached to him as a result of a remark about the ability of George Kauffmann to direct *Mice*: 'What would a wiseacre New York Jew know about people like George and Lennie?'[43] In fact, the remark was not uncharacteristic of the provincial Steinbeck of the early phase. After a bohemian gathering in Carmel attended by some commercial writers from the East, he made a slur against Jews redolent of the prejudice of the period.[44] In his writing, moreover, as French notes, Steinbeck displayed 'a stronger element of Nordic supremacy than one might expect'.[45] In 'Johnny Bear' it is seen as degrading for a Caucasian woman to have a Chinese baby. In 'The Murder' the customs of Slavs regarding marriage are presented in a way that 'it is difficult to believe that most Americans would not read as an illustration of racial superiority'. In *Once There Was a War*, published as late as 1957, Steinbeck would brand the Arabs as 'the dirtiest people in the world and among the smelliest'. *The Forgotten Village* (1941) shows his tendency to be condescending, if compassionate, in treatment of Mexican natives. So too, arguably, does *The Pearl* (1947), in which the hero must flee to save himself and his family. 'Their Blood is Strong' (1938) and *Grapes* both emphasise that the migrants have 'good old names . . . English, German, and Scandinavian'.[46] Steinbeck took on the creed of Everymanism during the war, but his prolonged stays in Europe in the 1950s and his praise of English culture while adapting *Le Morte d'Arthur* reveal a sentimental bias toward white Northern races only a few steps removed from the proud supremacism of London and Norris. When it comes to the *paisanos* of *Tortilla Flat*, then, what is in question is a racial affection as abstract as it is real. Danny and his friends are versions of the 'noble savage'. They are sympathetic precisely because they are racial Undermen. Given commerce and money, like Torelli or Lee Chong of *Cannery Row* (1945) or Jesus-and-Maria of *Sweet Thursday* (1954), they would no doubt be seen as usurious comic villains.

Danny and his friends are not free of native racism themselves. Descendants of the original inhabitants of California, they have a pride far outstripping their present status. A slightly extortionary price for wine from Torelli earns the Italian their contemptuous sobriquet 'that Jew'.[47] A jilting by one Arabella Gross, for whom Danny has gone so far as to buy a bra, provokes the declaration, 'These cheap white girls are vicious' (73). Coming from the mouths of motley lumpen-prols, such remarks are doubtless realistic. Steinbeck seems content to accept them as humorous; and one sometimes wonders if in them, as in other opinions advanced, he is not passing off insults of his own under the guise of the foolishness of people less sophisticated. This is still the period in which Al Jolson was painting his face black to sing 'Mammy' to well-heeled audiences who would never breathe a word against a 'Negro', and the fact may help explain the popularity of a book which seems to purvey such an anti-Establishment philosophy. Danny and his friends live a life of chasing loose women and drinking cheap wine. Theft in service of these pastimes is viewed with toleration. Acts of charity, such as stealing beans from the railroad to feed Teresina Cortez's children, are seen as eminently honourable. The irony of the mock-heroic form protects the author from over-identification with these subversive values; but, in fact, Steinbeck's 'slumming' infatuation is apparent. Chapter 14, which sums up Danny and his friends' code, is an accurate statement of the values which ruled Steinbeck's early adulthood at its happiest – values which he yearned, adolescently, to perpetuate through later life: (1) 'Love and fighting, and a little wine. Then you are always young, always happy'; (2) always laugh, though remember that laughter can be 'something like a hand that squeezes your heart'; (3) watch out for women who laugh – 'they will drive you crazy, make you want to hang yourself'; (4) 'Old men should not run after babies. They should sit in the sun.' Homespun, simple-minded, good – values of an eternal childhood are advanced here. It is not a mature world, but, for a moment, it is a beautiful one: charged with 'sweetness and joy, philanthropy, and, in the end, a mystic sorrow' (9).

Tortilla Flat is in the lyric, pastoral vein of a Shakespearean romance. Happy and sad, light and heavy by turns, it is, for all its suspect qualities philosophically, a little masterpiece of atmosphere,[48] demonstrating an ability, hinted at in Bret Harte and carried on in contemporary times to some degree by Richard Brautigan, of the Californian to create a fairy-tale. Danny and his friends may in the end be taken as spirits, Danny himself transcending finally, as Fontenrose argues, into not only the mock-heroic spirit of King Arthur at Avalon but also the sun of the pagan myth behind that legend: 'Danny is the sun that rises, rules the sky and the wind, has its high noon and brilliant afternoon, and then sets into darkness ["Danny is now a god . . . the clouds flamed and spelled DANNY in tremendous letters . . . the moon dripped blood"].'[49] On a less exalted plane, Danny and friends are also bumpkins ruled by spirits: comic types like Bottom and the rest in *A Midsummer Night's Dream*, constantly being led into errant amusing situations by forces they cannot apprehend. Superstition rules their actions, as with so many of Steinbeck's characters. But, where superstition can turn ominous as in *To a God Unknown*, in *Tortilla* it is consistently charming and a force for the good. Pirate once pledged a gold candlestick to St Francis if a sick dog of his got well. It hardly matters that the dog got well to be run over by a truck; the superstition has created a heard that is holy. Danny and friends guard Pirate's collection of quarters when they would steal with impunity from unspiritual types such as Torelli. The quarters are 'the symbolic center of the friendship'. The friendship transcends all worldly considerations. It is the mystical motif that shimmers behind the order of Tortilla Flat in the way that brotherhood and the knightly code shimmer behind Malory's Round Table or Wagner's Grail Order. At Danny's funeral the bereft company is, as one, 'struck by a celestial thought' (312): they burn down the house that brought them together yet embodied the materialism that threatened to drive them apart. 'Thus it must be, oh, wise friends of Danny', Steinbeck concludes in nostalgic benediction. 'The cord that bound you together is cut. The magnet . . . has lost its virtue' (313).

Holy friendship independent of the trappings of material success was a theme that so moved Steinbeck that he would return to it at the end of the war. In the intervening years, however, came something quite different: success, enormous success. First there was the acclaim of *Tortilla*, which, combined with the death of his parents and a modest inheritance, removed Steinbeck from the beans–wine–rejection slip diet forever. Two years later came the yet greater success of *Mice*, leading to associations with New York which would make his Californian provincialism a thing of the past. Two years after that came the sensation of *Grapes*, the Pulitzer Prize, huge sums for film-rights, international celebrity. The simple anonymous life of the writer, which had produced such varied works of promise, would never exist again. The old life began to slip away. Ricketts was not madly admiring of *Grapes*: it seemed to him overly moral, teleological, redolent of the righteous impulses in religion, government and business which Steinbeck had attacked.[50] Carol was uncomfortable with the crowd John was mixing with in Hollywood, and with good reason: unknown to her, a young torch-singer, Gwyn Conger, who liked to appear by the piano with 'a pet white mouse placed on her lovely shoulder',[51] was undermining the Steinbeck marriage. Conscious of this slippage in the two most important relationships in his life, Steinbeck bought half-interest in Rickett's laboratory and threw himself into an exploratory voyage to the Gulf of California, signing Carol aboard as cook. During this expedition he resuscitated the 'non-teleological thinking' he shared with Ricketts and spent many a twilight harmonising on harmonica as Carol played her piccolo. But Carol slept in a forward cabin while Steinbeck slept aft, and the log of the voyage co-authored with Ricketts proved by Steinbeck's own account a culmination of work done in the past more than a preview of aims for the future. Back in the States, Steinbeck hurried to Hollywood, where he continued his courtship of Gwyn, either in person or by an elaborate system of signals. The house in Los Gatos went up for sale. Carol followed Steinbeck to New York to fight for him – 'none of this noble little woman stuff'. Soon, however, she realised the extent of his yearning for a break with the past and returned to California to get a divorce.

This stormy unwrenching inaugurated the second phase of Steinbeck's career. Gwyn, Hollywood and New York replaced Carol, the pen and the Salinas Valley. Meanwhile, the War had begun. Adapting to the change this seemed to call for, Steinbeck wrote a play novel set in a vaguely Norwegian town about the resistance of the individual spirit to the oppressions of group-man. *The Moon is Down* (1942) won acclaim for its timeliness and hurtled Steinbeck into the role of writer-as-propagandist. It was not, however, the *tour de force* that *Mice* had been. Steinbeck had entered an uncertain phase artistically; the attempt to reproduce a previous success was a symptom; criticism began to beset him; so too did requests for services. After finishing *The Forgotten Village*, a documentary on conditions in rural Mexico, he was asked by the Air Force to script an information film. Complying with *Bombs Away*, he published it in book-form as well and donated the proceeds to military relief. Contact with the Roosevelts since the success of *Grapes* had made him a name to conjure with in Washington, and officials induced him to script a propaganda film. *Lifeboat* was the result; Alfred Hitchcock directed. While this was being finished, Steinbeck was asked to go to Europe as a war-correspondent. Welcoming the chance to 'see action', he left his young wife in a flat on the East Side and travelled to North Africa. There he wrote the dispatches later to be collected in *Once There Was A War*. In an England preparing for

D-day, he rummaged for materials he would use in his reworking of *Le Morte d'Arthur*. All the while he wrote letters to Gwyn betraying homesickness and war-weariness. In her husband's absence Gwyn had started drinking rather heavily; this, however, did not dusturb Steinbeck on his return. Soon she was pregnant. Not until their break-up four years later did she tell him of the affair she had with a younger man. Apprehension may have stirred in Steinbeck at the time; if so, apart from an increase in drinking himself, this was only manifested by a homesickness for California and a zest for novel-writing not felt since *Grapes*.

He wanted to move back to Monterey to research a great novel. Gwyn was reluctant. Meanwhile, on the suggestion of a soldier that he write something to lift the troops' spirits, he threw himself into 'a funny little book that is fun'[52] and completed in six weeks *Cannery Row*. 'A dense allegory about the folly of misplaced human ambition'[53] is how Thomas Kiernan, Steinbeck's biographer, describes the book. Gwyn had trapped Steinbeck in the very 'symbols of security and respectability' that had caused him to leave Carol: house, status and so forth. *Cannery Row* was a yearning back toward the life of Ricketts, who appears as Doc. Steinbeck himself appears as the maritally beleaguered captain, liberated from his gloom only by the intrusion of Mac and the boys and the drunken melée which follows: 'It is doubtful whether the captain had ever had so much fun. . . . When the curtains caught fire and were put out with the little towels, the captain told the boys not to mind. . . . "My wife is a wonderful woman . . . ought to of been a man . . . [then] I wouldn' of married her." '[54] The captain wants to drop out and take up residence with Mac and the boys in 'The Palace Flophouse'. He doesn't in the end; nor did Steinbeck leave his wife until two sons had been born, the alcohol-problem had intensified, and Gwyn had made it clear that she resented his friends – she impugned the association with Ricketts – and his work. *Cannery Row* nevertheless is the creation of a man disappointed in marriage. No extended male–female relationship is depicted as successful: Mac is divorced; the painter Henri is a perennial loser in love; Doc is wedded to a dream princess. The only praiseworthy females in view work for Dora, the madam of the Bear Flag restaurant. It is a dream of the Wild West, brought up to date. Men are comrades; women are whores-with-hearts-of-gold. Respectability is conscientiously subverted – Doc's method for getting revenge on a bank: 'Rent a safety-deposit box . . . deposit in it one whole fresh salmon and go away for six months' (17). The good people are those like the Malloys, who live in an abandoned boiler; Hazel, the dim-wit, who loves to hear Doc talk but can't understand a word; or Frankie, the 'Holy Fool', who prepares with grand care to serve Doc's girl a glass of beer only to end up spilling it in her lap.

Cannery Row is in fact a version of *Tortilla Flat*. Mac and the boys are Danny and friends returned to the clothing and accents of Mac and the pickers of *In Dubious Battle*. Like Danny and friends, Mac and the boys live in a ramshackle structure, despise steady jobs, and contrive to avoid paying rent. Like Danny and friends, their inebriation, thus happiness, is at the mercy of an ethnic grocer: Lee Chong instead of Torelli. Like Torelli, Lee Chong becomes an object of wrath for his meanness. Unlike Torelli, Lee proves himself one of 'the boys' in the end by his generosity in the cause of Doc. Like Danny and friends, Mac and the boys enjoy canine companionship: the health of their dog, Darling, is a bellwether of the spiritual health of Cannery Row in the way that the baying of Pirate's dogs provides a chorus on the well or ill-being of Tortilla Flat. Like Danny and friends, Mac and the boys must go on a journey into the woods to find the lucre to pursue their good deeds – in this case the frogs to pay for the party for Doc. To throw a party for the most admired male is the ultimate purpose of both brotherhoods, and the party Mac and the boys throw for Doc ends in fights and hallucinogenic poeticising just as does that last party Tortilla Flat throws for Danny. Mac and the boys subscribe to the code of Danny and friends, but 'Old Tennis Shoes' whisky has taken the place of red wine for them, and the pursuit of loose women has been tempered by age. Mac's brotherhood operates more successfully as a protection against female 'viciousness' than Danny's ever did. Not since *In Dubious Battle* has essential puritanism proved quite potent. Dora and her girls have little more prominence than London's daughter-in-law in the strike novel; and the Galahad code of Jim Nolan, while never stated, is observed by that paragon, Doc. Mac and the boys, Fontenrose points out, may be a burlesque of Mac and the pickers. Steinbeck had become an FDR Democrat by this time, a patriot rather than a radical; and 'though the power of the Word', which Fontenrose contends is the principle mythical idea of the book, 'the Party is rendered innocuous'.[55]

Doc of *Cannery* has a position roughly similar to Doc of *In*

Dubious Battle; but, as Mac's position is reduced, so Doc's is exalted. Doc remains the man-of-thought to Mac's man-of-action, but no substantive philosophical dispute any longer exists. Doc in fact voices the apology for Mac and his kind which is the moral of the book:

> It has always seemed strange to me. . . . The things we admire in men, kindness and generosity, openness, honesty, understanding and feeling are the concomitants of failure in our system. . . . Those traits we detest, sharpness, greed, acquisitiveness, meanness, egotism and self-interest are the traits of success. . . . While men admire the quality of the first they love the produce of the second. . . . Everywhere in the world there are Mac and the boys. (98)

Doc's character is defined by the fact that he, a professional man acceptable to the 'respectable' world, prefers the company of these blithe Undermen who, in Steinbeck's words, are really 'the Virtues, the Graces, the Beauties' (9). Doc shares in his creator's antibourgeois bias: 'What can it profit a man to gain the whole world and to come to his property with a gastric ulcer, a blown prostate, and bifocals?' (10). As a symbol of his trust, Doc leaves his laboratory and home open to the town at large. In evidence of his generosity, he feeds and liquors all comers and ministers to their pain, spiritual or physical. When Mac and the boys nearly destroy his property by throwing a party in his absence, Doc proves forgiving. If he seems something of a sucker, that is in his favour. If he is too literal to understand some jokes and pranks, that merely dilutes his appearance of superior intellect and makes him seem down-to-earth. Doc's melancholy and his lack of success with women are touching, so too his difficulties in getting his work done amid so many small acts of kindness. His love of music confirms the general belief in his goodness, though neither Dora nor Mac any of their minions can understand the distinctions apparent to him between *Daphnis and Chloe,* an Eleusian Chant, or a piece of Monteverdi. The aesthetic sensitivity of the man, however, is apparent to all. This Steinbeck sums up by the arresting image of Doc's reaction to the drowned girl with dark hair and a pale pretty face whom he discovers staring up at him from a La Jolla tidepool where he is collecting octopuses: 'Music sounded in Doc's ears, a high thin piercingly sweet flute carrying a melody he could never remember. . . . The flute went up into regions beyond the hearing range and even there it carried its unbelievable melody' (75).

Doc's trance over this 'drowned Ophelia' is disturbed by the comment of a resident of the materialistic Californian beachtown: 'Say — . . . you get a bounty for finding a body' (76). We are in the realm of the philistine comments of the boozing American tourists on the skeleton of Santiago's marlin in *The Old Man and the Sea*, or of the cacophonous grindings and whirrings of the modern city which obscure the precious vision of the hyacinth-garden in Eliot's *Waste Land*. The ideal versus the real, art versus life – conflicts typical of the aesthetic tradition of the Romantics, Decadents and even Modernists in Europe make an appearance in *Cannery Row*. The form itself is a piece of 'intricate music', French points out:[56] not plotted so much as patterned by a series of contrasting or analogous incidents. The conclusion, in which Doc chases the melancholy of the dying party by a recitation of the highly sensual Sanskrit poem 'Black Marigolds', represents a statement of faith in the power of Art. 'Doc', French observes, 'is a man who has learned to find compensation for the frailties of human nature and other aspects of physical nature in what Yeats called "monuments of unaging intellect". . . . The novel is a defense of the creative spirit, a defense of poetry.'[57] Aestheticism has provided, at least temporarily, a replacement for the creed of socialism. As with Edmund Wilson, who bore down on Steinbeck for the sentimentality of the book yet called it his most enjoyable read,[58] Steinbeck was experiencing the pendulum-swing between political activism and ivory-towerism – between *To the Finland Station* and *Axël's Castle* – which was broadly characteristic of his generation. 'All the discontented heirs of Henry James,' Maxwell Geismar observed, 'middle class bohemians . . . in their belated efforts to escape from Lardner's dead end found themselves suddenly along the road to Leningrad.'[59] As Wilson shortly would, Steinbeck was now returning back down that road. The absorption of the anger of his earlier books into the greater morality of the New Deal and anti-Hitler America may also have convinced him of another of Geismar's salient observations: 'It is not inconceivable that in the end the US will bring about its great sweeping social changes as a sort of new popular fashion.'[60]

Popular. In spite of its aesthetic conclusion, *Cannery* was a popular book, not a critical success. Steinbeck was teetering between art and commerce, and the huge sums and paltry kudos he had received since *Grapes* were encouraging him toward the latter. His reputation had been established firmly by his eye for populist culture, and *Cannery* replays in innumerable vignettes and details the scenes in earlier books which had charmed a large readership: the diurnal motherings of Ma Joad, her concern for cleanliness, her worrying over her little children who have never seen a porcelain toilet-bowl; the rituals of eating, the sizzling dough-cakes and smell of coffee in the morning, Tom's longing for 'side-meat' and the getting of milk for the pregnant 'Rosasharn'; Uncle John's getting drunk, Al's tom-catting, Tom's avoidance of running over small animals; the ritual of life on the road and the poetry of the jalopy. In *Cannery* Steinbeck stops to praise a minor character, Gay, as 'the little mechanic of God, the St Francis of all things that turn and twist and explode, the St Francis of coils and armatures and gears' (43). A few sentences later he looks down from on high to suggest,

> Someone should write an erudite essay on the moral, physical, and esthetic effect of the Model T Ford on the American nation. Two generations of Americans knew more about the Ford than the clitoris, about the planetary system of gears than the solar system of stars. With the Model T, part of the concept of private property disappeared. Pliers ceased to be privately owned and a tyre-pump belonged to the last man who had picked it up. Most of the babies of the period were conceived in Model T Fords and not a few were born in them. The theory of the Anglo-Saxon home became so warped that it never quite recovered.   (45)

The irony here is grand, almost pompous. The author realises the trick he is playing, the response he is trying to manipulate. The spontaneity of such observations in *Grapes* has given way to a calculation which leaps toward the general after only the briefest glance at the specific. At some point this kind of omniscience becomes know-it-all-ism. At some point an author who lauds humility should not dare to play God. In *Cannery* Steinbeck, sure of his art but no longer so sure of his purpose, just avoids turning into a posturing, insincere crowd-pleaser.

Soon after completing *Cannery*, Steinbeck moved back to Monterey. His plan was to research a great novel on the Salinas

Valley. This was held in abeyance while he travelled to Mexico to work on yet another film, *The Pearl*, the story of which was published as a novella. A parable of the self-defeating nature of material success, *The Pearl* proved popular for its simplicity though again was no hit with the critics. *Cannery* meanwhile was proving unpalatable with 'respectable' types in Monterey; Gwyn felt hostility and agitated to move back to New York. Steinbeck, though eager to embark on a new big novel – an expansion of the *Lifeboat* scenario transposed to a bus – was also hurt by the 'knife in the back' he felt he was receiving from his home and agreed to his wife's entreaties. 'I was happier in New York. . . . This isn't my country anymore. . . . It won't be until I am dead.'[61] New York, however, was hardly more adequate to the writer's needs. Two baby boys and increasing marital feuding robbed the flat of peace, and Steinbeck found himself forced to retreat to the basement to work on *The Wayward Bus*.[62] Despairing of being able to make the novel a masterpiece, he decided to shelve it. His publisher wouldn't hear of this, however; and, shortly after Steinbeck returned from a journalistic trip to Russia, a 'paste-up job' was released. Once again came great sales yet disparaging reviews. Once again Steinbeck, restless to produce a great novel, returned to California to do research. This time Gwyn and the babies didn't come with him. This time he moved back into association with old friends such as Ricketts. He may have amused himself with local prostitutes. His marriage in any case was foundering. His change of personality from shy country-fellow to sophisticated wit annoyed Gwyn. She accused him of being pompous. After Ricketts's death in a car accident she declared drunkenly, 'Now your public will see you as you really are.' Her jealousy of the male bond bubbled to the surface: 'Without him you are nothing. You will be the failure you were before you met him, and I don't want to be married to a failure!'[63]

A bitter divorce followed. 'She took every goddamn thing I had', Steinbeck complained; 'by a curious trick she even got all of my books – and certainly not because she wanted to read.'[64] Back to Monterey he went. He moved into the little summer-house which his father had built and he and Carol had lived in in struggling days. With Ricketts gone and his love marriage crushed, he floundered in his attempts to get on with the big novel. Much drinking took place. There was 'a kind of crack-up'. One night, insomniac, Steinbeck wrote 'a little story that was so evil, so completely evil that when I finished it I burned it' (336–7). The errant libido that had been unsatisfied through his first marriage and frustrated in his second now led him as it would: 'When my pants are hot, I get out and get a girl *when* I want her and if that one is not available another one is ' (332). A 'binge of fornication' gave birth to what friends noted as some 'peculiar ideas about women'. American females, Steinbeck contended, were 'part man, part politician'; they had 'the minds of whores and the vaginas of Presbyterians'; eventually they would 'succeed in creating a race of homosexuals' (343). This madness continued until he met Elaine Scott, a Texan who had worked for the Theatre Guild in New York and was married to a Hollywood actor. 'She's not like American women . . . doesn't want to be a man. . . . I guess, in other words, she's a well-adjusted girl' (400). Through Ann Sothern and other Hollywood mutuals, Steinbeck played the game of cryptic messages and notes under false names he had played while courting Gwyn behind Carol's back. Where Gwyn had promised bright lights and sex to chase the rural humdrum with Carol, Elaine promised urban charm and sophistication without psychoses. Putting his self-pitying debauchery behind him, Steinbeck, now forty-seven, prepared for respectability and his third and final phase. Elaine divorced her husband; she and Steinbeck married; they moved back to New York – 'I am sure that she belongs here rather than in that despondent paradise of Hollywood' (399).

Once before he had moved to New York with a new wife. Once before he had begun his new life by attempting to reproduce the theatrical success of *Mice*. This time, armed with Elaine's contacts from the Theatre Guild and his own status in the Hollywood–New York nexus, he tried again. *Burning Bright*, his third and final play novel, was produced by Rogers and Hammerstein, better known for their popular musicals. Like *The Moon is Down* a philosophical work in a non-specific setting, *Burning Bright* brought down a host of critical barbs and closed after a brief run. Steinbeck lashed out at his critics. Later he admitted that the play was flawed and dismissed it as little more than a respite from his 'marathon novel' of a quarter-million words, *East of Eden*. This book, for which, Steinbeck contended, all his previous works, including *Grapes*, had been practice, was published in 1952. Two years later the last section of it was made into a film vehicle for the young James Dean, an idea of Elia Kazan's, who had recently made a success of Steinbeck's *Viva Zapata!* (1950) by using the young

Marlon Brando. Film kudos and book-club sales had to sustain the author: *East of Eden* was the greatest critical disappointment yet. Steinbeck turned at once from the writing of a serious novel to the subject and form designed best to entertain. Rogers and Hammerstein wanted to do a musical version of *Cannery*. A brief attempt to adapt the book as it was proving impossible, Steinbeck set about to write yet a third version of the tale he had told first in *Tortilla*. *Sweet Thursday* was the novel, *Pipe Dream* the musical produced from it. The latter flopped on stage in 1955, ending Steinbeck's theatrical career. Undoubtedly it was a grave disappointment. A New Yorker at last, he aspired to be that man-about-town that had never existed in the province of his youth. Like Bernard Shaw, he wrote witty opinionated articles. Like Frank Harris, he was a boastful proponent of heterosexual performance. Like Oscar Wilde, he like to appear dandified – with a silver-knobbed walking-stick and red-lined opera cape.[65] Friend of presidents and Nobel laureate-to-be, Steinbeck was not any longer, however, the writer of quality he had been.

Sweet Thursday is the index. 'Through the treatment of certain personal symbols Steinbeck seems to confirm that relaxation of attention,' one critic wrote, 'that surrender, which first became evident in *Burning Bright*, where it resulted in an irresponsible sentimentality, and in *East of Eden*, where it resulted in disintegration of form.'[66] Another critic wondered if Steinbeck were groping for growth: 'Whether the important changes in key symbols effected by *Sweet Thursday* truly comprise a capitulation to romantic sentimentality or whether, like the changes in Hemingway's *Across the River and into the Trees*, they constitute a purposeful destruction heralding a new period in his art, is in question.'[67] *Sweet Thursday* is 'warm, romantically melancholy, nostalgic', observes the sympathetic English critic Watt, and 'there is a kind of zany musical comedy charm'; but 'there is none of the "poison" or the cutting-edge of *Cannery*, where such playfulness would be out of the question'.[68] Irresponsible play such as Wilde might have lauded seems to have been Steinbeck's object; but the playfulness presented involves a kind of vulgarity, viciousness, and anti-intellectualism that would have appalled Wilde. The book is a 'sell-out', contends Warren French: 'It is genuinely anti-intellectual if we define anti-intellectualism as a belief that problems are solved by force and violence rather than reason. . . . The anti-intellectualism is that of the fatuously melodramatic nineteenth century road-show, which was based on the assumption that if one is sweet, one doesn't have to be bright.'[69] Doc in *Sweet Thursday* does not end by enunciating that love of old art which redeems *Cannery*: he drives into the happily-ever-after in a clattering Model T with his whore-with-a-heart-of-gold. *Cannery* walked a tightrope between serious art and crowd-pleasing; *Sweet Thursday* falls headlong into the latter. Steinbeck himself had no illusions about this. 'I'm so fascinated by everything about the theatre,' he said of *Pipe Dream*, 'I don't really care if the show's a flop.'[70] Recently he had defended Tennessee Williams's *Camino Real*. His Californians now were at least as remote from reality, his Cannery Row as much a make-believe 'anywhere' as Shakespeare's 'Italy of the imagination'.

Like Harte and Twain after the Gold Rush, Steinbeck had turned his back on his homeland, loudly declaring its provincialism, treachery and unsophistication. Now, however, he had the temerity to exploit the old picturesque types that had brought his early successes. Whereas in those successes the tendency to make stage-Californians instead of living characters had been tempered by everyday experience, here the tendency goes unchecked. The result is both arrogant and inaccurate. James M. Cain in his preface to *Three of a Kind* pointed out that there is a substantial difference between the grammar of Western and that of Eastern lower classes: in California the sensitive ear will immediately pick up the absence of ghetto accents and the signs of more uniform education.[71] Steinbeck, whose ear for dialect had once been a source of pride, fails in *Sweet Thursday* for the first time, and fails distressingly. He forces the pompous 'I and the boys' into the mouth of Mack, where in *Cannery* it was always the more natural and accurate 'me and the boys'. Fauna, the revision of Dora, speaks in down-home-isms more typical of Eighth Avenue than California and most typical of all of a Hollywood version of how a whore is supposed to speak: 'I guess if you laid all the hard luck I've ever heard end to end, why, the Bible would look short.'[72] These inaccuracies are symptoms of the final breaking-away from the California Steinbeck had so loved in his youth. Amid the nostalgia, one might detect the giddy sense of devilishness that often attends the severance of an umbilical tie. The seer that so impressed Joseph in *To a God Unknown* is now reduced to an old bum whom Doc has to bail out of jail for stealing meat from the market. Steinbeck no longer finds the anti-material life so blithe and credible. The seer's belief in the mystical power of sunset over Big Sur is now, like all such Lawrentian attitudes, depicted as silly: 'I'm a seer . . . I live alone . . . I live in the open. I hear the waves at night and see the black patterns of the pine boughs against the sky. With sound and silence and color and solitude, of course I see visions. Anyone would' (66).

Sweet Thursday has been called Steinbeck's farewell tribute to Ricketts, and it was the last time the Doc figure was to appear. Ostensibly this Doc is the same as the one in *Cannery*. He has the same exalted position as 'healer of the wounded soul and the cut finger' (55). His laboratory is a place to which people make 'pilgrimages', there to hear classical music and recitations from Lao-Tse, Isaiah or the *Bhagavad-Gita*. There is a new element of passivity in Doc, however, almost a laziness. His laboratory is described as having ' a designed and lovely purposelessness' (21). He himself is afflicted with severe writer's cramp – a biological report which he is unable to finish. This gives birth to an adolescent flight-wish: 'Doc desparately wanted to go back to his old life – the hopeless wish of a man wanting to be a little boy, forgetting the pain of little boys' (64). In fact, we are observing a very different Doc, one harassed by discontent and given to brooding self-analysis: 'Where does the discontent start? You are warm enough, but you shiver. You are fed, yet hunger gnaws you. You have been loved, but your yearning wanders in new fields. And to prod all these there's time, the bastard Time. The end of life is now not so terribly far away' (20). This Doc is less Ricketts than a version of Steinbeck, fearing the demise of his powers and, beyond that, death. It is the persona of a man confronting middle age and wishing for a doting, mothering world to salve his existential malaise. Magically, for *Sweet Thursday* remains in the realm of friendship-fantasy of *Tortilla* and *Cannery*, the Macks and Faunas know precisely what to do: throw a party and, beyond that, find Doc a *dame*! The popular tune from Rogers and Hammerstein's *South Pacific* might indeed have provided Steinbeck with an alternative title: 'There Ain't Nothin' Like a Dame!' The enthusiasm of Mack and the boys and Fauna and the girls to set Doc up with the cute, pert little new whore in town, Suzy, is straight out of the most crowd-pleasing Broadway–Hollywood formula. To call it insincere, however, would be remiss: since his marriage to Elaine, as his letters show, such sentimental enthusiasm had gripped Steinbeck as well.

What kind of dame? What kind of Grail does this last Danny seek? 'Doc don't want no dame that knows as much as him', Mack proclaims, chauvinistically; 'What would he have to talk about?' With the force of her experience Fauna adds, 'When a man falls in love it's ninety to one he falls for the dame that's worst for him' (114). Jesus-and-Maria, proprietor of Torelli's–Lee Chong's, further qualifies this new Steinbeck ideal: 'A healthy woman [is] a broke woman. . . . Dame with money [is] a kind of half-assed man.' So enter cute Suzy. She doesn't smile, she grins. She isn't smart, but she's tough. 'You ain't never going to write that paper', she blurts to Doc with her instinctive horse-sense; 'you're just sitting here like a little kid playing wish games' (104). Doc is struck. Preparing for the date Fauna has set up, he starts to listen to the overture to *Don Giovanni*, then snaps it off: 'Is that what I think of myself?' (157). Later he psychoanalyses his attraction: 'Not only is she illiterate, but she has a violent temper. She has all the convictions of the uninformed. She is sure of things she has not investigated, not only sure for herself, but sure for everyone. In two months she will become a prude. Then where will your freedom go? Your thinking will be like tennis against a bad player' (228). Against this Doc's vulnerable side argues, 'I know if I should win her I'll have many happy times. . . . If I fail I'll never be a whole man. I'll live a grey half-life, and I'll mourn for my lost girl every hour of the rest of my life' (236). Suzy meanwhile is schooling herself in a 'S-L-O-W-N-E-S-S' that will make everything 'royal', the 'maidenly' qualities, and 'a kind of lonely and terrible modesty' (145). These are the virtues in a woman, even if achieved by artifice. 'When I get friends with myself,' she tells Doc, 'maybe I can get friends with somebody with no chip' (203). She moves out of Fauna's into the boiler the Malloys inhabited in *Cannery*. Doc visits and, seeing that she has pasted up curtains, he marvels, 'My God! What a brave thing is the human!' (240). Domestic respectability triumphs where once it was mocked. 'I want a guy that's wide open', Suzy tells Doc; 'he's got to need the hell out of me . . . got to be the kind of guy that if he ain't got me he ain't got nothing' (242). Once an embodiment of male self-reliance, inner balance and peace of mind, Doc now pledges his being to this cliché of tractable-practical femininity, part kewpie-doll and part nanny, claiming that he can never be happy – nor even continue his work – without her.

III   *FEMME FATALE*

Fontenrose calls Suzy 'a splendid example of the Virgin Whore'.[73]
He borrows his term from Claude-Edmond Magny, who uses it in
reviewing *East of Eden*. The Virgin Whore is 'the mythical
prototype of all Steinbeck's women'. Traditionally she may be a
nymphomaniac or frigid, Aphrodite or Artemis or Hecate, Helen
or Judith or the *Giftmädchen*. Cathy Ames Trask of *East of Eden* is
one aspect of her, particularly deadly. Others appear in La Santa
Roja, Curly's wife, and Camille Oaks. The only additional major
type of woman in Steinbeck, Magny contents, is the wholly
different and nearly sexless mother-figure, of which Ma Joad is the
great example. Magny's review was the second piece the French
writer produced on Steinbeck. The first, published in 1948,
emphasised the cult of nature and 'noble optimism' in the opus and
suggested that Steinbeck 'sadly lacks' a sense of evil.[74] 'America has
no soul and will not deserve one until it consents to plunge into the
abyss of human suffering and sin', Magny quotes from Walter
Rathenau. Could it be that this opinion encouraged Steinbeck,
always admiring of the French, to press on with the most ominous
of his fantasies? Publicly he claimed to pay no attention to critics;
yet it is curious that he should have begun to create his monster of
evil and sin just as he was being accused of deficiency in this
regard. Cathy Trask is both the blot on Steinbeck's career and his
most revealing creation. In her one can find the ideological link-up
he was moving toward yet recoiling from throughout his previous
career, a link-up typical of the puritan imagination from the
Jacobeans to Hawthorne to Tennessee Williams: sin equals desire;
desire equals woman; woman equals sin. Cathy is the Eve in
Steinbeck's Eden. All his women, however, have been Eves to some
degree. The fact is central to his art, and typical of the stage of
cultural development in which that art appeared. Steinbeck has
been associated predominantly with male or general social
concerns. This imagination was ravaged by 'erotic compulsions',[75]
however; and, like that of another sexually haunted artist, it
oscillated between a chaste Elizabeth and a seductive Venus until
the two were synthesised finally in an alluring yet guilt-ridden
and ultimately tragic Kundry.[76]
    Steinbeck's first novel, *Cup of Gold* (1929), a historical romance
written in his twenties about Henry Morgan the pirate, previews
this aspect of his work in all its permutations. Young Henry grows

up in a Welsh valley – the valley, with its Freudian significance
(and Freud is usually significant in Steinbeck), is the emblematic
'figure on the carpet', Californian valleys forming the venue of
most of Steinbeck's early work.[77] Morgan's mother, like some
portentous Hardy character, is associated with necromancy, the
'mystical scissors', and war of women against male foolishness.
Morgan's father once 'fancied himself Orpheus',[78] but his wife
insisted he attend real things and become a success in life. Gwenaliana Morgan 'considered marriage with a diety as some manner
of a crime against nature'; gradually 'her ridicule gnawed off
[her husband's] wings'. Young Henry does not comprehend fully
the threat to his fantastic impulses this female reality-principle
represents; subliminally, however, he feels the valley 'smothering'
him. He goes to a surrogate father-figure, Merlin, for advice and
Merlin counsels pursuit of his dreams: 'You want the moon to
drink as if from a golden cup, and so, it is very likely that you will
become a great man – if only you remain a little child' (27).
Resolving to leave his valley, Henry goes to bid farewell to a girl,
Elizabeth, he has admired from afar. A mysterious self-assurance
in Elizabeth intimidates him, however ('All girls and women
hoarded something they never spoke of' – 29–30) and he retreats
without speaking and goes home to dream a dream in which 'a
shadowy composite of Elizabeth and his mother came to him'. The
next day he feels 'a loathing of himself and her'. He considers
himself 'a kind of unnatural monster and her a kind of succubus'.
Nevertheless, with Proustian surreption, he returns to Elizabeth's
house and spies on her as she stands in the doorway. He sees 'the
fine curve of her legs and the swell of her hips'; a 'wild shame' fills
him; he runs away into the dark (33). The next morning he steals
off for Cardiff. His mother grieves at his departure; but via 'white
Druids' she prophesies that he will have riches and sovereignty, and
will marry 'a white-souled maiden of mighty rank' (39).

In swift succession woman has been identified as realist, sexual
object, succubus, witch, and pure maiden. These identifications
persist throughout the novel, nor would Steinbeck ever entirely
shake them. The perception of woman as 'other' – as somehow
an order of creature different from man – is latent in the
generalisation 'All girls and women hoarded something they never
spoke of'; and motifs of secrecy and deception are attached to the
female disturbingly. In fact young Henry, with his masturbatory
fantasies, is the secreter and deceiver. His suspicion of woman is a

projection. His own lack of integrity is revealed by his boast to the first sailor he meets that, before leaving home, he was visited in the dark by his 'girl with gold hair' (57). Confusion over sex and woman contributes to the flight of this adolescent 'romantic liar';[79] nor is it surprising that in the wind of the open seas, where such issues of civilisation are removed, he exults 'like a young god'. It is a London-like initiation into manhood. Like Van Weyden or Burning Daylight or Wagner's Siegfried, Henry comes to maturity beyond the pale of femininity. An eternal feminine is supplied by quietistic nature: 'There is a peace in the tropic oceans which passes a desire for understanding' (70). Only after being indentured in the West Indies and becoming the indispensable lieutenant of his master, does Henry, in his twenties, meet females again. Buccaneering in a cargo boat he has named the *Elizabeth*, he starts going to 'brown-eyed prostitutes'. At length he buys a slave, Paulette, of 'Spanish and Carib and Negro and French' blood. Paulette exercises a fascination over him reminiscent of Jeanne Duval over Baudelaire. Henry speaks of her 'sensuous, passionate beauty'; of lips that 'could writhe like slender, twisting serpents or bloom like red flowers' (89). Here is a mixture of pagan and Christian elements, with a touch of evil: 'She was a Christian, but she worshipped wood-spirits and sang low chants in honor of the Great Snake.' Henry describes her explicitly as a sex-object: 'a delicate machine perfectly made for pleasure, a sexual contraption'. He imagines her, again, in terms of a succubus: 'like those tall, cool women of the night who ride with the wings of sleep – soulless bodies'.

As Gwenaliana Morgan broke the wings of her husband's Orphic genius, so Paulette comes to threaten her rival: Henry's spiritual attachment to the sea. 'As the year went on, the soil of her love thrust up strong vines of choking fear. . . . She knew that when he finally deserted her she would be far more than just alone' (91). To keep him and avoid having to marry a Negro, Paulette plots get Henry to marry her. She contrives to make him drunk. Henry does not succumb to her purposeful deception, however; he attacks the basis of her attraction: 'May one worship a god merely because he is big, or cherish a land which has no virtue save its breath, or love a whole woman whose realm is her flesh?' In a burst of Baudelairean spleen he cries, 'Ah, Paulette! You have no soul at all!' (96). The body–soul split of the puritan is upon him. 'Elizabeth had a white winged soul', he declares, with no more basis in reality than there was for his youthful boast of the gold-haired girl visiting him in the night. 'I love you – yes – with what you have to be loved -the body,' he concludes, like Tannhäuser to Venus; 'but Elizabeth – I loved Elizabeth with my soul.' Elizabeth has suddenly ascended in fantasy to become the embodiment of *das Ewig Weibliche*, and the vision emboldens Morgan to reject his sexually–racially impure mistress in brutal, misogynistic terms: 'Hush! Or I box your mouth and have you whipped on the cross. . . . What can you know of love that lies without your fleshly juggling?' One might note the motif of the whip, which will reappear in the brothel of Cathy Ames Trask.[80] One might note too the sudden contempt for the sex-object that the hero has wallowed in and consider it beside Steinbeck's sudden and complete recoiling from Gwyn Conger, which preceded his creation of his 'monster'. One might note as well that this melodramatic scene is followed immediately by a sentimental farewell between Henry and his master, another surrogate father-figure. The chaste male bond replaces the sordid connection with woman, as it does repeatedly, however comically, in as apparently innocent a book as *Tortilla Flat*.[81] Here is another puritan motif characteristic of Steinbeck. Its most blunt expression comes in *Mice*, where Curly's wife destroys the precious and fragile male bond, cemented by dreams of an Edenic little farm, between George and Lennie.

Morgan goes to Port Royal and seeks out his uncle, the lieutenant-governor; the elder Morgan turns out to be a snob in fancy waistcoats and offers no assistance; his fourteen-year-old daughter, ironically name Elizabeth, is equally haughty; Henry is forced to proceed by his wits among pirates, gyp-artists, and buccaneers. Back in the all-male world of the sea he now becomes the great figure of legend: *primus inter pares* of 'the Free Brotherhood of the Coast'. He grows rich from plunder; his hair turns grey. 'He had thought the adulation of the Brotherhood might salve the wound of his desire'; but, like the stirring of Venus's music in the mind of Wagner's Tannhäuser, 'the nameless craving in him grew' (122). He is told the legend of Santa Roja, the 'red saint' who lives in 'the Cup of Gold', the city of Panama. Symbol of the richest stronghold of the Indies, Santa Roja represents an exotic strain of sophistication: she is rumoured to have been to Paris and Madrid. Seamen pray to her. Women curse her as a devil: 'Cup of Gold may go the way of Troy town on account of her' (131). Morgan falls under the spell of this mythical

Helen: 'The legend of the Red Saint grew in his brain like a powerful vine, and a voice came out of the West to coax and mock: "There is a woman in the Cup of Gold, and they worship her for unnameable beauties"' (134). Five times this phrase is repeated, as Morgan grows obsessed. He sacks every port in the Indies. Finally he turns his attention to Panama. The lure of Santa Roja is invoked to attract an army of buccaneers. 'The magnet of unseen beauty' is appealed to during the hot hungry march through the jungle. Morgan exhorts the reluctant with promises of gold, female slaves, beef to gorge upon, glory in history. Meanwhile, to himself he argues, 'There is more than lust. . . . This woman is the harbour of all my questing . . . a moment of peace after turmoil' (175). Longing for the quietistic *Ewig Weibliche* belies the weariness that lurks behind Morgan's obsessive quest. A local old woman is disappointed by the buccaneers as they approach: 'These aren't devils, only men like the Spanish' (185). On this foreshadowing note Morgan enters the city, takes the palace, and prepares to meet his mythic enchantress.

It is a case of the ideal versus the real which so haunted Decadents from the era of Baudelaire. Ysobel, Santa Roja, comes challengingly into the palace. Instead of the shy girl with 'blue, seraphic eyes' she turns out to be harsh and mocking: 'Hers was the harsh, dangerous beauty of lightning' (192). Morgan is nonplussed. Still, having sacrificed lives and destroyed a city to gain her, he feels compelled to make love to the woman. Partially repelled by her, he deliberately confuses her with Elizabeth as he recites a melodious speech of passion: 'You would vibrate to my touch like the fine body of an old violin. . . . I know by the dark sweet music of your eyes . . . the throbbing heart-beats on your lips. . . . Your lips are like twin petals of a red hibiscus' (194). As often in his erotic writing, Steinbeck sounds almost like Wilde; and there is much to compare between a writer whose females oscillate between the mother-figure of Lady Bracknell and the destructive object-of-desire, Salomé, and one whose vary from Ma Joad to Curly's wife. In response to Morgan, like Wilde's Hérodias in response to Herod, Ysobel laughs. She has heard speeches of the kind too many times: 'Is there some book with which aspiring lovers instruct themselves?' She wants to be brutalised. She has envisioned Morgan as one man who might command her, not beg her as so many others have. Morgan is brought up short. He tries to change course and become brutal, but Ysobel laughs and says it is too late.

In a rage against his ineffectuality, Morgan kills a man in cold blood (in a parallel to Wolf Larsen scapegoating Mugridge, the victim is a Cockney cook). Shortly after, he shoots his most favoured lieutenant for merely asking if he had 'conquered' Santa Roja. Dazed and remorseful, Morgan realises that he must get rid of the woman and arranges for her husband to ransom her. Confronting her for the last time, he confesses that he does not in fact love her as he imagined he would and now he simply wishes to return to 'the black mountains of his homeland'. Ysobel for her part says that she must lose her youth since he has not lived up to her vision (222).

Cup of Gold is an uneven novel, sometimes precocious, sometimes adolescent; but as a prophecy on Steinbeck's own career it is remarkable.[82] The mysterious early years in the native valley are followed by a long and ardent pursuit of a 'grail': success, whether in plunder or art, that will provide an essentially 'ugly' man (Morgan thinks this of himself as Steinbeck did of himself) with the power to win the mythic female of his dreams. The trick of using woman as a lure in this way may work in so far as it gains the material reward; but no material reward can transform the real into an ideal; real woman thus becomes a disappointment and a source of mockery. Still, Morgan lives on. He marries Elizabeth, daughter of his uncle, because of 'the orderly nature of her harp-playing' and because 'she was so little and so helpless, he thought' (241). In fact Elizabeth, now an orphan, plots to win the wealthy buccaneer with as much premeditation as Paulette once employed. This self-seeking philosophy of the new governor's wife has been her guide: 'Don't you know by now that almost any woman can marry almost any man as long as some woman doesn't interfere? . . . I captured the Governor when sitting in a garden. . . . A little water-snake ambled along the path and terrified me into his arms' (238–9). The perfidies of Eve. They would be more depressing if the Adam they were perpetrated upon were more noble. But Steinbeck's first hero is a disppointing figure, who 'splits up' before the pressures of civilisation. When Charles II asks him to relate his adventures, Morgan lies that he both had Santa Roja and took a hundred thousand pieces of eight in ransom for her; then he breaks down, confesses his lie, excuses himself with age and illness, and backs out of the monarch's presence. One might see here a foreshadowing of the aging Steinbeck in New York, who, according to Kiernan, became full of the bile and pomposity of 'a man profoundly unhappy' with his career.[83] As Morgan dies, he imaginatively enters a grotto of great pillars and glittering crystal. There little Elizabeth from Wales enters to 'the low, sweet tone' of organ music. *Das Ewig Weibliche* remains at the end of his vision, like the 'voix des enfants' at the end of Wagner's most misogynistic music drama, *Parsifal.*

Like Wagner's last work, *East of Eden* is a ponderous essay into the nature of good and evil. Conceived during the breakdown with Gwyn and finished under a blanket of support from Elaine, the book is more uneven than anything else Steinbeck wrote. Non-teleological thinking has given way to moralising. The determinism of the author of *In Dubious Battle* and *Mice* comes up against the straining after hope and belief in free will of a man who has gained material success, yet feels increasing guilt and disappointment in human relations. Gone almost entirely is the belief in the necessity of togetherness of *Grapes*. The New Deal is over; Communism is a world conspiracy; Steinbeck is now declaring that the only great creations are those made by lonely individuals.[84] Contemplation has replaced action. Self-analysis in the wake of divorce has proceeded to the point of neurotic inversion. Steinbeck goes back to Salinas to research the history of his ancestors, where fifteen years earlier he had gone out to the central valley to observe the suffering of the migrants. Where *Grapes* sprang out of inspiration, *East of Eden* derives from years of calculation. The issue is forced; the conscious effort shows; the artist has failed to conceal his props and dismantle his scaffolding.[85] *East of Eden* is half-dead in comparison to its great predecessor and, as befits a novel half-dead, its concerns are the morbid and perverse. The good and evil depicted are the values of an essential puritan who has tasted the forbidden fruit of his suppressed desires, has recoiled, and now – with a superstitious fear of damnation lurking at the back of his mind – is trying to teach a lesson to others.[86] The convention Steinbeck adopts is as banal as that of a French operetta in which the ardent and guileless youth is lured to destruction by the calculating and wicked Eve. His subject is Satan: the impulse toward error in mankind. But, while error in his life was produced by his own crooked desire, he contrives in his art – with little more integrity than a 1950s pop song – to paint the devil as a woman.

'I believe there are monsters born in the world to human parents. . . . And just as there are physical monsters, can there not be mental or psychic monsters born?'[87] *East of Eden* comes from an era when the teachings of Freud were invading American suburbs in the form of high-priced psychoanalysts, and Steinbeck spends the better part of the book's first four sections detailing the early case-history that has so twisted his heroine. Cathy Ames has a face of innocence and the figure of a child, which remains unaltered as she grows. Before puberty her nipples 'turned inward'; her body 'was a boy's body'; there 'must have been some steel cord in her throat', for her voice 'cut like a file' (73). The perverse in her figure is carried on in her mind: She 'interlards' her lies with truth and 'tells a truth as though it were a lie'. At an early age she discovers that 'sexuality with all its attendant yearnings and pains, jealousies and taboos, is the most disturbing impulse humans have'. At fourteen she is found in the barn with two young boys, naked, her wrists 'tied with a heavy rope'. At seventeen she is implicated with a young teacher of Latin, a 'pale intense young man' reminiscent of Hawthorne, who cannot abide scandalous whispers and ends in suicide. Cathy's mother responds to her daughter's vagaries by 'settling down to a steady hysteria'. Cathy's father, a Yankee puritan and himself a 'covert' man, is less resigned. He confiscates a copy of *Alice in Wonderland* which he finds his daughter reading: 'You're too big for that' (82). He lectures her on the authority God has given him: 'A little sternness never hurt anybody.' When she runs away from home and is returned by the Boston police, he whips her until she screams and writhes. A few days later his office and house are consumed in flames. Chicken-blood painted around the places Cathy was known to frequent is taken as evidence that she has been either kidnapped or murdered. Gypsies are blamed. 'At length a bumbling hairy half-wit was brought in for questioning' (88). Cathy, free of her parents and her repressive youth, has embarked to the city; Boston, and her career of crime.

It is a fantasy of dark nineteenth-century New England fabricated by a Californian transplanted in New York City: a fiction as transparent as a tale of old Monterey by an Easterner who has only just crossed the Sierras. Catherine Amesbury, as she is now called, turns up in the service of one Mr Edwards, a whoremaster who is known to 'take a heavy quirt from his suitcase, and whip the girls unmercifully' (91). Catherine avoids such brutal treatment by

making Edwards fall as hopelessly and miserably in love with her as
Steinbeck with Gwyn Conger. She keeps him anxious: 'She gave
him the impression of restlessness, as though she might take flight
at any moment' (94). She manipulates him sexually: 'She convinced
him that the result was not quite satisfactory to her, that if he were
a better man he could release a flood of unbelievable reaction in
her.' She puts him thoroughly off balance until one night, after he
has plied her with drink, she declares, 'You fat slug. . . . What do
you know about me?' (96). One might be reminded of Gwyn's
drunken attack on Steinbeck after Ricketts's death, and Edwards
writhes in an agony such as Steinbeck apparently experienced:
'Love to a man like Mr Edwards is a crippling emotion . . . ruining
his judgment, cancelling his knowledge, weakening him.' The
melodrama reaches a feverish pitch: Edwards threatens the whip;
Cathy fingers a knife concealed in her purse; Edwards finally gives
way to madness: 'His chest and stomach turned to molten metal
and a redness glowed in his head behind his eyes' (97). He beats
Cathy nearly to death and tries to bury her. He then goes back to
his wife, who nurses him as Elaine nursed the wounded Steinbeck,
and after a time returns to his business, respectable, composed,
'never to let the insanity of love come near him again'. Cathy
meanwhile crawls from her grave, 'a dirty bundle of rags and
mud'. She finds her way to the home of Adam and Charles Trask,
the original Abel and Cain of the overall Eden tale. Nursed by the
good Adam and suspected by the devious Charles, Cathy agrees to
marry the one and, on her wedding-night, seduces the other. Her
laughter at Adam's expense is diabolical.

   Here as in so many places in this book the depiction of evil seems
gratuitous, contrived, pandering to the taste for sensation of a
mass audience jaded by the War and fascinated by covert sex. In
her seduction and betrayal of Adam, Cathy has no apparent
motive. She does not want to go to California with him; she does
not want to be a mother; she has no zest for his Eden dream.
Confusion over her motives now even troubles Steinbeck: 'When I
said Cathy was a monster it seemed to me that it was so. Now I have
bent close with a glass over the small print of her and re-read the
footnotes, and I wonder if it was true. The trouble is that since we
cannot know what she wanted, we will never know whether or not
she got it' (184). This is clearly inadmissible, especially in an
omniscient narration. Steinbeck should have stopped the novel on
the spot and sorted out the motives. As it is, he asks the reader to

follow his vixen for another 500 pages bearing on his back the burden of uncertainty. Why, for instance, does Cathy, after giving birth to twin sons, turn on Adam, shoot him, and vanish? Is it merely a deepening of that aversion she felt for Edwards; a contempt for any man too easy to manipulate? 'I can do anything to you', she says to Adam; 'any woman can. . . . You're a fool' (201). Or does Steinbeck agree that there is some inherent moral deficiency in her, as Adam's Chinese houseboy, Lee, and his neighbour, Sam Hamilton, and Sam's wife, Liza – good Californians all – are ready to suspect of this creature from the East? 'Her hands, Samuel, her hands – what was she doing with her hands? . . . Not sewing, not mending, not knitting? . . . I don't know that it's a good idea for you to go over there. Riches and idleness, devil's tools' (182). Steinbeck puts little ironic edge on these provincials' suspicions. The fact that the Hamiltons were his own highly revered grandparents suggests his bias toward their opinions. Combined with his latent misogyny this encourages the building of a one-sided case against Cathy: 'A woman was likely to have strange tastes. . . . It was set down to the Eve nature still under sentence for original sin' (184).

The Eve nature again. What does this catch-all actually mean? In Cathy's case, it seems, an endless habit of vicious deception in favour of her own ill-defined ends. Going to Salinas, she cajoles herself into the service of the best madam in town, Faye. Is this strictly in character or is it in part motivated by Steinbeck's desire to wax verbose about the profession that had come to fascinate him, at least superficially, in middle life?[88] The question bears asking. The novel might have been more credible had Steinbeck allowed his heroine, even as wicked as he makes her, to follow a more conventional line of development. If the portrait has import-ance, it must be as a revelation of a pathological tendency in the American female; but, where revelation of the pathological obsession of Ahab in *Moby Dick* actually sheds light on the character of the American male at that stage in his development, the significance of Cathy's behaviour often seems obscure.[89] In general it is hard to sustain 'suspended disbelief' when a novel is as structurally flawed and inconsistent as *East of Eden*. Yet, reading on, one cannot be certain that there is not something significant being said, in spite of all the luridness, in the depiction of how Cathy, now renamed Kate, makes her way to be one of the most powerful women in the valley. She manipulates Faye's affection in the way that she once manipulated Edwards's. Once Faye has declared her as beneficiary, she begins to poison the woman, both literally and psychologically. Though plotting continually, Kate does not hurry: she is 'mistress of a technique which is the basis of good wrestling – that of letting your opponent do the heavy work toward his own defeat' (240). As Faye nears death, Kate falls into a delirium so intense that no one could possibly suspect her. The best-laid plans of evil women go better than those of mice and men apparently. Inheriting the whorehouse, Kate encourages a clientele of civic and social leaders. Catering to their darkest sado-masochistic fantasies, she gathers evidence on the fleshly weakness of those who rule. This confirms her fatal prejudice that the world is depraved and without good.

Kate has the moral despair of Wagner's Kundry. At the centre of her progress comes a scene which echoes the scene in the Decadent magic garden in which Parsifal defeats his *femme fatale*. Adam Trask goes to visit Kate's establishment, whose existence Sam Hamilton on his deathbed has revealed. It is night and the atmosphere is portentous:

> The paint had long disappeared from the clapboard walls and no work had ever been done in the garden. . . . A soft voice said, 'Won't you come in?' . . . Adam got a quick impression of richness and order. . . . He tried to think of what animal, what night prowler, [the voice's owner] reminded him . . . some secret predatory animal. . . . She picked her words as one picks flowers in a mixed garden   (315).

Adam is ushered into Kate's private chamber. The walls are 'clad in saffron silk'; the curtains are 'apple-green'. Kate, dressed severely, still has her childlike figure; but her hands have aged, her abdomen bulges slightly, her ankles have swollen from use of drugs. 'You were such a fool', she begins, pouring drinks; 'like a child. You didn't know what to do. . . . I can teach you now. You seem to be a man' (319). Adam, having learned the lesson of Parsifal and experienced the Amfortas wound, is proof now against taunts and flattery. 'I wonder what it is you hate so much', he muses. 'It isn't hatred, it's contempt' – Kate's tongue now loosens with liquor: 'You're a fool. . . . That's what I hate, the liars, and they're all liars. . . . I love to show them up.' Adam: 'Do you mean in the whole world there's only evil and folly?' Kate: 'I'll

have you begging to get in here . . . screaming at the moon. . . . No
one has ever escaped. . . . I'd rather be a dog than a human. . . .
But I'm smarter than humans. . . . Nobody can hurt me' (323).
Rage and intimidation failing, Kate tries seduction: 'Don't go,
dear. . . . My sheets are silk.' Adam drops his eyes to a hand
'wrinkled as a monkey's paw'. Presumably this impresses Kate's
degeneracy on him. When at length she reveals that his brother is
father to one of his sons, Adam declares, 'You are a devil.'
Impotent hatred gleaming in her eyes, Kate utters 'a long and
shrill animal screech'. Adam departs, released at last from all
thraldom to this, his personal, Satan.

The last quarter of *East of Eden* weaves the spectacle of Kate's
demise into the story of the new Cain and Abel,[90] Caleb and Aron
Trask. From a narrative point of view this is the novel's most
effective section: Steinbeck's intentions are at last clear and his
language and structure reflect as much. Interior monologues
reveal Kate's haunted fears of having her murder of Faye
discovered and being blackmailed. These are moving and lend her
character stature. Operating under duress for the first time, Kate
is less an evil manipulator than an errant soul struggling for
survival. A belated obsession with her fair-haired son, Aron, shows
her to have some capacity to love, however stunted. Her last
important relationship serves to elevate her as well, if only by
contrast. This is with her assistant and hit-man, Joe Valery, a stock
criminal tough who has perfected 'a lonely set of rules which might
have gone like this: 1. Don't believe nobody. . . . 2. Keep your
mouth shut. . . . 3. Keep your ears open. . . . 4. Everybody's a son
of a bitch. . . . 5. Go at everything roundabout. . . . 6. Don't never
trust no dame. . . . 7. Put your faith in dough' (501). Whereas Kate
has finally developed a bleak existential rationalisation for her
viciousness, Joe has no capacity for considering morality at all. His
world is as purely dog-eat-dog as Thomas Mugridge's; and, when
he spies an opportunity to blackmail Kate, Joe falls to it with as
much application as Mugridge cutting the *Ghost*'s ropes. Like
Wolf Larsen, Kate subscribes to a philosophy which only weakens
her and encourages her doom. But, also like Larsen, she has the
tenacity, cleverness and will to fight her opponents to the death;
thus, even as she prepares her suicide, she sets Joe Valery up for
arrest. In the face of premature arthritis, drug-induced weariness
and psychological torment, Kate's clinging to life has a kind of
courage. In the face of her unstated realisation that her career has

amounted to nothing but evil, her escape through overdose into an *Alice in Wonderland* quietus has a flicker of nobility. But in the end sensation triumphs over sense in her story. As French says, 'Steinbeck seems to have written with his eye on the lending library rather than the concentration camp.'[91]

Hideous though she may be, Cathy Trask should not be overlooked when considering Steinbeck. In terms of the male principle he was striving after, she might be taken as a goad: a projection of his self-contempt – thus the association with whips. When she attacks men as fools, liars and hypocrites, Kate represents to some degree Steinbeck's inner voice attacking himself for weaknesses always latent but most painfully revealed during the break-up with Gwyn; also his social critic's voice attacking the male principle in America, of which preceding and subsequent novels show him to be sceptical.[92] Cathy in this way is an unconscious feminist: a woman struggling to liberate herself from domination by a puritan male order, represented first by her father and the Latin-teacher, later by Adam Trask and Sam Hamilton. Cathy naturally gravitates toward criminal types such as Edwards, Charles Trask and Joe Valery, because they too are subverting the dominant puritan male order. Steinbeck for once appears clearly on the side of that order: Adam and Sam are almost excessively 'good' characters; the Chinaman, Lee, who becomes spokesman of their values in the end, is beguilingly quaint. The fact that Steinbeck loads the dice in their favour – gives way to the sentimental male chauvinism and reactive Manicheanism that the episode with Gwyn had released in him – is what makes the novel incredible and in the end bad; and Cathy is evidence not only of Steinbeck's wounded libido warring against his superego, but also of his artistic instinct struggling for survival against imposed moralism. Having recognised as much, one should also note that Cathy does reveal something important about the Californian woman at this stage in the culture's progress. The growing urban–suburban society is no longer a world for Ma Joad. Fundamental needs for food, shelter and sanitation are for the vast majority now taken care of. Life is no longer elemental. Boredom and desire are phenomena all have to deal with. Success is dependent on salesmanship in a competitive world – Cathy providing kinky East Coast perversions for Salinas is an inversion of Adam trying to provide refrigerated Salinas lettuce for the East Coast.[93]

In one of her essays in *Slouching toward Bethlehem* Joan Didion describes a type of woman characteristic of the late 1940s and 1950s, living in San Bernardino and perhaps of migrant stock, who through the temptations of the new suburban civilisation engages in an adulterous affair which finally, like the affair of Phyllis Nirdlinger with the insurance man in Cain's *Double Indemnity*, leads on to murder.[94] The woman has frosted, teased hair. She is conscious that her youth and sexual attractiveness are ebbing. Covertly jealous of her children and resentful of men, she drinks. Perhaps she takes drugs. In the new culture of California she has no religion or moral principle to restrain her. The spectacle of Hollywood, conveyed through the 'silver screen' and fan magazines, is her primary guide. Cathy Trask was conceived in this era. The war over, prosperity was widespread. Satiety and anomie were settling in even among people who had lately been farming dirt. The new Californian – particularly the woman, because the sanction that she should be a housewife was still in effect – had the new affliction of undirected wanderlust, of *Amour de l'impossible*. Steinbeck was suffering a version of this when he left Carol for Gwyn and his native valley for Hollywood and New York. It is the impulse that moves Faye to dream aloud to Kate about the trip to Europe they will take, and Kate to declare to Adam that she will move to New York as soon as she has enough money to live in grand style on Park Avenue. The wanderlust and desire that ruled the great dramatist of the era, Tennessee Williams, in works from *Streetcar Named Desire* to *Night of the Iguana*, grew out of kindred impulses in the cultural mind; impulses still threatening because the older provincial order and standards behind them were not yet fully dead. It is no accident that Cathy Trask's story was written in the sophisticated and corrupt pleasure-dome of New York City, by a man insistently nostalgic for a pastoral ideal of a homeland he had left; nor is it any mistake that the story is on one level an attempt to extirpate that past and, with questionable success, exorcise the guilts associated with it.

Cathy is a black version of the whores-with-hearts-of-gold who had been prominent in Steinbeck's work since the War. *Cannery Row*, *Burning Bright* and *Sweet Thursday* all reflect this peculiar obsession. Another work of the period, *The Pearl*, is set in the unconventional and exotic context of primitive Mexico; and the woman, Juana, is mysterious and remote. The other major work of the period, *The Wayward Bus*, was conceived in Mexico and drafted first in Spanish, and has a Mexican American for its hero. The heroine is yet another version of the whore-with-a-heart-of-gold, Camille Oaks, a Betty Grable/Marilyn Monroe/Jayne Mansfield 'blonde bombshell' who supports herself by swimming nude in wine bowls at stag parties in businessmen's clubs. The rebellion from the traditional American puritan order that these motifs indicate should be obvious. The perverse and primitive obsess Steinbeck's imagination in the period as much as Tennessee Williams's, though prostitution substitutes for homosexuality and a persistent streak of proletarianism for a Lawrentian philosophy of the primitive. The male chauvinism is extreme because the male persona, in a state of renovation, is insecure. The characterisation of woman as sex-object is extreme because the male persona, insecure, is consumed by desire; and, in the absence of knowing precisely what that desire is for, some objective correlative seems necessary. Desire, born of discontent with the status quo, is the dynamic principle. When desire threatens to destroy the security of the status quo entirely, as in the case of Cathy, the objective correlative for the desire must seem evil. But, when desire offers an interest in life, a *raison d'être* to eclipse a status quo grown entirely too tedious, the objective correlative, however disturbing, will in the end be seen as good. Camille Oaks of *The Wayward Bus* is in this sense a 'good' character, even a redemptive one. She comes of the phase preceding the break-up with Gwyn, when Steinbeck's desire had reached an apogee but had not yet so undermined the status quo as to send him scrambling to the past for images of male perfection and dominance.

The Wayward Bus is Steinbeck's most delicately balanced production.[95] On the subject of sex it is the one book in which he succeeds in presenting the many attitudes of which he was capable without loading the dice in favour of one or another. The Whitmanesque anti-puritanism of Jim Casy is shown in practice to achieve less than idealists might wish. The reactive puritanism of *East of Eden* is shown up for its hypocrisy and satirised with skill in such characters as the Pritchards and old Van Brunt. The brutal tendency that led the young Steinbeck to dangle a girl out of a window is confined to the one partially justified instance of marital rape by Mr Pritchard. The suspicion of marriage that lurks behind *Cannery* is out in the open in the miserable state of affairs between Juan and Alice Chicoy; but in this picture the woman is sinned against as well as sinning, and both husband and wife prove willing to make further attempts to carry on, even in the face of the ominous drinking-problems of the one and persistent wanderlust of the other. The adolescent tom-catting that afflicted Al Joad is reproduced with virtuoso brilliance in 'Pimples' Carson, who derives his name from a skin problem equal to Steinbeck's own as a youth (Pimples may constitute Steinbeck's best picture of himself in immaturity, Jody of *The Red Pony* notwithstanding). Norma, the waitress at the Chicoy's lunch-counter in Rebel Corners, is Steinbeck's most complete expression of the tendency he depicts in Curly's wife, of being obsessed with the life-style of Hollywood; and Norma's pathetic lies about her relationship with Clark Gable demonstrate Steinbeck's sentimental humanism at its most self-detected. Mildred Pritchard provides a portrait, largely unique in Steinbeck, of the political–sexual rebellion bubbling under the surface in the new upper-middle-class American *femme savante*. Her coupling with Juan at the book's climax provides realistic comment on what can be expected by those who indulge in romantic fantasy *à la* Lawrence's civilised woman/primitive man.

Camille Oaks is introduced getting on a Greyhound bus bound for Rebel Corners. The driver, who wishes he were Bing Crosby or Bob Hope, spots her, the moment she walks into the depot, as a 'dish', a 'looker', one who 'smelled of sex'.[96] Eyeing her big breasts and the make-up job that looks 'like some of the picture stars', he parades his style for her. The 'pig', however, fails to respond, and the driver wreaks his revenge by noting her flaws in his rear-view mirror: the split ends of her hair, the faint signs that her jaw was once broken. Camille doesn't miss any of this. In interior monologue she reveals that she always provokes such reactions ('There was always trouble') and that she is in flight from her excessive attractiveness. Resistance to the ability to manipulate distinguishes her from Cathy Trask. Experience has blessed her with gonorrhea, bad teeth, and sadness; but these 'hard knocks' have taught her sympathy, not cynicism. At Rebel Corners as on the Greyhound she sends electric waves through everyone: Pimples is lust-struck; Pritchard, who doesn't recall a certain stag-party, wonders where he might have seen her before; Mrs Pritchard, Mildred, and Alice Chicoy are suspicious; Norma is worshipful even before Camille asks her to share a seat on Juan's bus. As they journey up the back roads, Camille is called upon to handle uninvited attentions. This she does with a deftness, humour, and firmness that demonstrate that she both knows herself and has

mastered what Yeats would call her 'body of fate'. When Pritchard
careens into her lap with a swerve of the bus, Camille is gracious in
spite of general titillation. When Mildred questions her as to where
her father might have seen Camille before, she snaps off the line of
inquiry: 'He made a mistake. . . . You can take that any way you
want' (199). When Norma blurts a plea that they find a flat together in LA, Camille resists letting her down brutally, repeating
'We'll see how it goes', even though she can see how it would go with
painful clarity: 'Norma would meet a boy and naturally she'd bring
him home to show him off and the boy would make passes at
Camille and Norma would hate her' (143).

Camille is perhaps the most balanced woman in Steinbeck. Juan
Chicoy is an attempt for an equivalent male balance – something
Steinbeck had not achieved in a man of humble origins since Slim
in *Mice*. The extent to which Juan is successful is a matter of
debate. Watt accepts Steinbeck's description of his hero as 'all the
God the Fathers you ever saw driving a six-cylinder, broken down
world through time and space'.[97] Peter Lisca finds in him the three
cardinal virtues in a Steinbeck male: skill, self-reliance, self-
containment.[98] Charles Walcutt, however, complains,

> Juan's personal superiority is not justified. . . . He is set up
> before us as a noble savage who can repair a bus and haul it out
> of a hole better than a typical American. . . . [But] there is
> something phony in this sort of primitivism, for neither Juan's
> Mexican–Catholic roots nor his mechanical competence go
> deep enough to account for his superiority to the group of
> travelers.[99]

There is the note of falsity in Juan's Mexicanness that there is in all
Steinbeck's Mexicans, nor does the JC–Christ identification seem
appropriate here as in the case of Jim Casy. On the other hand,
Juan demonstrates a patience with his wife which is not
uncommendable and a gentleness with Pimples that matches
Camille's with Norma. His resentment of the Pritchards and
frustration with Van Brunt are not unjustified. Though he gives
way to the desire for flight which, curiously, afflicts all Steinbeck's
Mexican heroes,[100] in the end he recognises his responsibilities and
returns. Above all, like Camille, Juan is characterised by
self-knowledge:

He wondered why he stayed with [Alice]. . . . Just pure laziness, he guessed. . . . Didn't want to go through the emotional turmoil of leaving her. . . . He'd worry about her. . . . He'd need another woman right away and that took a lot of talking and arguing. . . . Besides, Alice was the only woman he ever found outside of Mexico who could cook beans. . . . But there was another reason. . . . She loved him. . . . You can't leave a thing like that without tearing off a piece of yourself. . . . If you want to remain whole you stay no matter how much you may dislike staying. . . . Juan was not a man who fooled himself very much. (136-7)

Especially in light of Steinbeck's biography, this is not entirely convincing. Still, Juan constitutes a commendable stab at a persona of balance amid domestic and cultural turmoil, superior to the forced heroes that succeeded him in *East of Eden*. In him desire and responsibility achieve that uneasy equilibrium that was always so tenuous in Steinbeck's own character. One may be reminded of the equilibrium London achieves in Dick Forrest. But, though they were only a generation apart, Steinbeck and London are enormously distant on sex and women. In London equilibrium is always attainable: women, even when their desires conflict with their men's, are never consciously·destructive or diabolical. The self-confidence of London's heroes may be one reason for this. But London's women as well are substantially proof against the inner conflicts that prey on Curly's wife and Cathy Trask. At base, Steinbeck's women seem to doubt their ability to find satisfactory men. His men, correspondingly, become disillusioned about their ability to find satisfactory women. Much of this may be blamed on a stage in cultural development where old sexual stereotypes were being propped up by increasingly artificial means. Radical change was known to be coming; what form that change might take was in doubt; the doubt could stimulate fear as well as desire; desire itself, forcing the consciousness half-blindly forward, could come to seem an enemy. Steinbeck was a fearful man in the realm of desire. He was confused about women because he was confused about what he wanted for and of himself. Art was the natural place for this confusion to be worked out. Art based on unresolved confusions, however – or on forced resolutions such as characterise *East of Eden* – is rarely satisfying. For this reason Steinbeck's career once he left his native valley failed, albeit in a most informative way, to live up to its original promise. Thus for his most worthwhile and enduring performances we must, with the possible exception of *The Wayward Bus*, look back to *In Dubious Battle* with its hard-cut, fiery-tempered artistry, and *The Grapes of Wrath* with its infectious inspiration and unique march-tempo style.[101]

4 The Tough Guys

I HAMMETT AND PURITANISM

The Maltese Falcon (1930) is only superficially a detective thriller. Ross MacDonald has called it 'a fable of modern man in quest for love and money'.[1] To Hammett as he wrote, it must have unfolded as a parable of what it took to succeed in the corrupt modern city. Caspar Gutman, like the Chinaman in Brecht's contemporary *In the Jungles of the Cities*, embodies the knowledge Sam Spade must gain and the twisted romanticism he must conquer in order to progress to honourable manhood. Spade fails with Gutman in the centre of the book; later he comes back to win against him. In this the novel is also about the necessity of the Parsifalian 'second chance'. Like Steinbeck and Chandler, Hammett took inspiration from medieval romance, and Spade is the seminal representation of the 'knight' required by California's 'mean streets'. Like von Eschenbach's *Parzival, The Maltese Falcon* is a *Bildungsroman* in which the young hero is stymied by his aggressive self-expression and incomplete understanding of his limitations. That it is a Grail story is obvious, the Grail being the ambiguous prize of the falcon, with its elaborate history stretching back to the Crusades and mingling with the legends of the Hospitallers and Templars which inspired Romantics from Scott to Wagner and Flaubert. The book parts company with the medieval epics in its dramatic unity: the time is limited to the days necessary to 'wrap up' the related murders, the place to a Gothic San Francisco. The perfection of the book lies in this density: the plot in which every incident is meaningful in terms not only of the mystery, but also of Spade's psychological growth ('It is a psychological novel with almost no psychology', Peter Wolfe says[2]); the architecture in which every scene is balanced against the whole, and development and dénouement form a completed arch ('Very few literary works manipulate the reader as much'[3]). Stylistically the book may lack some of the personality that appeals in Chandler, but there is none of the befuddled plotting that Chandler is so often masking by his brilliant asides. *The Maltese Falcon* is unparodistic, straight, muscular. It is so single-minded in purpose that it should perhaps be categorised as novella rather than novel. In its obsessional quality it is more like Wagnerian opera or Symbolist drama than the traditional novel (the jewel-encrusted falcon, Gutman informs Spade, was originally created by Grand Master Villiers de l'Isle Adam, a name Hammett could not have failed to associate with the Decadent author of *Axël*). Uncomfortable as a Marxist realist may have been with this 'Schopenhauerian' aesthetic tradition,[4] Hammett's art belies a persistent fascination with it. Chandler would suggest as much when he remarked that Hammett's style was 'almost as formalised as a page of *Marius the Epicurean*'.[5]

Spade is both the Nietzschean strong man posed against the Decadents and the new American posed against the old Europeans. The 'V' motif in his features, the hooked nose and high flat temples of his initial description, announce toughness and moral ambiguity: 'He looked rather pleasantly like a blond satan'.[6] From the first he is defined by contrast to other male characters: Miles Archer, his partner, 'as many years past forty as Spade was past thirty' (428), whose lip-licking attentions to women point up Spade's own restraint; Floyd Thursby, the tough guy as thug, whom 'Miss Wonderly' describes as loud, blustery, nervous, irritable, violent, and carrying himself 'erect' in 'what could be called a decidedly military carriage' (429–30). That Spade is antipathetic to the military style will be seen in his relations with the cops. That he is not psychologically compelled to assume the posture of an erect phallus is noted by his response when Joel Cairo comes in 'holding his small-boned body erect and stiff': 'In the comfortable slackness of [Spade's] body, in the easy stillness of his features, there was no indication of either curiosity or impatience' (476). Coolness, that quality Tom Wolfe would find so sought-after on the beach in *The Pump-house Gang* or among Kesey's redwoods in *The Electric Kool-aid Acid Test*, is what Spade is after; and from the first he has the superficial aspect of it. His language is replete with street-slang that the advent of 'talkies' would soon make familiar to the world: Miss Wonderly's hundred-dollar bills have 'brothers'; Miles is not to 'dynamite' her too much (430). The police are invited to 'turn the dump upside down', Spade 'won't squawk' (437). A dog metaphor introduced with the

cops early on ('I got up on my hind legs. . . . You birds coming in.
. . . You birds cracking foxy' – 439) is put to effective use in the final
scene: 'Expecting me to run criminals down and let them go free is
like asking a dog to catch a rabbit and then let it go.' Spade is
apparently as familiar with hunting as Hammett was.[7] This would
be consistent with the expertise on guns he demonstrates with the
cops and with Gutman's 'gunsel', Wilmer. Spade's urban
lower-middle-class origins enable him to speak the language of
cops and criminals with equal ease. He reads Wilmer on first sight
and addresses him in the appropriate New York sub-culture slang:
'Baumes rush? . . . You're not in Romeville now. You're in my
burg' (496). San Franciscan chauvinism is a motif he will repeat
twice with Gutman, the first time revealing the provinciality that
puts him at a disadvantage, the second the fixed identity that
sustains him in a way that Gutman's cosmopolitan wandering
cannot. Style, looks and language all converge to define Spade as
the California big-city tough. Then Hammett cuts across it all by
having the man correct his secretary's syntax: 'On the La Paloma?
. . . The *La* is a lousy combination' (544).

Spade has enough culture to set him off from 'the abyss'. His
foreign antagonists by contrast have too much. Joel Cairo, who
introduces the problem of the falcon, is the first of these Spade
must deal with. 'This guy is queer', Spade's secretary comments in
warning (456). Hammett goes on to detail Cairo's Levantine
features, narrow shoulders, slightly plump hips, trousers that 'fit
his round legs more snugly than was the current fashion', fawn
spats, chamois gloves, four baguette diamonds, fragrance of
chypre, high-pitched thin voice, and 'short, mincing, bobbing
steps'. Such details, particularly the last, reappear leitmotivally
each time Cairo surfaces; and Hammett's close attention belies
a fascination for that *rara avis* of the modern city, the type
dominating European Decadent society in figures such as
Diaghelev in Paris or those Martin Green refers to as 'children of
the sun' in England,[8] whom Proust following Balzac described as
tantes and produced the fullest literary specimen of in Charlus.
(The relationship of this detective genre and the voyeurism of
Proust, with which it was vaguely contemporaneous, is worth
noting: it receives its most pronounced expression in Chandler.)
The emphasis on the Levantine or Semitic is also in harmony with
the *Zeitgeist*: one might be put in mind of the Smyrna merchant of
The Waste Land, a work to which *The Maltese Falcon* merits

comparison as an evocation of the 'unreal city'. Cairo's pockets, which Spade rifles after knocking him out, continue the dissection by producing a collection of objects as random yet revealing as one of Joyce's lists in *Ulysses*. But Cairo is neither an artist-*manqué* like Stephen Dedalus nor a good-hearted 'chump' like Leopold Bloom; he is a *fin-de-siècle* dandy of a type Joyce himself aspired to be as a young man, unpredictable and amoral as a character out of Huysmans. As soon as he recovers from Spade's punch, Cairo pulls his gun again. Spade has to laugh: Old World guile proves superior for the moment to the physical force characteristic of a city less than a century away from the frontier. But Cairo has a flaw, and Spade has only to wait to capitalise on it. The Levantine's 'culture' disintegrates into a perverse romanticism which, on the one hand, provokes him to a 'bitch's rivalry' with Brigid for Wilmer and, on the other, to selling out Wilmer for 'the black bird'. The 'word of honour' Cairo gives Spade vanishes in the first conflict with self-interest; so too a love which is transitory and 'sinful'.

Cairo's spat with Brigid ends with his being taken in by the cops, Dundy and Polhaus, who are investigating Miles Archer's murder. The cops provide a second set of male figures, father–authority figures of a sort, with whom Spade must deal. Generally he is proficient in getting round them: he has dealt with cops for years and knows their psychology: his bafflement of them in the scene with Cairo and Brigid is an impressive display of his abilities: he provokes the young cop into losing his temper and charms the older one with 'horse-feathers'. But, thrown off stride by his failure with Gutman, Spade finds it trying to confront officialdom and becomes less impressive. When Polhaus gives fatherly advice about not provoking Dundy, Spade comforts himself by sneering at the cops' inadequacy: 'You mean a couple of high-class sleuths like you and Dundy worked on that lily-of-the-valley [Cairo] all night and couldn't crack him?' (535). In the scene that follows, in which Spade is ushered before the District Attorney, his impudence is pointless and immature. 'Hello, Bryan!' he opens over-familiarly; and, when the DA presses about his partner's murder: 'My guess might be excellent, or it might be crummy, but Mrs Spade didn't raise any children dippy enough to make guesses in front of a District Attorney, an Assistant District Attorney, and a stenographer' (536). Full of wisecracks, Spade pretends to be on top. In fact, his self-doubt at not yet being able to solve Miles's murder is stirring paranoia (there is an additional explanation for this

paranoia, which I shall come to in the next section); and, when the
DA spins out an elaborate pet scenario about how Eastern
mafia-types trying to horn in on San Francisco may have been
responsible, Spade misses the lunacy altogether and in a voice 'low
and hoarse and passionate' growls, 'Well, what do you think? Did
I kill him for his creditors? Or just find him and let them do the
killing?' (538). Eventually recovering his cool, Spade recognises
that the DA has 'Arnold Rothstein on the brain'. Meanwhile,
however, this nearly self-defeating tendency to provoke cops and
bureaucrats should be noted. A hallmark of Spade's style, it would
be inherited by Chandler's Marlowe in a greater dosage. It is a
motif Californian culture has often partaken of, Steinbeck's
passionate outbursts in *In Dubious Battle* and *Grapes* and the
radical insurgency of the 1960s being examples. Though
unidentified as such in Spade, the tendency is grounded on an
expectation of social injustice. The cops are not only father–
authority figures that must be conquered for psychological
growth; they are also stupid and inefficient and unjust. Polhaus's
redeeming humanity is the exception rather than the rule. The
powers-that-be deserve to be mocked with as much ardour as
Baudelaire would *épater le bourgeois*.

Such is not the case with Gutman. The 'fat man' must be taken
with respect, and Spade's initial lack-of-deference proves
thoroughly counterproductive. Gutman is ruthless, totally. Apart
from being responsible for the murders of innocent Miles and the
captain of *La Paloma*, he allows the 'accidental' burning of that
ship and, worst of all, the drugging and near-fatal death of his
daughter. In superficials, by contrast, Gutman is the complete
gentleman – host, *raconteur*, wit in the grand style – and Spade
must grudgingly admire him for these qualities, just as he in turn
must admire Spade for his guts, resourcefulness and individualism. The introduction of Gutman is as grand a visual feast as that
of Cairo:

> As he advanced to meet Spade all his bulbs rose and shook and
> fell separately with each step, in the manner of clustered
> soap-bubbles not yet released from the pipe through which they
> had been blown. . . . He wore a black cutaway coat, black vest,
> black satin Ascot tie holding a pinkish pearl, striped grey worsted
> trousers, and patent-leather shoes. His voice was a throaty purr.
> . . . His hand [was] like a fat pink star. (504–5)

There is Johnnie Walker whisky on a tray and a box of cigars, Coronas del Ritz (Hammett is quite specific here), symbols of civilised manliness; and Gutman himself appears from the first as high-priest of the civilised manly code:

> I distrust a man who says when. If he's got to be careful not to drink too much it's because he's not to be trusted when he does. . . . I distrust a close-mouthed man. He generally picks the wrong time to talk and says the wrong things. Talking's something you can't do judiciously unless you keep in practice. . . . I do like a man who tells you right out he's looking out for himself. Don't we all? I don't trust a man that says he's not. And the man that's telling the truth when he says he's not I distrust most of all, because he's an ass that's going contrary to the laws of nature. (506)

Here is something approaching a confrontation between the extremes of Anglo-Saxon culture: the old boy, vaguely English public-school, man-of-calculation; the cowboy of the mean streets, solitary, man-of-action. Spade's response to Gutman's peroration is typically taciturn: 'Uh-huh. Now let's talk about the black bird.' But distaste for nonsense is masking confusion. Gutman assesses ('His face was a watchful-eyed smiling mask held up between his thoughts and Spade') and concludes that he can use this man with little more difficulty than he has used others in pursuit of the falcon. In the end this assessment proves both right and wrong.

The first meeting between Gutman and Spade is in the former's lavish hotel suite, the last in the latter's unpretentious apartment. As the venue shifts, so does the advantage. Gutman and company have surprised Spade by entering his apartment while he is off on one of their wild-goose chases, but he is prepared. He understands now where Gutman's flaw lies: much like Cairo, the fat man is subject to a perverse romanticism whose human expression is affection for Wilmer but whose obsession is to possess the falcon. Alone knowing the whereabouts of the bird, Spade demands Wilmer as fall-guy before parting with the information. This is psychologically telling: 'Wilmer's high voice and scrawny wrists, his beardlessness and his youth, bar him, along with his cowardice, from manhood. . . . Yet manhood is what he craves most. . . . Spade knows that he blocks Wilmer's drive to manhood. . . . Spade isn't safe with

Wilmer prowling around.'[9] As Wilmer embodies immaturity, so willingness to get rid of him signals resolution to grow. Spade wants to get rid of Wilmer and exorcise for once and all the punk in himself; the others, by contrast, want to cling to their emotional immaturity. Cairo resists the sacrifice of his catamite by throwing a lover's tantrum, trying to fight Spade and then trying to convince him to frame Brigid, the woman, instead. Gutman resists framing his 'son' by making a masterful sequence of appeals (563–7): to Spade's vanity ('We can leave the handling of the police to you. . . . You won't need our inexpert help'); to his courage ('You can't expect us at this late date to believe you are the least bit afraid of the police'); to his wisdom ('You've got a system that's got a lot to recommend it, sir. . . . But there comes a time when you've got to make exceptions, and a wise man just goes ahead and makes them'); to his wits ('Now maybe it will be a little more trouble than if you had your victim to hand over . . . but you're not a man that's afraid of a little trouble'). Through the flattery and veiled dares, Spade stands firm. As Gutman falls prey to the snipings of Cairo, he can't resist mocking: 'I thought this was your show. . . . Should I do my talking to the punk?' Gutman is only temporarily reduced, however. Agreeing to sacrifice Wilmer, he recoups a dignity that sets him apart from the whimpering Cairo and even that more lovely partner-in-crime, Brigid. When the bird arrives and is found to be fake, Cairo breaks into tears and curses. The fat man, however, responds with the unflinching commitment of the purest romantic questor: 'Everybody errs at times and you may be sure this is every bit as severe a blow to me as to anyone else. . . . Shall we stand here and shed tears and call each other names? Or shall we . . . go to Constantinople?' (584).

As a parable of the making of a man, *The Maltese Falcon* occupies a place in Hammett's opus much like that of *The Sea Wolf* in London's. Like London, Hammett was in process of leaving his wife as he wrote – the book is dedicated to her. London, however, was leaving Bess Maddern for his beloved Charmian, and *The Sea Wolf* moves from the making of a man to the making of a couple. Hammett was leaving Josie and his daughters (like London he had two) to be on his own; Lillian Hellman had not yet appeared in his life, and *The Maltese Falcon* takes a puritan line on women. Of the things Spade must do to achieve mastery, resisting the lure of

women ranks highest. Sex is seen as temptation, as a means of
lowering one's guard. 'Sex can kill you dead', is Wolfe's
summation; 'To show a woman love is to ask for trouble. Survival
in the urban jungle requires toughness, practicality, and clarity of
mind.'¹⁰ These things in turn require solitary, not dual,
perspective; and in this the tough guy, ironically, must, like Wolf
Larsen, be a kind of androgyne. 'The mannish talk and people
mask a feminine appreciation of what is indirect, intangible, and
unrevealed.'¹¹ The limitations to the *macho* are reflected in the
description of Spade's physique, which, also like Larsen's, is
delicate as well as strong: 'The smooth thickness of his arms, legs,
and body, the sag of his big rounded shoulders, made his body like
a bear's . . . a shaved bear's. . . . His chest was hairless. His skin was
childishly soft and pink' (432). The feminine note here is not to be
confused with the effeminancy of Cairo. Homosexuality is a
concern inasmuch as it is a symptom of the city corruption Spade is
combating. It is not surprising that Hammett should have paid
such attention to it at a time when he was leaving the security of a
conventional marriage: psychologically it is as apt as the fact that
he was preoccupied with what it took to be an effective man. The
attention does not belie a latent predilection, however. Spade is
attracted to women – indeed, too much so. That is the source of
his guilt and paranoia. Renunciation of what he desires most is the
key to his fatalistic melancholy.

Spade has been involved adulterously with his partner's wife,
Iva. The relationship was a mistake; Spade is ashamed of it;
particularly with his father-figures, the cops, he is defensive. At
3 a.m. the night after Miles's death he is lighting his fifth cigarette
and pouring his third Bacardi when Dundy and Polhaus come in to
grill him. 'I don't know anything about women', is his less-than-
candid retort (436). As the cops get tough, 'his upper lip, on the
left side, twitched over his eye tooth', and he chooses words that
suggest that his true annoyance is sexual: 'Here's something for
you not to forget, sweetheart. . . . What's itching your boyfriend
now? . . . Keep your damned paws off me' (438). It is almost as if,
in his half-drunken sleepless state, he were mistaking the cop for a
predatory woman. Fittingly, the next chapter, 'Three Women',
begins with Iva invading his office and trying to coerce his
affection. A 'blonde woman of a few more years than thirty', Iva
has a 'facial prettiness . . . perhaps five years beyond its best
moment' (441-2). Contrasted to her is Spade's secretary, Effie,

who has a 'boyish' face and is trustworthy, but sharp: 'Are you
going to marry Iva?' Spade: 'Don't be silly. . . . You're a
rattlebrained angel.' Effie: 'That louse wants to marry you, Sam'
(444). Iva wants Sam indeed: Miles was a 'chump' who chased
every 'skirt' in sight, and the evidence suggests that Iva laid traps to
snare his young partner. Spade's depth of involvement is indicated
when he consults his good father-figure, the cigar-chomping
Jewish lawyer Sid Wise (a sort of Gurnemanz figure in the *Parsifal*
scheme): 'Are you going to marry her, Sammy?' Wise queries,
echoing Effie. Spade clearly has some obligation to Iva. That he
feels more honour-bound than the book explicitly states is revealed
in the last scene. 'Iva is here', Effie announces (Brigid has just been
sent off to jail) (596). Spade shivers, then takes his medicine: 'Send
her in', he says. The 'awful daring of a moment's surrender' has,
one is left to suppose, saddled him with the worst of his possible
female partners.

Of the 'three women', Effie Perine is least threatening. She
wants Spade as much as Iva; instinctively, however, she
understands the necessity of renunciation and sublimates her love
into devoted friendship. Effie operates as Spade's good conscience:
a kind of practical anima who warns about the people who come
through his door. Continually he is asking her to consult her
'woman's intuition'. On Brigid in particular she provides
commentary. Perhaps she senses that here at last is a woman able
to absorb Spade's attention; in any case, her liking for Brigid is a
factor in Spade's involvement with that *femme fatale*. His own
male intuition suspects Brigid from the first; Effie, however, is so
foxed that, in the finale when Spade tells her that he has sent
Brigid up, she responds, 'You did that to her, Sam? . . . Please,
don't touch me' (595). The woman who has renounced love has
been living vicariously via the woman who has not – that is why
Effie is so appalled that Spade puts law over love. Effie's recoiling is
what leaves Spade with no one but Iva. The price a man must pay
for justice is enormous, it seems: not only his happiness but even his
well-being. Effie, however, is probably a type who will calm down
and settle back into her role as supportive girl Friday: doing
errands for Sam in the wee hours, covering for him with those he
does not want to see, nagging and chiding when he's feeling
ineffective, enlisting her mother and cousin to do favours for him.
All this Effie does without applying the slightest pressure for
amorous reward. Most important of all, she runs his office with an

efficiency that gives it a quite different atmosphere from the
low-rent, whisky-bottle-in-the-drawer, musty-middle-aged-man
surroundings of Chandler's Marlowe. Effie is the tomboyish,
non-demanding woman-as-pal that Ann Riordan aspires to be in
Farewell, My Lovely. Marlowe in the end prefers his cynical
self-absorbed solitude. Spade, via Effie, retains a vital, if minimal,
link to the world of decent females.

'Spade's behaviour with women belies Somerset Maugham's
description of him as an "unscrupulous rogue" ', Wolfe writes;
'Does his compassion [for Gutman's daughter] befit a rogue? . . .
He even acts the gentleman in his sexual relationships [with Iva
and Effie].'[12] As for Brigid:

> Not only does Spade love [her]; he also believes they are well
> suited. . . . Both of them enjoy communicating through
> nuance; both skirt the fringes of the law. . . . The subtle verbal
> by-play they generate amid wavelets of sexual arousal prefigures
> the loving, sparkling repartee of Nick and Nora Charles in *The
> Thin Man.* . . . As shrewd and crafty as she is, Brigid keeps pace
> with him most of the way. Not only is she a fine actress; like
> Spade, she also knows how to time her best effects.[13]

In the realm of women Brigid is the great challenge, the noble
enemy, the counterpart of Gutman in the realm of men. Her
aliases set her up with a magical aura – first Miss Wonderly, then
Miss LeBlanc. 'Miss Wonderly called up', Effie reports; 'She wants
to see you . . . at the Coronet, on California Street, apartment one
thousand and one' (447). The suggestion of Scheherazade is apt:
Brigid has an endless supply of exotic fictions about herself, several
with Oriental venues. At her first private tryst with Spade she tries
one of these on him. When it doesn't work, she appeals to the
knight-in-shining-armour: 'I want you to save me from – from it
all' (449). She goes down on her knees and in a tremulous voice
confides, 'I haven't lived a good life . . . but I'm not all bad. . . . Be
generous, Mr Spade. . . . You're strong, you're resourceful, you're
brave.' Brigid is transparent; still, she is very attractive ('cobalt-
blue' eyes are the leitmotival feature), and her Art Nouveau posture
as damsel-in-distress flatters the tough guy with a vision of what,
ideally, he sees himself to be. Brigid will not be discouraged by
Spade's imperviousness either. Alone with him again after the spat
with Cairo, she adopts an 'immortal weariness of beauty' attitude

out of Arthur Symons or Baudelaire: 'Oh, I'm so tired, so tired of it all, of myself, of lying and thinking up lies, and of not knowing what is a lie and what is truth' (492). At the close of this scene Spade apparently sleeps with her. No doubt he is motivated by desire, but there is also a good professional reason: in the morning, with 'as little sound as might be', he steals her key, slips out, and searches her room at the Coronet. Returning with an armful of groceries, he makes out, charmingly, that his sole intention has been to procure her a hearty breakfast.

Gutman's hubris is imagining that he can outwit Spade; Brigid's, fitting the beautiful woman, is imagining that her sexual attractiveness can overpower Spade's commitment to justice. Following his triumph over Gutman in the matter of the bird comes the chapter 'If They Hang You', in which he is put to the ultimate test: can he renounce this woman? The most passionate and brutally frank passages of the book show Spade pinning Brigid for her crimes: 'You had Thursby hooked and you knew it. He was a sucker for women. . . . His record shows that. . . . Once a chump, always a chump. . . . Miles hadn't many brains, but, Christ! he had too many years' experience as a detective to be caught like that by a man he was shadowing. . . . But he'd've gone up [that dark alley] with you, angel' (588–9). Too many bones of previous victims lie at this Venus's feet. 'I would have come back to you', Brigid replies, trying to convince Spade that with him it was different; 'from the instant I saw you I knew'. Spade is proof against this, however: 'You angel! Well, if you get a good break you'll be out of San Quentin in twenty years.' Brigid: 'You didn't - don't - love me?' Spade:

> I think I do. . . . What of it? . . . I won't play the sap for you. . . . When a man's partner is killed he's supposed to do something. . . . Maybe I love you. . . . Maybe next month I won't. I've been through it before. . . . I'll have some rotten nights – but that'll· pass. . . . If that doesn't mean anything to you forget it and we'll make it this: I won't [shield you from the cops] because all of me wants to – wants to say hell with the consequences and do it – and because – God damn you – you've counted on that with me the same as you counted on that with all the others. (593–4)

Honour over desire is the code. To put it in the less exalted phrase that Spade repeats leitmotivally: 'I won't play the sap for you.' It is the ultimate and typical perversity of the puritan psyche: renunciation. '*Falcon* leans heavily on the head–heart dualism', Wolfe says; 'but Hammett opposes Hawthorne and Faulkner by rating reason over emotion.'[14] Hawthorne and Faulkner were reacting against cultures where puritan repression was all too ascendant. Hammett, via Spade, is responding to a culture where, by contrast, licence was beginning to run amok.

Hammett was born eighteen years after London, eight before Steinbeck, in 1894, in Baltimore, a city which, curiously, also gave birth to two of the other most notable immigrant California writers, Upton Sinclair and James M. Cain, and whose greatest literary figures, Poe and Mencken, both had significance to London's work, the former for inspiration, the latter as mentor (London himself gave one of his few non-Californian heroes, Pathurst of *The Mutiny of the Elsinore*, a Baltimore origin, a detail which must have seemed appropriate to the decadent strain in Pathurst's character, anomalous among London's heroes). Scottish on his father's side, French on his mother's, Hammett, like London, spent his youth in the tough urban milieu, working from an early age as newsboy, messenger, freight-clerk, timekeeper, stevedore and yardman, before, at twenty, becoming a Pinkerton. Like Chandler, he served in the First World War in Europe. Like Hemingway, he drove an ambulance. Like Cain, he suffered from tuberculosis. In and out of army hospitals in Tacoma and San Diego, he met Josie, married her in 1921, moved to San Francisco. To support a nascent family, he wrote advertising copy for a local jeweller (shades of *McTeague*) and went back to work as a Pinkerton. In 1922 he published his first story in *Black Mask*, the mystery magazine which was conceived by Mencken and George Jean Nathan to support the more highbrow *Smart Set*, and which in the next decade would give Chandler his start as well. Within nine years Hammett had completed all his major work save *The Thin Man* (1934): sixty-odd stories and four novels – *Red Harvest* (1929), which Wolfe classifies as a 'western'; *The Dain Curse* (1929), a 'Gothic' thriller; *The Maltese Falcon*, a 'hidden treasure' story; *The Glass Key* (1931), a dissection of the corrupt city.[15] *The Maltese Falcon* is by consensus considered Hammett's great accomplishment, though Gide and some Marxists have favoured the violent *Red Harvest* and A. Alvarez *The Glass Key*. Neither of the latter has a Californian setting nor any specifically Californian aspect. Apart from *Falcon*, the only novel which does is its awkward yet revealing immediate predecessor, *The Dain Curse*.

In her brief impressionistic memoir of Hammett, Lillian Hellman misrepresents when she suggests that he only started writing after a series of severe haemorrhages; that, thinking he had just a few months to live, he quit the Pinkertons, left his wife, and recouped his spirits by a bohemian existence of art, cheap restaurants, 'dago red wine', and the affections of 'one girl on Pine Street, another on Grant'.[16] Miss Hellman did not know Hammett until after he left San Francisco in the early 1930s; and, possibly to protect memories of his marriage and family, he appears to have been mysterious about his past to her. Probably it is for reasons having to do with her personal myth of her young life with the great writer that Hellman over-romanticises. What is most important in her representation is that leaving Josie was tied up with Hammett's best work. *The Maltese Falcon*, as we have seen, indicates a sense of connection between renunciation and success. *The Dain Curse*, parts of which may have been written simultaneously, shows this sense at a more rudimentary stage with the puritan resolution not yet fully achieved. Both Brigid O'Shaughnessy and Gabrielle Dain must, on some psychological level at least, be versions of Josie. Both exercise an attraction over the detective that he must break free of in the end. Gabrielle is more victimised and less calculating than her successor, a less sure embodiment of the woman as 'other'. She increasingly absorbs the detective's attention as *The Dain Curse* proceeds; and in the final, 'Quesada' (Carmel), section there are several scenes of just the two of them together. Ostensibly the detective is putting the girl through a cure for morphine addiction; the dialogue in many places, however, reads like a dramatisation of the conversations in a difficult marriage. Even before the *Falcon* begins, Spade has reached a point in his relations with women that he knows he must resist and renounce. In *The Dain Curse*, by contrast, his predecessor has not given up hope that, through a strong tutorial–fatherly line, he might be able to 'save' the woman. Young husband still trying to 'master' young wife?

The motif of the 'curse' suggests the identification of woman as the wicked Eve that hovers behind the book. Like Cathy Trask, Gabrielle Dain has a history of murder in her background. She also has signs of physical degeneracy: 'She's about twenty; five feet four or five; looks thinner than she really is; light brown hair, short and curly; big eyes that are sometimes brown and sometimes green; white skin; hardly any forehead; small mouth and teeth; pointed chin; no lobes on her ears, and they're pointed on top; been sick for a couple of months and looks it.'[17] Why does Hammett choose to depict his heroine as degenerate? Why, further, does the detective pay such attention to these signs, especially when he will try to convince her that the idea of 'degeneracy' is a myth? Don't these things indicate some doubt at the deepest level about the full humanity of woman? Gabrielle herself believes she is 'cursed'. During her morphine cure–exorcism she asks the detective, 'Can't there be – aren't there people who are so thoroughly – fundamentally evil that they poison – bring out the worst in – everybody they touch?' (349). This is a remarkably similar proposition to the one Steinbeck advances about Cathy. Hammett, however, appears to be in some doubt. He raises the issue, then has his detective combat it, only to be proved wrong in the end. In a twist of the Steinbeck situation, the woman protests her essential evil while the man tries to convince her of her good. All, meanwhile, is projected from the man's point of view. The detective's opinion, even by the girl, is granted precedence; and Hammett's bias is already toward the cool, individual male reason that the *Falcon* would celebrate. The detective's fatherly comfortings indeed have a disturbing way of suggesting that she (most people, in fact) is not really capable of intelligence at all: 'Thinking is a dizzy business, a matter of catching as many of those foggy glimpses as you can and fitting them together as best you can. That's why people hang on so tight to their beliefs and opinions; because, compared to the haphazard way in which they're arrived at, even the goofiest opinion seems wonderfully clear, sane, and self-evident' (347–8).

There is a degree of 'goofiness' throughout *The Dain Curse* that makes its creator seem confused at times, silly at others. Patches of evocation are brilliant: the picture of California cultism at this early stage in the Haldorns' phony cult of the Holy Grail, which lures the already effete of the Golden State and prefigures a motif that would become standard by the time of *Farewell, My Lovely*. Often, however, the Gothic ornamentation seems extrinsic: the Devil's Island escape-story and French aristocratic history of Gabrielle's father, which intrude from the realm of decadent literature to which Hammett felt such an attraction–repulsion. Personal disquiet with the book may be indicated by the fact that the author makes a writer into the evil genius behind Gabrielle's continued 'possession'. Owen Fitzstephan is author of *The Pale Egyptian* and *Eighteen Inches*, Aleister Crowley-like essays into the occult presumably: they 'bear all the better known indications of authorial degeneracy' (378). Fitzstephan is a precursor of Gutman on the one hand: the cultured gentleman, sedentary, full of quips and witty conversation which stimulates the detective. He seems a portrait of Hammett at this stage in other respects:

> a long, lean, sorrel-haired man of thirty-two, with sleepy grey eyes, a wide, humorous mouth, and carelessly worn clothes; a man who pretended to be lazier than he was, would rather talk than do anything else, and had a lot of what seemed to be accurate information and original ideas on any subject that happened to come up, as long as it was a little out of the ordinary. (227–9)

The apartment Fitzstephan inhabits suggests Spade's in *Falcon* (both were probably based on Hammett's in life) and his ease of posture Spade's detumescent, 'cool' attitude. Fitzstephan, however, represents the aesthetic side of Hammett's persona to the detective's practical: 'I fantasise Dumas and you reduce it to the level of O. Henry' (263). In the end this side, the more Decadent, must give way to the other, the more New World; for to the latter it seems deeply disturbed:

> As a sane man who, by pretending to be a lunatic, had done as he pleased and escaped punishment, he had a joke – if you wanted to call it that – on the world. But if he was a lunatic who, ignorant of his craziness, thought he was pretending to be a lunatic, then the joke – if you wanted to call it that – was on him. And my having such a joke on him was more than his egotism could stomach, even though it's not likely he ever admitted to himself that he was, or might be, actually crazy. (380)

Wolfe sees Fitzstephan as an indication of Hammett's dissatisfaction with his career.[18] He sees the novels, two of which have leading characters suffering from tuberculosis, Dan Rolff of *Red Harvest* and Ned Beaumont of *The Glass Key*, as working out a struggle between 'the ideal of physical suffering of the artist from Schopenhauer' and 'the 'Marxist bias against intellectualism'. The latter phrase seems loose, and Hammett probably would have thought it inaccurate; nor should one rush to accept Wolfe's thesis that Hammett's turning-away from writing represented a conscious rejection of 'the novel's built-in endorsement of individuality'.[19] *Grapes of Wrath* is one of many works which confutes this characterisation of the novel; and Hammett's turning away, in any case, is more complex. Antipathy for the values in his novels and inability to see how to change them is a possible explanation. Illness is a probable one: 'The fact of breathing, just breathing,' Hellman recalls, 'took up all the days and nights.'[20] A third may be that, having moved from the budding culture of San Francisco to the established one of New York, Hammett lost the compulsive atmosphere, the sense of the new place crying out for literary treatment. *The Thin Man*, his New York book, is in fact the most difficult to reconcile with his Marxism, and its main value may be as a revelation of what a happy relationship might constitute. Hellman apparently fulfilled Hammett in a way that Josie had not. With her he was able to play the tutorial father, artistically and politically as well as domestically. This of all factors may have done most to quell the daemon that had driven him through the 1920s. Having realised in Spade a character who succeeds in renouncing women for the sake of honour, individualism and success, Hammett appears to have done the reverse. As a successful artist he was finished shortly after meeting Hellman – much of his creative energy was thereafter devoted to her work. As an individual he turned to Marxist collectivism, defended the American Communist Party, and ended up cleaning toilets in jail in the McCarthy period. As a man of honour he put himself in the precarious position of having the Grail of his legacy guarded by a sceptic who felt deeply ambivalent about his code: 'He made up honor early in life and stuck with his rules, fierce in protection of them.'[21] About Hammett altogether this last *femme fatale* of his career would conclude, 'Proud men who can ask for nothing may be fine characters in life and novels, but they are difficult to live with or understand.'[22]

II THE *ZEITGEIST* AND CAIN

Puritanism and socialism, separately and in relation, are factors of considerable importance in the literature we are discussing. In the popular mind, Jack London was an advocate of free thinking, advanced sexual morality, drinking and parties and 'living living living', as well as a political ideologue; still, in *John Barleycorn*, London wrote his own 'de Profundis' rejecting much of this, and the book may have been a major stimulus to Prohibition. Like George Bernard Shaw in England, the socialist writer in America at the beginning of the century was often morally conservative. The wedding of Whitmanesque free love and radical politics was still only in the theoretical stages when Steinbeck wrote *Grapes of Wrath*. The intercourse of these two strands of progressive thought in the late 1960s led, arguably, to a misalliance which has left the idea of socialism in America impotent. Some prophetic writers of the early century might have predicted this development. One whose case we might consider at least in passing is Upton Sinclair.[23] Born two years after London, in Baltimore as noted, Sinclair grew up on the mean streets of New York. His parents were fallen aristocrats, genteel but penniless, who found it 'cheaper to move than pay rent'. Sinclair as a teenager wrote for boys' magazines: 'While other youths were thinking about "dates", I was pondering the jokableness of Scotchmen, Irishmen, Negroes, and Jews.'[24] The young man fell under the influence of a minister who felt that repression of sexual desire enhanced one's mental and spiritual powers. He developed the idea that 'ecstasy' was the condition to be sought for in art. Jesus, Hamlet and Shelley became his literary idols. Art took the place of religion for him and the artist that of the priest. At age twenty-one Sinclair wrote in the theosophist *Metaphysical Magazine*, 'Art presages a future heaven on earth.'[25]

Sinclair believed in the notion of 'genius' current among Europeans of the epoch, and his early novels reflect as much. *Springtime and Harvest* (1900) preaches platonic love and the necessity of avoiding materialism; rejected by publishers, it was printed and distributed by the young enthusiast himself. *Prince Hagen* (1903) demonstrates a sympathy with Wagnerian metaphysics: a gold-seeking Nibelung turns up in America, becomes a Tammany organiser, then a Republican orator, finally an unscrupulous Wall Street lawyer. There is a relation here to Norris and the metaphysics of *The Octopus* and *McTeague*. There is a relation to London as well as Norris in connection with *The Overman* (1907), which continues Sinclair's exploration of European ideas by dramatising a Nietzschean awakening: a young musician is shipwrecked on a Pacific island; there he learns that 'each individual soul is a microcosm self-sufficient'; through 'indescribable fear' and 'a sudden rending away of barriers', he enters a state of mystical ecstasy in which he stands 'transfixed with the glory of an endless vision of dawn'.[26] This and other early work was written during Sinclair's troublesome marriage to Meta Fuller. The young idealist, following Shelley, had undertaken the marriage in part to 'save' the woman from the wickedness of the world. But, once his code of chastity was challenged by Meta's opinion that sexual intercourse constituted 'an utter blending of two selves, the losing of one's personality in another', he suffered from 'feelings of shame and entrapment'.[27] In spite of his Wagnerism, such *Tristan*-like love appeared as threatening to Sinclair as to his contemporary Shaw; and the emotional shambles his marriage became may have contributed, as with London and *The Sea Wolf*, Steinbeck and *Grapes*, and Hammett and *The Maltese Falcon*, to the intensity of his most celebrated work, *The Jungle* (1906).

Certainly the conflict between traditional puritanism and the licence and materialism which characterised the new century contributed to Sinclair's turn to socialism. He began publishing articles in *Appeal to Reason*, the socialist journal that originated in Kansas and established the essentially agrarian and Western character of the movement, which London and Steinbeck would reflect in their blendings of socialism with doctrines of return to the land. Sinclair's attraction to socialism, however, came more like Wagner's from his frustrations in early years as an artist: his article 'On Bourgeois Literature' (1904) responds to Gertrude Atherton's complaint that the American arts were 'timid' by echoing the message of *Art and Revolution*: 'Society must change before art can.'[28] For the rest of his long and eccentric career, Sinclair oscillated between art and social action. He used the profits of *The Jungle* to found Helicon Hall, a 'cooperative living experiment' which, in some respects, prefigured the radical communes of the 1960s. He experimented with fasting as a panacea for all ailments and wrote *The Fasting Cure* (1911). He wandered to Carmel, met George Sterling and the bohemian 'Crowd', set up a drama group to perform didactic plays, and wrote *Samuel the Seeker* (1910) to show that, after all, socialism was 'the only true faith'. In this period he professed considerable sympathy with the work of London, and his *Industrial Republic* (1907) shares motifs with *The Iron Heel*, including the indentification of 1912 as the critical year in the curtailment of capitalism and William Randolph Hearst as a pivotal figure. When these predictions failed to come true, Sinclair, like London, spent some years paying more attention to personal morality. *Love's Pilgrimage* (1911), *Sylvia* (1913) and *Sylvia's Marriage* (1914) attempt to objectify his feelings about marriage and women by dealing with subjects of separation, flight, venereal disease, infatuation and true love. Such outings demonstrate in greater degree than in London, perhaps even in Norris, a tendency to interweave 'extreme rationality in matters of sex and love' with 'subjectivity, idealism, and sentimentality' in approach and diction. The combination can mar Sinclair's work. His energy could breed over-enthusiasm.

The Cry for Justice (1914), which Sinclair edited and convinced London to contribute an introduction to, has been said to constitute 'the last, most comprehensive statement of the older, eclectic attitude toward socialist art'.[29] Sinclair, however, continued on as a muckraker; and, while world attention was focused on the War, he wrote *King Coal* (1917) in appeal to Vincent Astor and John D. Rockefeller to improve the mineworkers' conditions following their strike in Ludlow, Colorado. By the 1920s, with London dead and the first American anti-Red witch-hunt on, Sinclair 'almost was radical American literature'. Having moved permanently to Pasadena, he was again publishing his own works. These included *Upton Sinclair's: A Magazine for a Clean Peace and the Internation* (1918–19); *Jimmie Higgins* (1919), which attacks Western intervention against the Bolshevik Revolution; *100%* (1920), a reaction against the Palmer Raids, in which false patriotism is satirised; and the 'Dead Hand' series of sociological studies of the pernicious effects of capitalism on religion, journalism, higher education, secondary education, literature, and art. Novels of this period include Sinclair's most important California books, *They Call Me Carpenter* (1922) and *OIL!* (1927). Both have to do with the burgeoning new capitalist order of Los Angeles, established by General Harrison Gray Otis's union-busting at the turn of the century and advanced by the machinations of the Dohenys and others, leading to the Elk Hills scandal of the early 1920s. Both novels demonstrate that Sinclair's brand of socialism was individualistic and Christian; both include pure, sympathetic working-class heroes who become martyrs for the 'Cause'. *OIL!* is perhaps Sinclair's masterpiece. 'It's curiosity and ease and power are Tolstoyan', remarked Floyd Dell, the socialist, Bohemian, and friend of London.[30] *OIL!* is remembered as a piece of muckraking; but, as a novel, it is an advance over earlier efforts such as *The Jungle*. Now class-antagonisms are viewed as tragic for the rich as well as for the poor: Dad Ross, the semi-literate quickly rising southern Californian oil executive, is himself a character who merits serious consideration – even our sympathy.

The sheer bulk of Sinclair's opus may be one reason why he has not been taken seriously as a literary artist. The speed and carelessness of his adolescent apprenticeship in journalism never wholly left him; and his renunciation of aestheticism in favour of causes is apparent from *The Jungle* on. The fact that he would leave off literature to form EPIC (End Poverty in California) in the early 1930s and run, nearly successfully, for governor of the state, underlines the point that his commitment to art had lost its primacy. One might argue too that, where London had the human misfortune to die young, Sinclair had the artistic misfortune to live too long. The ten best-selling Lanny Budd novels that he wrote in his sixties link him in retrospect to the facile, commercial side of American letters; and the anti-Communism and prejudice in favour of high birth and breeding increasingly apparent in these novels must suggest to many that there was a dubious element in his socialism from the start. Like Norris, Sinclair is not a writer whose work will endure for its fineness and readability. The case of Sinclair, however, illuminates something about the *Zeitgeist* in which all of the figures under discussion operated. It raises essential questions about the interplay of morality and utterance. How much, for instance, were art and anger at the apparent breakdown of social justice functions of internal changes in the puritan psyche? How much, in specific, was the socialistic urge a projection of inner existential and sexual discontents? How much, conversely, were these a result of the capitalism and materialism decried?

In a lull in the action of *The Maltese Falcon* Sam Spade tells Brigid O'Shaughnessy a story which Hammett may have intended as an emblem of modern man's existential condition (Wolfe finds it sufficiently indicative of Hammett's own outlook to title his critical study after it).[31] Flitcraft is a successful businessman in Tacoma. He has a perfectly normal home-life with wife and children and

seems happy. One day he is walking down the street and a beam
falls from a building site and nearly kills him, and on the spot he
realises that life is not the 'clean orderly sane affair' he has taken it
to be; that 'in sensibly ordering his affairs he [has] gotten out of
step, and not into step with life'; that breath itself remains his only
so long as 'blind chance [spares] him'. Thereupon he disappears,
changes his name, and drops out. He has 'no feeling of guilt'; he
has 'left his family well-provided for, and what he [has] done
[seems] to him perfectly reasonable'. He thus succeeds in acting
out a fantasy of individual rebellion against the strictures of
modern civilisation. Hammett, however, via Spade, is fatalistic
about his chances for anything different. A few years later Flitcraft
is living in Spokane, doing well in business, enjoying a perfectly
normal home-life with a new wife and baby. This resolution belies
Hammett's suspicion that his own marital break would produce
nothing better – *plus la même chose*. It also implies that Spade will
fall back into association with Iva or someone like her – 'Once a
chump, always a chump.' Yet the possibility of release from past
patterns has been hoped for, the desire to transcend oppressive
responsibility and law registered. In Flitcraft there is a shadow of
London's nature-man, who left his factory-job in Portland,
regained health in the California foothills, and went on to make a
new life in the South Seas; also an anticipation of the motif of
escape that drives so many in Steinbeck, the Mexican heroes of
'Flight', *The Pearl* and *The Wayward Bus* notably. One might go
so far as to see a version of the urge to escape overpowering
civilisation that moved European Decadents of the turn of the
century, symbolised for literati by the flight of Rimbaud to black
Africa and summed up in fiction by the case of Kurtz in Conrad's
Heart of Darkness.

Wolf Larsen loves to play pranks. Good or evil, the successful
prank is an act of defiance against man's helplessness *vis-à-vis* the
gods and proves his power over mortal destiny. Tricks, acts of
bogus magic, anarchic subversion of the superego of the law typify
Steinbeck's comedic characters from *Tortilla* to *Sweet Thursday*.
The identity hoax is a *sine qua non* in the detective genre; and
Hammett's Fitzstephan, alias Dain, demonstrates the urge of the
author to play the invisible mover. A strong element of what
Jungians identify with the Trickster is present in the *Zeitgeist* of the
period, and no case illustrates this better than the mysterious
B. Traven's.[32] Among the many identities ascribed to this multi-

national author is that of Jack London. He might not have died in
1916, it is argued, but disappeared to Mexico, where, according to
one version of the story, Traven first turned up in 1914 in
Tampico, the time and place of London's sole visit to Mexico, to
report on oil and the revolution. Tampico in 1914 was visited by
another California writer, Ambrose Bierce, who was also
intending to report on oil and the revolution but disappeared
under mysterious circumstances that have yet to be explained.
Bitter-tongued Bierce has been offered as another identity for
Traven; but Bierce was in his seventies when he disappeared, and
Traven's books did not begin to surface until over ten years later.
Preoccupation with ships, labour conditions and the 'Cause' make
London more credible; but London's proletarian zeal was in
eclipse at the end of his life, and in any case Traven's vision is more
inferno-like than anything London ever wrote, *The Iron Heel*
included. These identifications with Californians prove only that
the real Traven was taken with the mystique of the furthest, wildest
reaches of Western civilisation. This animated contemporary
German thought as much as things Eastern, and a man who took
the name 'Marut' from the chariot-drivers of Hindu mythology
tried several times in the 1910s to obtain a US passport. He claimed
to have been born in San Francisco in 1882. As municipal records
had been destroyed in the earthquake of 1906, this could not be
disproved. Marut's description of where friends and family had
lived, however – south of Market, west of Chinatown, under 'Blue
Mountain', etc. – failed to convince the State Department.

Marut's knowledge of San Francisco came from reading. Those
who knew him in Munich during the First World War recall that
he was self-taught in English and numbered Jack London among
his favourite authors, along with Whitman and Shelley. The
detective work of Will Wyatt, following the studies of Judy Stone of
the San Francisco *Chronicle* and Martin Baumann of California
State University, has proved recently that Marut was really Otto
Fiege. Born in a disputed strip of land in Eastern Europe, Fiege's
de jure nationality changed twice in the early years of the century
(the savage hostility Traven later expressed against boundaries
and passports, particularly in *The Death Ship*, emanates from
this). Fiege studied theology in Germany before taking on the identity of Marut. As the latter, he became a disciple of the nineteenth-
century philosopher Max Stirner, whose 'unique ideas of individualistic anarchism were proclaimed in his book *The Ego and*

Its Own'. Marut adopted Stirner's philosophy that 'personal
indignation was the most powerful agent for change'. In *Der
Ziegelbrenner*, a journal which he edited for a short time in
1917–18, he proclaimed, 'THE NOBLEST, PUREST AND MOST
SIGNIFICANT HUMAN LOVE IS THAT TO ONESELF! I want to be
free!'[33] *Der Ziegelbrenner* was associated in the public mind with
Vorwärts!, mouthpiece of the Jewish radical Kurt Eisner, who led
the left-wing putsch in Munich in 1918; and Marut was hounded
out of Bavaria by the Freikorps and lived the rest of his life in some
paranoia of retribution from the German right. In the McCarthy
era in America publishers were reluctant to push his work because
of allegations of Communism; at the same time, East German
publishers were expurgating editions out of fear of earning trips to
Siberia. In fact, Marut–Traven's creed was devoutly anti-
political: 'I cannot belong to any party because to be a member of
any party would be a restriction of my personal freedom, because
the obligation to follow a party programme would take away from
me all possibility of developing into what I consider to be the
highest and noblest goal on earth: *to be a human being.*'[34]

Aided by the type of willing woman who would occasionally
appear in his novels, Marut escaped Germany for Rotterdam. He
became a seaman. Eventually he turned up in the East End
described in *People of the Abyss* and was arrested, ostensibly for
failing to register with the police, in fact for being 'a foreign
radical'. After leaving Brixton Prison, he changed his name to
Traven (a German ship, the *Trave*, was docked across from his digs
on the Commercial Road) and made his way to Mexico. There in
the next decade he published through a contact in Germany the
bulk of his work, including *The Death Ship*, *The Cotton Pickers*,
The Wobbly and *The Treasure of the Sierra Madre* (all circa
1925–8); also the Caoba, or Mahogany, Cycle of *The Bridge in the
Jungle* (1929), *The Carreta* and *Government* (1931), *The March
from Caobaland* (1933), *The Troza* and *The Rebellion of the
Hanged* (1936) and *The General from the Jungle* (1940). In the
early 1930s Bernard Smith, an editor at Knopf's, discovered *The
Death Ship* and, finding it more authoritative than the 'bourgeois'
proletarian novels of the day, undertook to revise and publish it.
The Traven mystery thereupon began. The appeal was to a
generation preoccupied with social injustice but also having a taste
for hoax and hidden identity. It also fed on the attractions of a
Mexico that seemed more Californian than California in its pro-

mise of sun, freedom, treasure, outlawry, *machismo*, and pagan sensuality like that touched on by D. H. Lawrence in *the Plumed Serpent*. This Mexico was not the old homeland of California *rancheros* celebrated by Helen Hunt Jackson and other nostalgists for missionary feudalism, but a wild place which many socialists after 1911, London included, looked to as the home of the revolution. It was the land of escape and transformation that Bierce had intimated, Steinbeck would romanticise, and latter-day bohemians such as Jack Kerouac would make pilgrimages to. In some respects it anticipated the mystical Indian Mexico that Carlos Castenada tries to interpret in his Don Juan books. Mythically it provided a dark underside to the bright new civilisation growing up in California and elsewhere in the West, a further frontier where a man could still belong to no one but himself – could still be a romantic loner, like Lecoud in *The Treasure of the Sierra Madre*, whom the old man, Howard, dubs 'The Wandering Digger', partly in reference to his equally lonesome and dogged precursor, the wandering Indian.

Hollywood, the antennae of the 'New West', discovered Traven in the 1940s. John Huston, fresh from success with *The Maltese Falcon*, went south to film the greatest of Traven's parables. A mysterious old-timer called Hal Croves surfaced to look after Traven's interest in the script. Croves claimed to be an American, born in Chicago in 1890, but Huston suspected him to be the author. Eventually Croves fell out with Huston over a *macho* prank of trying to paint his testicles silver, and Huston ended by reckoning that Croves did not match up to the boisterous, gutsy personality behind Traven's books. Croves was Traven, however, the creator distinct from the creation; and after the film was released he wrote bitterly, 'Traven does not need Mr John Huston. . . . Never again will Mr John Huston have an opportunity to direct a picture based on any other of Traven's books.'[35] Of all those books *Treasure* is the most applicable to this study. Its driving force of quest for gold derives not only from Otto Fiege's native German tradition (cf. Wagner's *Ring*) but also from the Gold Rush and works of Harte and London in which Ret Marut was well versed. Transcendental lust for adventure, commitment to the big gamble, vicissitudes of male comradeship, and the pernicious influence of greed are its great themes, as in books such as *Burning Daylight*; and the dialectic between Dobbs's Social Darwinist-

Nietzschean self-assertion and Curtin's Christian–socialist belief in morality recalls the dilemma London continually dealt with, in *The Sea Wolf* and *Martin Eden* most notably. What may have drawn Huston to *Treasure* above all is the character of Howard.[36] This cantankerous, rebellious, boyish yet wise old man leads Dobbs and Curtin out of their demoralising struggle for oil-rig jobs amid the labour contractors of Tampico into pursuit of the gold. He knows beforehand every stage of delight and degradation the pursuit will entail. He is neither surprised nor condemning when Dobbs attempts to kill Curtin. He laughs at himself and at all human striving when in the end the gold is blown away by sandstorm. Providing something lacking in Californian mythology (the old Kanakas of London's last stories and Sam Hamilton of *East of Eden* are gropings in this direction), Howard is a bold and intensely human type which confutes the impression that heroism is possible only in youth and that age must produce either capitalist predators like Shelgrim, criminals like Gutman, or pathetic resigned victims like Pa Joad.

Women are hardly a memory in the *macho* world of *Treasure*: 'Women were seldom mentioned among them, unless with contempt. . . . One always speaks contemptuously of what cannot be had.'[37] Ideologically, like the wearers of sealskin coats by Wolf Larsen, women are identified with capitalist rapacity: 'The gold that a beautiful and elegant woman wears on her finger . . . has been in strange company and washed in blood as often as soap and water' (98). Sex with such creatures is beyond conception, and the only sexual note in the novel comes in this Lawrentian tableau:

There were Indians by the dozens splashing in the water as well as white men of the same social level as Dobbs. . . . No one was in bathing drawers, but there was no one who worried. . . . Women and girls went passed the bathing-places and thought nothing of men bathing entirely naked. . . . Only the smart American and European women would have thought it beneath their dignity. . . . They watched the bathers with good prismatic glasses from the balconies and windows of the houses high above. . . . This is why the colony here had the name of Bella Vista. (15)

Open sensuality of the low versus sexual hypocrisy of the high is a motif of the *Zeitgeist* reflected as well by James M. Cain. When the hero of *Serenade* (1937) goes to a posh Hollywood party with his Mexican girlfriend, who wears a simple *rebozo* instead of a gown from Bullocks, he is told by the hostess never to bring 'a cheap Mexican tart' again. Belting the hostess, John Howard Sharp takes Juana off for an evening in the Chicano district of LA. 'It was the first time I had ever had a friendly feeling toward Mexico', he says.[38] In fact Mexico, embodied in the simple yet sex-wise Juana, offers the very primitive gutsiness necessary to restore full manhood to the over-civilised Sharp. At the climax of the novel in a symbolic struggle for Sharp's being, Juana murders Winston Hawes, homosexual dilettante and scion of one of the richest Yankee families, after Hawes, who is more subtle than the Hollywood hostess but no less motivated by sexual competition and class contempt, has contrived to have her deported. Juana's heroism in this act is left in no doubt. Passionate individualistic assertion is the highest value in Cain, as in Traven. Only those Promethean souls who are willing to risk damnation are worthy of full attention.

Sharp is introduced as a failed opera-singer bumming around Mexico City. Weaving Hemingway with George Moore with anticipations of Chandler, *Serenade* opens in a cantina with a bullfighter, a whore, and the singing of an aria from *Carmen*. Through a boldness that will be the leitmotiv of his success, Sharp wins the whore from the bullfighter and returns to her establishment with her. Juana asks him to sing. Something in his tone makes her suspect that he 'no like to entertain señoritas', and she asks him to be her pimp ('No have any trouble') (42). The implication of homosexuality makes Sharp seethe; and, as he drives Juana to Acapulco where a *politico* john is going to set her up with a brothel, a vengeful heterosexual passion grows: 'I could smell her', Sharp repeats in a line typical of that element in Cain which made Chandler remark that he wrote 'like a billygoat'.[39] Caught in a torrential rainstorm, Sharp drives through the doors of a deserted church. While Juana abases herself in front of the altar to beg forgiveness for *sacrilegio*, he exchanges his wet clothes for a priest's cassock (Cain, who had Irish Catholic heritage, delights as much as James Joyce in adapting divine ritual to the earthy and sensual). As thunderclaps sound and Juana screams in superstition, Sharp plays an *Agnus Dei* on the organ and sings. Again hearing that suspect note, Juana remarks that he sounds like a priest. Again seething over the implication, Sharp now stalks the woman: 'She was crouched down, on her knees, her face touching the floor and her hands pressing down beside. . . . She was stark naked, except for a *rebozo*. . . . She had been sliding back to the jungle ever since she took off that first shoe. . . . I blew out the candle, knelt down, and turned her over' (78). After the act, the storm abates and Sharp ventures outside. In a Hemingwayesque ritual more suggestive of Steinbeck than Chandler, he captures an iguana, guts it, cooks it, serves it to Juana and eats. In the moonlight later he sings for a third time: 'It didn't sound like a priest anymore.' Manhood is regained: Sharp has his *cojones* back. 'That was very beautiful, *gracias*', Juana says. Sharp: 'I used to be a singer.' 'Yes', Juana says; 'Maybe I made a mistake.' Sharp: 'I think you did.' Juana: 'Maybe not' (91).

At his best, which much of *Serenade* is, Cain writes with an energy like Balzac's; and, like Hammett, he has affinities to nineteenth-century Romanticism. The magical figure of Captain O'Connors, who ferries Juana and Sharp from Acapulco to LA after Sharp has belted Juana's *politico* in a fit of jealousy, might have stepped out of Dumas; and his mellifluous description of Beauty might have come from Wilde or Symons:

> I think much about Beauty, sitting alone at night, listening to my wireless, and trying to get at the reason of it, and understand how a man like Strauss can put the worst sounds on the surface that ever profaned the night, and yet give me something I can sink my teeth into. . . . True beauty has *terror* in it. . . . Beethoven has terror in him. . . . The eternities and infinities are in it, they strike at the soul, like death.   (123-4)

Though more of a God than a Lucifer figure, O'Connors has a good deal of the harsh lyricism of Wolf Larsen in him: 'The waters, the surf, the colors on the shore. You think they make the beauty of the tropical sea, aye, lad? They do not. 'Tis the knowledge of what lurks below the surface of it . . . that carries death with every move that it makes. . . . So it is with all beauty' (124-5). The shark, which O'Connors refers to specifically here, is an important symbol for Cain in this connection. At the end of *Double Indemnity* (1936), just before they commit suicide, Walter and Phyllis, that book's partners in crime, see the flash of a black fin through the 'dirty white'. Phyllis says: 'We'll have to wait. Till the moon comes up. . . . I want to see that black fin. Cutting the water in the moonlight.'[40] When the hour comes, Walter describes Phyllis thus: 'She's made her face chalk white, with black circles under her eyes and red on her lips and cheeks. She's got that red thing on. It's awful-looking. . . . She looks like what came aboard the ship to shoot dice for souls in The Rhyme of the Ancient Mariner .'[41] Beauty is related to death; both find their objective correlative in the *femme fatale*. This is a consistent motif in Cain, and Phyllis sums it up yet more dramatically than Captain O'Connors: 'There's something in me that loves Death', she tells Walter when seducing him into murdering her husband. 'I think of myself as Death, sometimes. In a scarlet shroud, floating through the night. I'm *so* beautiful, then. And sad. And hungry to make the whole world happy, by taking them out to where I am, into the night, away from all trouble, all unhappiness.'[42]

Cain's enthusiasm for this sort of decadence can mar his books. Phyllis has an incredible, stagy aspect, even more than her precursor, Cora, in the similarly structured *The Postman Always Rings Twice* (1934); and Captain O'Connors's opinions are almost as jarring as his *deus ex machina*-like appearances. When Cain strains after aesthetic effects, he can be bad. When he depicts the struggle of the arts in his contemporary world, however, he can be excellent. Shortly after arriving in LA, Sharp jumps on stage at the Hollywood Bowl and takes over singing the Toreador song – *Carmen* again. On the spot he is signed by a high-powered agent, and the following pages offer a bitingly critical introduction to the philistines ruling the film *Xanadu*: 'To them, singing is just something you buy, for whatever you have to pay, and so is acting, and so is writing, and so is music, and anything else they use' (157). Sharp makes a B-feature into a box-office hit with his voice, then holds out for a big contract for three films. He wins this gamble; subsequently, however, he decides to go to New York to realise his lifelong dream – that of a legitimate artist rather than a hack – to sing at the Metropolitan Opera. The Hollywood establishment is shocked: 'Grand Opera is through', the producer Gold tells him; 'Pictures have stepped in and done it so much better than they can do it that they can't get by any more' (182). This argument incenses Sharp and, in defiance, he breaks contract. His comeback at the Met is clinched by singing *Don Giovanni* (it was singing the 'serenade' from this that moved Captain O'Connor to rescue Sharp and Juana from Acapulco). He starts doing radio broadcasts and is

on his way to becoming the biggest star in New York when
Hollywood takes its revenge: Gold gets on to the Sceen Actors'
Guild, which gets on to the Musicians' Union; they compel the
orchestra at the Met to inform the management that it will walk
out if Sharp is allowed to continue to sing. Sharp consults a theatrical lawyer only to be informed, 'Show business is all one gigantic
hook-up, Gold knows it frontwards, backwards, crosswise, and on
the bias, and you haven't got a chance. You're sewed' (199).

  Serenade is one of the first novels to dramatise the talent-
devouring habits of the Hollywood monster; it remains one of the
most artful depictions of that much-painted subject. What makes
it more memorable than most is the way it shows the vast 'hook-up'
in action. It is not only the union-pressuring and contract-
manipulating ex-ragtrade Jews of Hollywood that can make the
artist twist in the wind but also, more crucially in the end, the
successor to the Yankee swindlers of *Burning Daylight* and brother
to the Wall Street sharpies that Traven and other radicals were
openly blaming for the misery of millions in the Depression.
Through a bank that his family owns, Winston Hawes is able to
'fix' Sharp's contract and shut up Gold at virtually a moment's
notice. All he asks in return – and here enters an American version
of the motif of perverse romanticism that Hammett imports – is
that Sharp sing for his, Hawes's pet camp band. It was singing for
this band in Paris and living under the unnerving pressure of
Hawes's homosexual admiration that caused Sharp to lose the
manliness in his voice and flee to Mexico in the first place.
Returning to sing for Hawes once again makes the syndrome recur.
'Have no *toro* in high voice', Juana complains; 'no *grrr* that
frighten little *muchacha,* make heart beat fast' (227). It is a
fabulous version of the radical argument: concentration of money
and power in the hands of a few capitalist decadents effectively
unmans those who must live under their sway. For a time Sharp
agonises over his career, then he renews his commitment to the
primitive woman who gave him his manhood back. 'All of a
sudden she broke from me, shoved the dress down from her
shoulder, slipped the brassiere and shoved a nipple in my mouth.
"Eat. Eat much. Make big *toro!*" ' (232). The symbol is not unlike
the one Steinbeck would shortly select to conclude *Grapes*. But
Cain does not end his *Serenade* on this note. His principals, unlike
Steinbeck's peasant victims, are romantic overreachers. The
murder of Hawes, ironically committed in a mock bullfight, puts

them on what Cain referred to as the 'love-rack' and leads to their destruction as well.

Edmund Wilson is one of the few critics to have recognised the qualities as well as limitations of Cain, and his remarks in *The Boys in the Back Room* deserve to be quoted at length:

> Let us begin with Mr Cain and his school. . . . The whole group stemmed originally from Hemingway, but it was a Hemingway turned picaresque; and it was allied also to the new school of mystery writers of the type of Dashiell Hammett. . . . Mr Cain remained the best of these novelists. . . . The hero of the typical Cain novel is a good-looking down-and-outer, who leads the life of a vagrant and rogue. He invariably falls under the domination – usually to his ruin – of a vulgar and determined woman from whom he finds it impossible to escape. . . . Cain's heroes are capable of extraordinary exploits, but they are always treading the edge of a precipice. They are doomed, like the heroes of Hemingway. . . . But whereas in Hemingway's stories, it is simply that these brave and decent men have had a dirty deal from life, the hero of a novel by Cain is an individual of mixed unstable character, who carries his precipice with him like Pascal. . . . In the meantime he has fabulous adventures – samples, as it were, from a *Thousand and One Nights* of the screwy Pacific Coast. . . . All these writers are also pre-eminently the poets of the tabloid murder. Cain himself is particularly ingenious at tracing from their first beginnings the tangle that gradually tightens around the necks of these people . . . even at showing – in *Serenade*, at any rate – the larger tangles of social interest which these deadly little knots represent. Such a subject might provide a great novel: in *An American Tragedy*, such a subject did. But as we follow, in a novel by Mr Cain, the development of one of his plots, we find ourselves more and more disconcerted by knocking up – to the destruction of illusion – against the blank and hard planes and angles of something we know all too well: the damned old conventions of Hollywood. . . . Mr Cain is actually a writer for the studios. . . . These novels have been produced in his off-time; and they are a kind of Devil's parody of the movies. Mr Cain is the *âme damnée* of Hollywood. All the things that the

Catholic censorship has excluded: sex, debauchery, unpunished crime, and sacrilege against the Catholic Church – Mr Cain has let all these loose, with a gusto as of pent-up ferocity that the reader cannot but share. What a pity that it is impossible for such a writer to create and produce his own pictures![43]

Cain was born in 1891, of Irish stock as noted, in Maryland.[44] His father was president of Washington University and later an insurance executive; he made a foray into letters by writing *A Financial History of the United States*. Cain's mother was a coloratura soprano, and as a youth Cain's own ambition, like James Joyce's, was to become an opera-singer. His mother blocked his singing-career, however, and the musical urge went under cover to reappear in the subjects and styles of his novels. For some years the young man attempted to follow the footsteps of his father: he sold accident-insurance; he taught and served as a dorm-master at Washington University; finally he went to work for the Baltimore *Sun*. As with Hemingway, the budding career in journalism was interrupted by the First World War. After returning from the trenches, Cain rose to become state editor of the paper. A major influence in this period was Mencken; and essays Cain wrote under the grand old man's tutelage were published in *Our Government* (1931). In 1924 Cain's first marriage broke up. Alcohol was one disintegrative factor, as for so many of the Prohibition generation; tuberculosis was another. Illness, Cain later claimed, gave him the compulsion to 'be a success in life'. He moved to New York and for seven years wrote for Walter Lippmann on the New York *World*. Meanwhile, on the recommendation of Mencken he wrote a play about West Virginia for the impresario Philip Goodman. This foray into theatre was not a success. Through it, however, Cain met the 'play-doctor' Vincent Lawrence, who helped him arrive at his concise and dramatic formula for short novels. These he began to write after moving to Hollywood in 1931. A stint on the *New Yorker* ('no place for a man of action') made him look around for an exit, and screen-writing seemed a logical step from drama and journalism. Cain failed with the studios in a few months, however. Left with no income at age forty, in the middle of the Depression, he wrote *The Postman*. The book was an instant success. Eventually adapted for Broadway, it brought the theatrical acclaim that had eluded the younger man. It provided Luchino Visconti with the subject for his first film, *Ossessione*, and Albert Camus with a model for *L'Étranger*. It led to the writing of fifteen further novels, many in the same style, most of which became films.

In 1942, in a preface to an omnibus edition of three of his short novels, Cain summed up his approach:

> I have had, since I began writing, the greatest difficulty with technique, or at any rate fictive technique. . . . I couldn't write a novel. . . . But my short stories, which were put in the mouth of some character, marched right along, for if I in the third person faltered and stumbled, my characters in the first person know perfectly well what they had to say. . . . They were homely characters, and spoke a gnarled and grotesque jargon that didn't seem quite adapted to long fiction. . . . But then I moved to California and heard the Western roughneck: the boy who is just as elemental inside as his Eastern colleague, but who has been to high school, completes his sentences, and uses reasonably good grammar. . . . I began to wonder if *that* wouldn't be the medium I could use to write novels.[45]

Of his encounters with Lawrence, Cain continues,

> He talked quite a bit about the One, the Two, and the Three, not seeming to know that these were nothing but the Aristotelian Beginning, Middle, and End. . . . 'Who the hell *was* Aristotle, and who did he lick?' . . . Until then, my idea of writing was that the story corresponded with life. . . . He said that if truth were the main object of writing, I would have a hard time competing with a 3 dollar camera.

Of his own characteristic adaptation of the *Tristan* theme to the thriller, Cain concludes,

> Murder, I said, had always been written from its least interesting angle, which was whether the police could catch the murderer. I was considering, I said, a story in which the murder was the *love-rack*, as it must be to any man and woman who conspire to commit it. But, I said, they would commit the perfect murder. It wouldn't go, of course, quite as they planned it. But in the end they would get away with it, and then what? They would find, I said, that the earth is not big enough for two persons who share

such a dreadful secret, and eventually turn on each other. . . .
The whole thing corresponded to a definition of tragedy I found
later in some of my father's writings: that it was the 'force of
circumstances driving the protagonist to the commission of the
dreadful act'.

The purest realisations of this formula are *The Postman* and
Double Indemnity. Few novels have been written in a more direct,
obsessive manner. 'As a result of my first fiasco at novel-writing, I
had acquired such a morbid fear of boring the reader that I got the
habit of needling the story at the least hint of a let-down.' Dialogue
constitutes more than 50 per cent of *The Postman*, and it is a sharp
telegraphic dialogue uncluttered by 'he said'–'she replied'.
'Sometimes Cain's dialogue, typographically, has the impact of a
graph,' Madden writes;[46] indeed, there is a visual clarity to it that
reminds one that it belongs to the era of the hard lines of Art Deco
and the high polish of chrome hubcaps against white-sidewall
tyres. Aurally the dialogue suggests the chromatic progressions of
late Romantic opera, which had already been adapted to the
incremental progression of movie-scenes: 'Key words regarding
future attitude and action at the end of one scene are picked up
and developed in the next with almost mathematical precision.'[47]
Cain uses, moreover, the Modernist technique of omission to
achieve compression and concentration of effect. Foreshadowing,
echo-pattern and recapitulation are employed to provide context.
What is actually given are the bare bones of the story: an
Expressionistic grid against which the reader must flesh in the
details: a less obscure and lofty version of the style Eliot used in *The
Waste Land*. The reader, Madden says, finds his greatest
satisfaction in a Cain novel from observing the authorial control:
'He observes Cain manipulating his concept of the popular reader,
and in the process, he becomes a captive himself.'[48] The
confessional first-person generally has the result of implicating the
reader in the narrator's behaviour; this effect is deepened
considerably in Cain through use of dramatic irony. The reader of
The Postman, for instance, is considerably more knowledgeable
than the District Attorney, who invents several scenarios for how
Cora's husband might have been murdered. Aware of Cora's and
Frank's guilt from the first, the reader's concern is not with 'who
dun it' but whether and when they will be caught. Cain is quite
different from conventional detective writers such as Hammett

and Chandler: anticipation is the hook here, not suspense.

Cain's setting for three of his four best novels – *The Postman, Double Indemnity,* and *Mildred Pierce* (1943) – is a vivid southern California; Hollywood, as noted, provides a milieu for the other, *Serenade.* Suburban Glendale is Cain's favourite locale. The specificity with which he describes it makes one feel that, even more than Chandler (who gave fictional names to his suburbs – Bay City, Idle Valley, Esmeralda), Cain realises the thing in itself. With characters as well Cain at his best has a Naturalistic distinctness that Chandler's caricatures and projections lack. The beach-bum mentality of Frank in *The Postman* is underlined by the fact that, in native southern Californian fashion, his only intimation of divine power comes not from law or justice or love even so much as from the waves: 'We played in the sand, and then we went way out and let the swells rock us. . . . I looked up at the sky. . . . I thought about God.'[49] The details of insurance-swindling in *Double Indemnity* demonstrate a Balzacian grasp of the grotesque importance the bourgeoisie of the nascent Sun-belt would put on money that goes deeper than Chandler's lofty post-Balzacian contempt. Allied to these qualities, however, is the sensationalism that in later novels would make critics wonder if Cain had ever been more than a charlatan of purple prose. Suspension of disbelief is, after all, sorely taxed when Frank reports that Cora demands 'Bite me! Bite me!' and then sinks his 'teeth into her lips so deep [he] could feel the blood spurt into [his] mouth'.[50] Cora's 'snarling like a cougar' points up the fact Madden remarks on, that sex is 'purely animal' in Cain. In the end one suspects that much is the opposite of Naturalism: the fantasies of another aging puritan. Austerity of plot and style, not this sensationalism, recommended *The Postman* to Camus. The existential defiance of the lower-middle-class hero, his view of the world as absurd, the deeply psychological situation described without psychological commentary – these things, not slick commercial panderings, made European contemporaries, embroiled in the breakdown of their old order, find a 'superior savagery' in the work of the Tough Guys: an original expression more American and more stimulating than the sophistries of 'later-day Henry James' . . . *chiens qui fument*'.[51]

'*Serenade* is a definite improvement on *Postman*,' Wilson wrote.

It, too, has its trashy aspect, its movie foreshortenings and its too well-oiled actions; but it establishes a surer illusion. *The Postman* was always in danger of becoming unintentionally funny. Yet even here brilliant moments of insight redeemed the unconscious burlesque; and there is enough of the real poet in Cain – both in writing and in imagination – to make one hope for something better than either.[52]

In response to this and to Clifton Fadiman's criticism of his 'conscious muscle-flexing', Cain made a promise at the end of his *Three of a Kind* preface: 'Recently, I have made steady progress in the art of letting a story secrete its own adrenalin, and I have probably written the last of my intense tales of the type that these represent. . . . What was bad will continue to drop off the cart . . . until in the end most of it will be bounced off.'[53] Cain was at work on the book that may be his masterpiece; certainly it was his largest in theme and scope. *Mildred Pierce* was conceived during the period of his break-up with his second wife, Elina Tyszecka, a Finn, a fact which fits into the remarkable pattern we are discovering of a link between domestic failure and artistic success. Reflecting the autobiographical situation, the novel begins with the break-up of a marriage: 'They spoke quickly, as though they were saying things that scalded their mouths, and had to be cooled by spit. Indeed, the whole scene had an ancient, almost classical ugliness to it, for they uttered the same recriminations that have been uttered since the beginning of marriage, and added little originality to them, and nothing of beauty.'[54] The husband (like all the male figures in the novel) is relatively weak, and Cain concentrates on the toughness and talent of women. The narration is third-person rather than the usual first – Cain apparently did not feel up to the pyrotechnics of expressionist self-revelation. Particularly at the outset the book is more careful and quiet than its predecessors: an attempt at more honest, objective Naturalism. This quality about it is impressive. There is a problem of language now and then, however, which betrays not only the strain under which Cain was working but also the unresolved question of whether he was a man of literature or a writer of potboilers.

'Saying things that scalded their mouths', 'ancient, almost classical ugliness', 'uttered the same recriminations that have been uttered' – such phrases would not have passed the lips of Frank, Walter, or even John Howard Sharp. This is literary language:

more stilted, wooden and self-conscious. The first sentences of the book foreshadow the fact that prose and subject will be more complex than in the wonderfully direct, slick *Postman*: 'In the spring of 1931, on a lawn in Glendale, California, a man was bracing trees. It was a tedious job, for he had first to prune dead twigs, then wrap canvas buffers around weak branches, then wind rope slings over the buffers and tie them to the trunks, to hold the weight of the avocados that would ripen in the fall' (5). Here is an almost Nineties-ish use of commas, an unwonted specificity of time and place, a foreign use of the English English 'tedious'. The deployment of 'for' is uncolloquial; the placement of 'first' after the verb phrase instead of before is unnatural. Imagery is similarly revealing: 'dead twigs', 'weak branches' 'weight of the avocados that would ripen in the fall' all alert us to the probability that we are embarking on a drama that in some sense will be about the high, the falling and the dying. When the theme of the novel ultimately reveals itself as naturalness versus artificiality, middle class versus aristocracy, the matter of language becomes crucial. Mildred's daughter, Veda, speaks in a manner which underlines her pretentions and infuriates her hard-working mother; 'You know you had no business saying what you did, and you knew it at the time, I could tell by the cheeky look on your face.' Veda: 'Very well, Mother, it shall be as you say.' Mildred: 'And stop that silly way of talking.' Veda: 'But I remind you, just the same. . . . Things have indeed changed here, and not for the better, alas! One might think peasants had taken over the house.' Mildred: 'Do you know what a peasant is?' Veda: 'A peasant is a very ill-bred person.' Mildred: 'Sometimes, Veda, I wonder if you have good sense' (59).

Mildred becomes a waitress so that she can support her household, particularly Veda. Ostensibly the novel is a chronicle of the rise of a divorced mother to wealth and status as a canny restaurateur. The heart of the matter, however, is this dialectic of Mildred's humility and good sense versus Veda's haughtiness and ennui. Veda is an original of the Californian spoiled child that would traipse through the novels of Chandler and Ross Mac-Donald and become a cultural stereotype in the 1960s and after (cf. Patty Hearst). But the 'Generation Gap' had not fully split by this time, and Mildred is fatally attracted to Veda's worst as well as best quality: 'She has something in her that I thought I had, and now I find I haven't. Pride, or whatever it is. Nothing on earth could make Veda do what I'm going to do' (56). For all her down-to-earth Americanism and Protestant work-ethic, Mildred shares the *fin-de-siècle* sickness in which Cain enshrouds Phyllis Nirdlinger. She likes to climb into bed with her daughter, breathe 'tremulous teary sighs', blow 'into her pyjamas', break down into 'torrential shaking sobs' (119). Latent incestuous, homophiliac eroticism is a leitmotiv of Cain's Freudian configuration. Mildred's relationship with Veda is pathological. When her 'good' daughter, Ray, is whisked away by pneumonia, Mildred's deepest emotion is gratitude that it wasn't her 'evil' Veda. Veda has some musical talent, and Mildred pays sums she initially can ill afford to train it. She follows her daughter's progress with an avidity that belies her vicarious urge to succeed as a performer (like Cora in *Postman*, Mildred came to California with designs on making it in the movies). When Veda rebels against this oppressive maternal will-to-success and runs away to become a torch-singer, Mildred throws her energies into getting the girl back. She courts and marries Monty Beragon, a decadent aristocrat from Pasadena. She knows that the oldest, snobbiest element in southern Californian society is what Veda has aspired to ever since her parents' divorce and mother's descent into 'work-beastism'. As Veda's Italian voice-coach remarks: 'Dees girl, she live for two t'ing. One is to make a mother feel bad, odder is to get back wit' all a rich pipple she know one time in Pasadena' (224).

Beragon's pedigree reflects the 'old is good' principle of the upstart society by stretching back to the Hispanic *rancheros*: '[My great-grandparents] were the original settlers – you know, the gay caballeros that gypped the Indians out of their land, the king out of his taxes, and then sold out to the Americans when Polk started annexing' (95–6). Though not a WASP, Beragon is a debased West Coast version of Winston Hawes, with whom he shares a snobbery vicious and racist, cloaked under affable supercilious manners: 'If you ask me, the old coot [his great-grandfather] was really a wop. I can't prove it, but I think the name was originally Bergoni. However, if he Spanished it up, it's all right with me. Wop or spig, I wouldn't trust either as far as a snail can hop.' That Monty apparently doesn't care about his aristocracy is charming to democratic, naïve Mildred; that the pedigreed loafer scorns Mildred's work-ethic behind her back is charming to pretentious Veda. Monty appears to care less for money; he himself is consummately generous; apart from the family mansion, however, he hasn't an asset. This leads him to become Mildred's kept man.

At first the arrangement seems comfortable; gradually, however, it deepens Monty's cynicism, until he is referring to himself as a 'gigolo' and Cain characterising him as 'a jumble of sorry fictions, an attitude with nothing behind it but pretence' (149). The authorial comment here seems extreme: Beragon is as much a victim of the 'larger tangles of social interest' as the passionate criminals of other Cain novels; and a greater writer might have allowed him at least the level of sympathy that Henry James grants Osmond in *Portrait of a Lady*. Where Osmond becomes increasingly rarefied and attached to plot-weaving Madame Merle, however, Beragon becomes increasingly vulgar and partisan to Veda. This development is previewed in Cain's fetishistic description of what 'Monty brutally called the Dairy: that had appeared almost overnight on [Veda's] high, arching chest. . . . Mildred had a mystical feeling about them: they made her think tremulously of Love, Motherhood, and similar milky concepts. . . . Monty denounced them as indecent, and told Veda for Christ's sake to get a hammock to sling them in. . . . Veda laughed gaily, and got brassieres' (138).

The first half of *Mildred Pierce* is about 'the great American institution that never gets mentioned on Fourth of July, a grass widow with two small children to support' (21); the second is about the successful businesswoman's hubris – Mildred's obsession with that projection of her own repressed pride, Veda. Like Phyllis's daughter in the second half of *Double Indemnity*, Veda increasingly becomes a focus. But Veda is more than just the sex-object that Beragon's attitude encourages. Her identification with music is something 'rich', 'dark', 'exciting', and deeply romantic (141). As Mildred's religion is Veda, so Veda's religion becomes romantic art. Art, however, as Cain showed in *Serenade*, requires, in the Hollywood milieu, values different from the hard-headed honesty that leads Mildred to business success. Ambition alone is not enough, Veda discovers after her piano-teacher dies and she is rejected by 'the only man in LA who could replace him'. Mildred tries to console her, but Veda lashes back, 'You think I'm hot stuff, don't you? . . . Well, I'm not. I'm just a Glendale Wunderkind. . . . In this racket you've got it or you haven't' (192). Perhaps because of insecurity in the breakdown of his marriage, Cain takes the bourgeois position for the first time and views Veda's drive to success with less sympathy than Mildred's. In fact, Veda's struggle requires a courage of its own and in the end must earn sneaking respect. She becomes a tart: 'The shadows under her eyes gave her true beauty. . . . They were suggestive of the modern world, of boulevards, theatres, and streamlined cars' (195). She spends her time with Hollywood gold-diggers and tries to 'shake down' a rich family by maintaining falsely that its scion made her pregnant. When this doesn't work, she trades Beethoven for Hank Somerville and does a night-club act which is a comic send-up of opera. Mildred's philistinism is illuminated by her admiration for how Veda's talent shines through in these performances which abuse her artistic creed. When the girl finally achieves her Grail by singing at the Hollywood Bowl, Mildred proves unable to appreciate the classical arias offered and is horrified by the 'wan, stagey look that Veda had turned on the audience'.

The proud, artistic highness which Mildred has aspired to via Veda is repulsive to her in the end. That her view was partially shared by her creator is suggested in the fact that his subsequent books did not reach toward similar greatness. The melodramatic climax of *Mildred Pierce* shows the heroine trying to strangle her daughter after finding the girl *in flagrante* with Beragon. Veda's vocal chords are crushed; Mildred must turn from 'the beautiful thing that she loved most in the world'; Cain appears to recoil from variants of Old World decadence that he, like Hammett, was fascinated by. For this aesthetic cousin of Oscar Wilde, Life deserved affirmation over Art in the end. Cain closes his novel with the reconciliation of Mildred and her divorced husband. His benediction is the down-to-earth post-Prohibition American trendyism: 'Let's get stinko!' (264).

III RAYMOND CHANDLER

Chandler was an inheritor of the art-for-art's-sake tradition. In his hands the type of work that Hammett, Cain and others had invented was brought to its final stage. *The Big Sleep* (1939), prototype of Chandler's seven novels, makes a kind of social comment and is spattered with the requisite gore; in the end, however, it is really a comedy:[55] a parodistic comedy of manners having much in common in spirit with the plays of Shaw and Maugham which dominated London theatre when Chandler was a young romantic poet writing reviews for the *Westminster Gazette*.

One of the great men-behind-the-scenes whom Marlowe must deal with in *The Big Sleep* is a District Attorney named Wilde. Chandler does not intend a portentous allusion: he would call a cop Hemingway in *Farewell, My Lovely* (1940) to make mischief with literature rather than pay homage. Still, the name is no accident. District Attorney Wilde is dressed in a tuxedo and presented in an environment elegant enough to suggest the standard of the most famous Anglo-Irish aesthete. Chandler's 'true Penelope' in literature may well have been the Wilde of the comedies; and behind Chandler's commercially successful novels as behind Wilde's four comic plays stands a precious, narcissistic, fairy-tale-loving disposition that would compose purple and erotically suggestive pieces such as 'English Summer', analogous to Wilde's passionate gushings from the early poems to *Salomé*. 'Behind every pale pink indiscretion of the censorious Marlowe, may be a purple swelling of Chandler's', Russell Davies opines.[56] The maudlin, breast-beating, sorrowing Chandler of the final years, recalled so well by Natasha Spender, with whom he carried on a platonic affair that might have appeared comic had the California provincial in London not taken himself so seriously, shows a propensity to the confessional.[57] Chandler yearned to be as self-dramatising as Wilde in *De Profundis*. Los Angeles, however, was not a literary stage like London; nor did Chandler's personality ever 'come out' in the way Wilde's compulsively had to. The result is a more Proustian art: an art of peeping and reporting rather than of exhibitionistly 'declaring'.

Chandler's English origin, as many have pointed out, is essential to understanding his work. Youth was spent in Dulwich under the eye of a dominant mother of Irish–American background. Chandler went to a public school, a fact advanced to explain the code of honour to which Marlowe adheres. He was drenched from childhood in Victorian Romanticism – 'the self-control of the Arnold tradition, mingled with the chaste and deathladen-images of the Tennysonian Arthurian legends which inspired his own early poetry.'[58] His favourite books, to become models, included Merimée's *Carmen*, Flaubert's *Trois Contes*, James's *Spoils of Poynton* and *Wings of the Dove*, Conrad's *Secret Agent*, works of Dickens and (like Hammett) Dumas. The great events of his life, recounted excellently in Frank McShane's biography,[59] included serving in the trenches in the First World War; going to southern California and in the 1920s rising to become an executive for one of the largest oil-exploitation groups; marrying Cissy Pascal, twenty years his senior, who left her husband for him and played surrogate mother to him until her death in 1954 in her eighties; working for the studios in the 1940s as one of Hollywood's most sought-after screen-writers; drinking, which lost him the oil job in his early thirties, marred the Hollywood period, and contributed to his suicidal agony after Cissy's death. 'One sees nothing of life-material in Chandler', Patricia Highsmith suggests.[60] On the contrary, while *The Long Goodbye* (1954), written during Cissy's last days, is the only book which is overtly autobiographical, the entire opus reflects the pattern of Chandler's peripatetic existence after leaving the oil business and starting to support himself by writing for *Black Mask*. It is a world of godlike rich men and women, crooks and con-men heroically trying to wrest a share, blonde-haired women touched up with the artifices and paint that Cissy apparently reverted to to sustain the interest of a man so many years her junior; Hollywood *femmes fatales* who seem all-the-more dangerous because the detective resisting their fleshly allure was in fact the aging Chandler, emotionally bound to a withering wife; drunks, losers, attendant lords of various types, most suffering to some degree from Chandler's own chronic disease of self-contempt.

Chandler's response to his life was cynical; so was his approach to his art. Like all parodists, he was better at ornamentation than plot. When working on the screenplay of *The Big Sleep*, Howard Hawks and William Faulkner are said to have phoned Chandler to find out what actually happens in the book and Chandler is supposed to have retorted, 'Why ask me? I only wrote it.' In fact, the plot of his first novel can be detailed easily enough: Rusty Regan is murdered by Carmen Sternwood in a fit of temper at being rejected sexually; Eddie Mars hides his wife to make it seem that Regan has run off with her, thus is not dead; this makes it easier for Mars to fleece General Sternwood, which in any case is not hard considering that his daughters have vices typical of the LA rich, drugs and sex for Carmen, gambling and sex for Vivien. The origin of the Hawks–Faulkner story is a 70 cent telegram Warner Brothers sent Chandler (causing the notoriously tight Jack Warner to complain, an incident Chandler would recall in *The Little Sister*) to find out who had killed the Sternwoods' chauffeur.[61] One is reminded of the title Edmund Wilson put to his 1945 essay on Chandler and thriller writers: 'Who Cares Who

Killed Roger Ackroyd?'[62] Chandler didn't. Another of his
comments which has become celebrated is that he would have
liked to have been able to write a novel so compelling in style alone
that the last two chapters could be ripped out and the reader
wouldn't mind.[63] Who dun it? Who cares? The plot of *The Big
Sleep* creaks in comparison with that of *The Maltese Falcon*. The
story does not have comparable unity, nor does it flow
psychologically from the situation of the hero (*The Long Goodbye*
is the only Chandler novel to do this). There is no marked change
or growth in Marlowe; there is not even much sign that the
experience has been necessary to confirm for him, as for Spade, the
rightness of his code. Marlowe and his code are constant before,
within and after the novel. Compared with Spade, he is a cipher: a
fixed point, a kind of camera-eye, to use the image created by one
of the few other writers whose company Chandler enjoyed, his
fellow expatriate in southern California, Christopher Isherwood.[64]

Static though it may be, Marlowe's vision is brilliant, even
poetic. Billy Wilder, who collaborated with Chandler on the script
of *Double Indemnity*, has said that the only artists to have
captured southern California are two Englishmen, Chandler and
Hockney.[65] There is something to this. Splashes of bright colour
illumine both men's work; both have a two-dimensionalism and
superficiality which suggest the impossibility of great depths in a
land of such heat and hedonism. Chandler's canvas is vaster than
Hockney's, however. From the orchid-room of the Sternwood
mansion to the spittoon of the Fulwider Building, Chandler paints
Los Angeles high and low; and it is a city he knew well enough,
high and low, to paint with a detail that makes for comparison
with London and Dickens, Paris and Balzac.[66] In his piquant essay
'The Country behind the Hill', Clive James refers to another nineteenth-century master of the novel: 'Flaubert liked tinsel better
than silver because tinsel possessed all silver's attributes plus one
in addition – pathos. . . . For whatever reason, Chandler was
fascinated by the cheapness of Los Angeles.'[67] This aspect of the
new Western city is not much more congenial to Hockney than to
his contemporary in letters, in some ways Chandler's successor,
Joan Didion. While anticipating the preoccupation with style that
London predicted the 'iron heel' would inculcate among artists of
the future, Chandler was still a contemporary of the radicals we
have been discussing. Most of his work was written during
Depression and War; and, though inward by nature, he remained

committed to looking outward into a larger world, his viewpoint informed with the active concern and idealism of his age. Marlowe in fact has a Marxist tendency. In spite of his *machismo*, he is a consistent partisan of the underdog. The murder of ne'er-do-well little Harry Jones is the crime that most haunts him in *The Big Sleep*, goading him to brave the hoods and solve the mystery.

Chandler's books are not political, and Marlowe is not a prescription for a leader but the ideal projection of an artist who dislikes politics and wants above all to be assured of an orderly world in which to pursue his muse. Marlowe has a political implication, however, and it is akin to the one favoured by previous romantics who had wandered from fairy-tale to dreams of action: Wagner's good king, Yeats's mythic leader, Pound's strong man of justice. There is fascism as well as Marxism in Marlowe. The unattractive side of it shows in his racist and sexist comments, the appealing side in his steadfast moral confidence. Chandler's famous description in 'The Simple Art of Murder' suggests what he was after in its best light:

Down these mean streets a man must go who is not himself mean, who is neither tarnished nor afraid. . . . He is the hero, he is everything. He must be a complete man and a common man and yet an unusual man. He must be, to use a rather weathered phrase, a man of honour, by instinct, by inevitability, without thought of it, and certainly without saying it. He must be the best man in his world and a good enough man for any world. I don't care about his private life; he is neither a eunuch nor a satyr; I think he might seduce a duchess and I am quite sure he would not spoil a virgin; if he is a man of honour in one thing, he is in all things. . . . He is a relatively poor man, or he would not be a detective at all. He is a common man or he could not go among common people. He has a sense of character, or he would not know his job. He will take no man's insolence without a due and dispassionate revenge. He is a lonely man and his pride is that you will treat him as a proud man or be very sorry you ever saw him. He talks as a man of his age talks, that is, with rude wit, a lively sense of the grotesque, a disgust for sham, and a contempt for pettiness. . . . The story of this man's adventure is search of a hidden truth, and it would be no adventure if it did not happen to a man fit for adventure. He has a range of awareness that startles you, but it belongs to him by

right because it belongs to the world he lives in. If there were
enough like him, I think the world would be a very safe place to
live in, and yet not too dull to be worth living in.[68]

Chandler's deficiencies lie in content, plot, and architecture; his
genius lies in exposition, metaphor, and the art of story-telling. Of
this last, *The Big Sleep* provides outstanding examples. Its
opening and closing paragraphs must rate among the most
memorable in twentieth-century prose:

> It was about eleven o'clock in the morning, mid-October, with
> the sun not shining and a look of hard wet rain in the clearness
> of the foothills. I was wearing my powder-blue suit, with dark
> blue shirt, tie and display handkerchief, black brogues, black
> wool socks with dark blue clocks on them. I was neat, clean,
> shaved, and sober, and I didn't care who knew it. I was
> everything the well-dressed private detective ought to be. I was
> calling on four million dollars.

In five sentences, Chandler previews the character of seven novels.
In 'eleven o'clock' and 'mid-October' are the motifs of lateness,
suspense, nostalgia and despair. There is gloom in the sky, 'sun not
shining', but this is juxtaposed against the stoical manly values of
'hardness' and 'clearness'. The first two sentences create a
romantic atmosphere, latent with fatalism; the third introduces
the hero. The description is apparently superficial, totally
sartorial; and the impression is of an individual of insouciance,
almost a dandy. The 'powder-blue suit, with dark blue shirt'
suggests a reverse, typical of sunny southern California, of the
normal dark suit and light shirt; the fact that the handkerchief is
merely for 'display' emphasises the importance of external
appearances, both to the culture with its narcissism and to the
detective in his profession. The surface tells all the inner story one
needs to know. Psychology is given in the form not of sentiment,
but of attitude: the man might be dirty, but isn't; he might be
stubble-faced, but has chosen to shave. His cleanliness is a virtue,
but not a blind one. The man knows what it is to let himself go. He
may have a strong urge to let himself go, but resists in respect to
duty. He has a job to do, a function to perform in a society that
might not be well-ordered but ought to be. He is, the last phrase

tells us, like it or not, a self-employed servant in a land of tremendous wealth:

> The main hallway of the Sternwood place was two stories high. Over the entrance doors, which would have let in a troop of Indian elephants, there was a broad stained-glass panel showing a knight in dark armour rescuing a lady who was tied to a tree and didn't have any clothes on but some very long and convenient hair. The knight had pushed the vizor of his helmet back to be sociable, and he was fiddling with the knots on the ropes that tied the lady to the tree and not getting anywhere. I stood there and thought that if I lived in the house, I would sooner or later have to climb up there and help him. He didn't seem to be really trying.

The first paragraph has been Naturalistic enough. The second, after obscuring the pretentions with the joke about elephants ('Indian' carries a resonance, appropriate to Chandler, of the British Empire), offers a mythic–symbolical context. As in Hammett and Steinbeck, the principal allusion is to medieval romance. The particular image is quasi-religious: it appears on stained-glass. It is ambiguous in the way that Hammett's 'blond-haired satan' is ambiguous: the knight is wearing 'dark armour'. It is witty, and the object of the wit is the sexual hypocrisy of women: the hair may be beautiful and entirely natural, but it is placed with calculation to insure an illusion of modesty. It is also humorous: the knight is 'fiddling' with the knots, a genial but not impressive or competent approach. It becomes finally a narcissistic projection: sooner or later the detective himself must become the knight. When he does, one assumes, he will take on the ease of manner ('not really trying') that the knight shares with Sam Spade in his inerect posture or Wilde in his apparently effortless public persona. At the same time, if the author's accomplishment is not to be thoroughly comic, the detective will have to be more effective than his fiddling counterpart.

Indeed he is. Marlowe unties the knots and uncovers a truth in the end he might have divined by reading Shakespeare – *Hamlet*, or the Sonnets:

> What did it matter where you lay once you were dead? In a dirty

sump or in a marble tower on top of a high hill? You were dead, you were sleeping the big sleep, you were not bothered by things like that. Oil and water were the same as wind and air to you. You just slept the big sleep, not caring about the nastiness of how you died or where you fell. Me, I was part of the nastiness now. Far more a part of it than Rusty Regan was. But the old man didn't have to be. He could lie quiet in his canopied bed, with his bloodless hands folded on the sheet, waiting. His heart was a brief, uncertain murmur. His thoughts were grey as ashes. And in a little while he too, like Rusty Regan, would be sleeping the big sleep.

It is characteristic of the thriller to titillate with violence. To be 'half in love with easeful death' is in the realm of Romantic poetry. The 'big sleep' is a poetic image. Three times it is repeated in order to create a rhythm, an inner beat. 'Nastiness' is also repeated from sentence to sentence. There is a hint here of chromatic musical progression, where each new chord incorporates a portion of the one preceding. Riches and status, as in Shakespeare, are nothing in the face of death: king and peasant alike must dine with the worms. 'Out, out, brief candle' may echo faintly in the phrase 'His heart was a brief, uncertain murmur'. A ghostly chorus of the elements blows behind all that has been real: oil, from which the Sternwoods made their fortune, and water become 'the same as wind and air'. Through the paragraph runs a sense of life dissipating: the old man, dry and Eliotic, with thoughts 'grey as ashes', is the last living person to be noted; yet this is only to acknowledge that he, like the symbol of youthful vitality, Regan, will soon be dead as well. The old man replaces the knight of the first paragraph as the male icon in the detective's vision; 'silver wig' (Cissy tinted her hair silvery blonde and wore wigs in order to sustain some illusion of youth) replaces the damsel-in-distress. In a final paragraph, appended perhaps to chase the un-Naturalistic poeticising and morbidity of what has preceded, the detective tries to bid farewell to his vision with a more fatalistic version of Mildred Pierce's resolution, 'Let's get stinko!' Characteristically for Chandler's persona, he fails.

Between the beginning and end of *The Big Sleep* are two stories, cobbled together out of earlier pieces for *Black Mask*. These divide the book roughly in half, between the eighteenth and nineteenth chapters, which form an intermezzo. The first story has to do with the bribery of the Sternwoods over Carmen's drug-taking and the murders related to it, the second with the disappearance of Regan and Eddie Mars's cover-up. In overall structure the novel is not so well ordered as this description might indicate. Chandler's chapters are not units of meaning like Hammett's; they are conveniences for the progress of the reader, and perhaps the author. Chapters 1-3 are really one chapter about the Sternwoods, chapters 4-8 one chapter about the various activities surrounding the blackmailer, Geiger. Other chapters link in a similar way. But toward the middle of the book the linkage becomes less distinct; development from chapter to chapter loses sequential logic; purpose and subject-matter become less certain. This reflects the fact that the detective is no longer really sure what he is after, but it does not do so with the meaningfulness of the middle chapters of *The Maltese Falcon*. Spade gets confused, not Hammett. But, where Marlowe appears confused, the problem may well lie with Chandler. For long stretches he seems merely to grope, filling space, trying himself to figure out how in the world he is going to knit the one old plot to the other and forge a marketable whole. Then, suddenly, he strikes on a way; the pace accelerates; Marlowe stops sharpening pencils and swatting flies in his office and goes out to be effective again. What carries us over these architectural blunders is Chandler's masterful ability to write sequences of dialogue, conceived almost as narrative paragraphs and broken by intrusions of brilliant exposition or outcroppings of flashy metaphor.

Marlowe's eye for the denizens of Los Angeles is as keen as Dante's for the historical pantheon of the thirteenth century; and, having a world-view as absolutist as Dante's Christianity, Chandler's 'knight' is able to place all in the proper circles of his inferno. The characters placed are types, however: rarely developed, rarely even as rounded as the types of Cain. Lacking capacity for interesting growth, they begin to merge together after a few stories. This is a deficiency. Chandler overcomes it by his genius for the *bon mot*, the epithet that 'pins' Prufrock to the wall, the piquant image. This genius is a Modernist phenomenon, recalling Pound's dictum that *image* is the most important unit of poetry or Mailer's equivalent claim for metaphor in fiction.[69] Chandler's penchant for bizarre analogies also suggests the aging Henry James; or Steinbeck of later years – *Sweet Thursday* is laden with comic metaphors and *East of Eden* with portentous ones. In light of the fact that these men were over fifty when their propensity reached its apogee, one might wonder whether metaphorising is not a trick or tick that a certain type of writer tends to develop with the years, often when his talents for fine architecture and unity of effect begin to fade. In Chandler's case, the imagery sometimes has a silliness that at worst seems senile and more generally suggests the crabbings of a grumpy old man. He was, as Clive James says, prone to 'overcooking a simile';[70] and the problem arises that, when his similes work best, they confuse his plots further by causing the reader to stop, chuckle and marvel. Something of continuity and coherence is lost with most humour: Shaw's metaphysics are not particularly advanced by the jokes he felt compelled to get off in order to win audience forbearance; low humour in Shakespeare or the patter of wit in a Restoration comedy can deflect attention from the serious theme and seem to reduce its consequence. The brilliant asides can do this in Chandler. By the same token, they can provide the breathing-space that makes his otherwise bloody and claustrophobic melodramas habitable – indeed, comfortable.

The High Window (1942), the one of Chandler's four early novels not pieced together from stories for *Black Mask*, is the magic garden of his metaphors. Of an aristocratic pouff: 'His smile was as faint as a fat lady at a fireman's ball.'[71] Of an artificial beauty: 'The blonde laughed a silvery ripple of laughter that held the unspoiled naturalness of a bubble dance' (346).Of the aging poor: 'On the wide cool front porches, reaching their cracked shoes into the sun and staring at nothing, sit the old men with faces like lost battles' (359). This description of decadent Bunker Hill is one of the great evocations in the opus, comparing with the descriptions of LA by night in *The Little Sister* (1949). Nostalgia for the ebbing youth of the city is mixed with partisanship for its victims. The poor of Bunker Hill are juxtaposed against the rich of Pasadena: the Murdock family, whose wealth and respectability mask a secret not unlike that of Hammett's Dains. Marlowe's association with the Murdocks is marked by passages revealing his disgust both for them and for himself for serving them. The exchanges are circuitous and often empty; they have a perverse benefit, however: 'Meaningless talk had a sort of cold bracing effect on me, making a mood with a hard gritty edge' (365). Perhaps this is Chandler's rationalisation for allowing Marlowe to pepper the world with sarcasm. Nature itself escapes the acidity of this city-observer no less than in Baudelaire: the air has 'a touch of that peculiar tom-cat smell that eucalyptus trees give off in warm weather' (374). Imagine Burning Daylight describing the eucalyptuses he has lovingly planted in the Oakland hills as giving off 'a peculiar tom-cat smell'! Chandler, city-bred, foreign to California, city-prejudiced as an inhabitant, is as partisan to art over nature as Vivien in Wilde's 'Decay of Lying'. Wit makes a virtue out of irreverence. It transvalues. As an approach, it is opposite to the passionate glorifications of London and the early Steinbeck. The great poet of southern California renders his land attractive through derision, not praise. Chandler is godfather to the tradition of Los Angeles as 'the city everyone loves to hate': that terminally cynical place where you can ask the concierge of a great hotel where to find a decent breakfast and be told, 'Some other city'.

San Francisco, self-proclaimed 'everyone's favourite city', chauvinised as 'my burg' by Sam Spade, mockingly dubbed 'San Narcisco' by Thomas Pynchon in *The Crying of Lot 49*, finds its low-down corrupt *alter ego* in that waste land of Iowans, fascists and rubes 400 miles south. Chandler would reveal his own LA versus SF prejudice by his response to Harlan Potter in *The Long Goodbye*. But, though he preferred LA to any place save an idealised England, he did not hesitate to portray it as 'the Great Wrong Place'.[72] The tough LA cop whom the world has come to know through TV is largely his creation. The corrupt lily-white suburb just outside the metropolis was first captured by Chandler in Bay City. This amalgam of Santa Monica, Long Beach, where Chandler worked in the oil business, and South Bay beach-towns such as Hermosa, where he and Cissy lived in the 1920s, is the locus of the most unsavoury activities in *Farewell, My Lovely*, *The Lady in the Lake* (1944) and *The Little Sister*, providing a foil to, respectively, a more civilised Los Angeles, a hamlet in the San Bernardino Mountains, and Hollywood. Los Angeles may be 'the Great Wrong Place'; its cops, like Nulty in *Farewell*, may be racist, misogynist, lazy, changeable, humourless, backbiting, subjective and nepotistic; but in contrast to the cops of Bay City they seem capable of humanity, fairness, appreciation of talent, skill, and camaraderie. Constable Jim Patton of Little Fawn Lake in *The Lady* is slow, vulgar, unsophisticated and self-indulgent; confront-

ed with the hot-headed and vicious Sergeant Degarmo of the Bay
City Police Department, however, he seems a paragon of cool and
good sense. The mobsters of Hollywood in *The Little Sister* may
appear to the public as proof of the corruption of that decadent
pleasure-dome; but Steelgrave in fact is a rather dashing, romantic
figure; and nothing he does is nearly so gruesome as the attempt of
Orrin Quest, the 'good' kid come to Bay City from a small town in
Kansas, to blackmail his own sister, now a movie-star, for having
an underworld boyfriend.

Chandler is prejudiced in favour of the big city, in spite of its
warts. Bay City provides a constant reminder of how much worse a
small city can be. Things in Bay City are not hopeless, however.
Sergeant Degarmo may be a sex killer and the cops under him too
willing to cover up his brutality; their big boss, however, is a man
of humanity and sense. 'Police work is a hell of a problem', Captain
Webber tells Marlowe after apologising for Degarmo's excess. 'It's
a good deal like politics. It asks for the highest type of men, and
there's nothing in it to attract the highest type of men.' Marlowe
answers, 'I've always known that.'[73] He knows, in fact, in a way that
Sam Spade in the confines of *The Maltese Falcon* never quite
learns, and that Steinbeck's cop-haters would rarely acknowledge.
Chandler's opus provides an endless catalogue of police brutality;
but from Bernie Ohls in *The Big Sleep* to the Esmeralda
police-chief in *Playback*, it also provides the other side of the coin:
the sensitive, realistic cop with a potential for fairness – Polhaus of
Falcon amplified. Like so many others in Chandler, cops fall into
the category of humanity victimised by a large and largely
unchangeable system. Bad cops are symptoms of a greater evil.
'Hemingway', who beats up Marlowe in *Farewell*, later drives him
through a poor district of Bay City, singing as he does the classic
aria of the ordinary beat-cop's predicament:

> You hear a lot about crooked cops. . . . Okay, how many cops
> you find living on a street even as good as this, with nice lawns
> and flowers? . . . Cops live in itty-bitty frame houses on the
> wrong side of town. . . . Cops don't go crooked for money. . . .
> They get caught in the system. . . . You know what's the matter
> with this country, baby? . . . A guy can't stay honest if he wants
> to. . . . He gets chiseled out of his pants if he does. . . . A lot of
> bastards think all we need is ninety thousand FBI men in clean
> collars and briefcases. . . . You know what I think? I think we

gotta make this world all over again. . . . Me, I'm just a dumb cop. I take orders. I got a wife and two kids and I do what the big shots say.[74]

It is not likely that those kids may grow up to echo Everhard of *The Iron Heel*: 'Father . . . did all sorts of dishonorable things to put bread in [our] mouths. . . . He was a slave'?[75]

Farewell, My Lovely was Chandler's favourite of his books. Edmund Wilson has called it his most radical.[76] Were some of the extrinsic scenes and plot-confusions removed, it might proceed like *The Maltese Falcon* in a direct drive toward the truth of what constitutes power in city-life and chart a growth in Marlowe to full confidence in his struggle to defeat corruption. The Bay City cops, as Hemingway says, are mere tools. They are directed by a chief and mayor who are themselves tools of a gangster who has made his place by gambling and currying favour with the rich. Laird Brunette, as often the case with this type in Chandler, is not evil incarnate; he too is relatively powerless. Behind the scenes lurk calm, civilised, almost invisible beings of really immense wealth. In *Farewell* this type is represented by Lewin Lockridge Grayle, an investment banker worth $20 million, who lives in a mansion 'no bigger than Buckingham Palace' and with 'fewer windows than the Chrysler Building'. A mild, sad old fellow, Grayle is almost as sympathetic to Marlowe as General Sternwood in *The Big Sleep*. He too is a victim – not, like the General, of daughters, but also of woman, in this case a wife young enough to be his daughter. Mrs Grayle is the Helen of Troy who causes the mayhem in *Farewell*. Originally a torch-singer from the wrong side of the tracks, she has made her way up the ladder by the beautiful woman's version of the mobster's rackets, the wiles of sex and love. Mrs Grayle is also a victim: of a system that puts all emphasis on making it to a superior pinnacle of wealth and power and then covering up how you got there. In the end the book suggests that she too should not be judged wholly culpable for her crimes. Her aspiration, after all, has not been substantially different from the one which makes Hemingway resent his 'itty-bitty frame house'. The rich and poor in Chandler are often separated only by the fact that the former have made it and the latter still want to.

Mrs Grayle's bloody end demonstrates Chandler's Shakespearean moral that blind ambition leads also, often more quickly, to the most levelling condition: death. Realising the self-destructive futility of the system, Marlowe himself has dropped out to observe, wait, and do what little he can to help others like himself. In *Farewell*, unusually, he needs a couple of assisters to keep him on this path of good sense. The first is Ann Riordan, who discovers him unconscious after being sapped by some of Brunette's operatives, nurses him, and puts him on the track of la Grayle (as with the name 'Quest' in *The Little Sister*, 'Grayle' sounds the symbolic note so overtly as to alert us to the element of parody). Ann's father was once the police-chief of Bay City. Brunette hounded him out of office because he was insufficiently corruptible; he and his wife died shortly thereafter, and some oil-land they owned was swindled out of Ann's hands (Chandler's guilt for his own behaviour as an oil-executive?). Ann is looking for the vindication of her father's memory by a clean-up of Bay City; Marlowe's success will put this in motion. The second assister is the boatman, Red Noorgaard, who ferries Marlowe from Bay City harbour to Brunette's gambling yacht outside the three-mile limit, helps him mentally to overcome his fear and physically to overcome the thugs who block his path. Noorgaard is also an ex-member of the Bay City Police Department, and his status will also be resurrected by the clean-up Marlowe sets in motion. Noorgaard's place in the novel has a mythic resonance altogether rare in Chandler: physically he has the strength and delicacy of Wolf Larsen; functionally he provides the service that Captain O'Connors provides for John Howard Sharp. Noorgaard, however, is wiser, less aesthetic, and more probable than either Larsen or O'Connors. He is the one who sums up Chandler's sense of the human element in the cop: 'The tough cop is neither bad nor good, neither crooked nor honest, full of guts and just dumb enough, like me, to think being on the cops is a sensible way to make a living' (293). He is also the one who sums up Chandler's perception of the individual quality in the cop's natural enemy, the crook: 'The top men, like Brunette – they didn't get there by murdering. . . . They got there by guts and brains – and they don't have the group courage that cops have either. . . . Above all they're businessmen' (294).

A notable case of the man of ambiguous morals who has made it is the power-broker of Hollywood. Chandler met the moguls during his second career, as a screen-writer. The book that incorporates

this 'life-material' is *The Little Sister*. It was written after the
Chandlers moved from LA to La Jolla, for reasons of age and
health. It is the first book Chandler dictated. He feared the fate of
Henry James, who had started dictating at an advanced stage and
became prey to almost terminal garrulity. In fact, such excess does
not show in *The Little Sister*. At least for the first hundred pages it
is as tight as Chandler's most compressed book, its predecessor,
Lady in the Lake. Still, Chandler found it 'overripe' – '[It is]
beautifully written, [but] there is nothing in it but style and
dialogue and characters. The plot creaks like a broken shutter'[77] –
and most commentators have agreed. Billy Wilder maintains that
the Hollywood interlude finished Chandler as a novelist and that
the last three books show a progressive slackening of power.[78] In
fact, the post-Hollywood Chandler was consciously trying to
expand his subject-matter and deepen the novelistic aspects of his
work.[79] The evocations of LA in *The Little Sister* are part of this; so
are the extrinsic passages about the studios. Such experiments
would continue in *The Long Goodbye*, which, like Steinbeck's
contemporary *East of Eden*, is marked by lengthy asides on general
cultural phenomena and has the slowness of pace and psychological complexity of the traditional great novel. *The Long Goodbye*
was intended by Chandler as his masterpiece. It may well be. *The
Little Sister* may fail as a thriller, because Chandler was becoming
unenthused about that eminently parodiable genre; but it has
passages which are more compelling on their own that can be
found in the four early books. 'It is the one book of mine I have
actively disliked', Chandler wrote; 'It was written in a bad mood
and I think that comes through.'[80] But irritability, Jack London
said, is fundamental to all good writing;[81] and this new aspect of
authorial self-revelation gives *The Little Sister* bite and character.

Chandler's bad temper, expressed particularly in Chapter 13,
may arise out of his unsatisfactory relations with the Hollywood
femme fatale. Mrs Grayle in *Farewell* and Eddie Mars's wife in *The
Big Sleep* are mostly imagined (probably extrapolated from
aspects of Cissy), and Marlowe's feelings of disappointment at
having to resist them are theoretical. The sirens of *The Little Sister*
are substantially taken from life, by contrast; Chandler had
become an aging *enfant terrible* who could finally afford his
fantasies financially but was no longer really up to them physically.
Compromised morally by his marriage to a septuagenarian, he felt
oppressed; and Marlowe's new irrationality about women is a

result. One may be reminded of Steinbeck and Cathy Trask. Chandler's turmoil is particularly evident from the fact that in *The Little Sister* and its successors Marlowe becomes vulnerable to sexual urges in a way he never has been before. He touches Mavis Weld's hand with intent when alone with her in her dressing-room. He kisses her country sister, Orfamay, when that deceptively prim little creature takes her 'cheaters' off. He goes positively weak at the knees over Dolores Gonzales; and, as the canny *femme fatale* must, she plays on this from the moment of their first meeting. Tall and dark, Dolores appears in jodphurs, a white silk shirt, and scarlet scarf loose around the neck – the same garb with same sado-masochistic overtones that appears on Chandler's fantasy female in 'English Summer'.[82] There are suggestions here of the influence of Cain, whose work Chandler claimed to despise but was fresh in his mind from working on *Double Indemnity*. Phyllis Nirdlinger and Juana of *Serenade* lurk behind Dolores as she holds her 'long brown cigarette in a pair of gold tweezers', presses a nipple 'hard as a ruby' against Marlowe's chest, and vamps him in a phony Mexican accent.[83] 'She looked as hard to get as a haircut' (63), he cracks; later, 'as exclusive as a mailbox' (106). Marlowe admires her in the end, however: 'Nothing would ever touch her, not even the law.' She has a courage that a lover of the romantic ethos will always value, even when it is wrong: 'No matter how many lovers a woman may have . . . there is always one she cannot bear to lose to another woman . . . The man I loved is dead. . . . That man I would not share' (186).

Like Mrs Grayle, Dolores ends by her own hand, and with Mrs Grayle she must rate as Chandler's strongest female character. But what is really new in *The Little Sister*, as noted, is the picture of Hollywood. 'What Hollywood seems to want is a writer who is ready to commit suicide in every story conference. What it actually gets is the fellow who screams like a stallion in heat and then cuts his throat with a banana. The scream demonstrates the artistic purity of his soul and he can eat the banana while somebody else is answering a telephone call about some other picture.'[84] Spattering it with this kind of humour, Chandler paints in chaptes 17–19 one of the best pictures of the types essayed by Schulberg, Fitzgerald and Cain. In his quest for the moguls Marlowe must first go through a tough receptionist and a slimy 'protection' man named Spink. These scenes dramatise Hollywood's subscription to Huysmans's dictum that all power comes from making people

wait. One of the many cooling his heels with Marlowe in the foyer
of top agent Sheridan Ballou is 'a very tall distinguished-looking
party' wearing 'a pearl-grey Homburg at a rakish angle' and
'yellow chamois gloves'. At length this *rara avis* strolls up to the
receptionist: 'I have been waiting for two hours to see Mr Ballou.
. . . I'm not accustomed to wait two hours to see anybody.'
Receptionist: 'So sorry, Mr Fortescue, Mr Ballou is just too busy for
words this a.m.' Fortescue: 'I'm sorry I cannot leave him a cheque.
. . . Probably the only thing that would interest him. But in default
of that –' Receptionist: 'Just a minute, kid. [To 'phone:] Who says
so besides Goldwyn? Can't you reach somebody that's not crazy?
[Slams down 'phone]' Fortescue: 'In default of that I should like to
leave a short personal message.' Receptionist: 'Please do . . . I'll get
it to him somehow.' Fortescue: 'Tell him with my love that he's a
dirty polecat.' Receptionist: 'Make it skunk, darling . . . He doesn't
know any English words.' Adding a flourish, Fortescure exits,
saying 'to hell with Sheridan Ballou Incorporated'. The receptionist explains to Marlowe: 'He isn't getting any parts so he comes in
every day and goes through that routine. He figures somebody
might see him and like it' (89). This is one of Chandler's many
vignettes showing the irrelevance of the Old World manners he was
brought up on. It prepares the reader to marvel at the mix of
philistinism, vulgarity and psychological perception that succeeds
in the magic garden of contemporary capitalist culture.

Spink adds a racial tint to Marlowe's ambivalent fascination. He
is 'a plump white-haired Jew' who smiles 'tenderly' and greets
Marlowe by opening 'a thing that looked like a trunk' and
presenting him with a cigarette 'not more than a foot long . . . in
an individual glass tube' (90). Marlowe is unimpressed. He is
impatient to see Ballou and makes as much clear, punctuating his
statement with 'to hell with people named Spink'. The latter reacts
by waving 'a generous hand on which a canary-yellow diamond
looked like an amber traffic light': 'Anti-Semitic, huh? . . . Ok, I
ain't offended. In a business like this you got to have somebody
around that don't get offended.' In general, Marlowe exhibits the
constant low-level racial distaste typical of white lower-middle-
class males of melting-pot cities. He is not averse to referring to a
black as a 'dinge' in *Farewell*; he has considerable difficulty
warming to Roger Wade's Mexican houseboy in *The Long
Goodbye*; he feels no compunction about describing a Jew as 'fat',
'greasy' and 'sensual' in *The High Window*, in spite of the fact that

Hitler was sending millions to the ovens as Chandler was writing
the book. But Marlowe-Chandler in his racism, as in all his
sarcasms and attitudes, is an old grouch rather than a dogmatist.
'He does not pursue [his racially tinged observations] below the
level of physical distaste', Russell Davies says; 'Sheer unthinking
(hygiene-based) snobbery is all that is involved here.'[85] Chandler's
supreme distaste was for the hypocritical *haut-bourgeois* WASP:
he refused to join the La Jolla Beach and Tennis Club because it
would not admit Jews; and, when charged with anti-Semitism, he
retorted, much like Jack London: 'Jews should be mature enough
to demand the right to have Jewish scoundrels in fiction. . . . Look
for your enemies among the brutes and snobs who do not speak of
Jews at all.'[86] At base Chandler shared with Cain and many
contemporaries a dislike for the type of Hollywood Jew who was 'a
philistine, unscrupulous individual whose only interest was a fast
buck'. At the same time, like Hammett or aficionados of Proust, he
admired intensely, if not without trepidation, the type which
embodied higher attainments in style, sensuality, and culture.

Sheridan Ballou is such a type. His office has 'double doors of
heavy black glass with silver peacocks etched into the panels' (91).
It is 'two storeys high, surrounded by a balcony loaded with
bookshelves'; it contains 'a concert Steinway in the corner and a lot
of glass and bleached wood furniture and a desk about the size of a
badminton court and chairs and couches and tables'. Ballou,
reclined on one of the couches, is 'a big shapely guy with wavy dark
hair'. He has 'his shirt open over a Charvet silk scarf you could have
found in the dark by listening to it purr'. There is a cloth over his
eyes and a 'lissome blonde girl was wringing out another in a silver
bowl of ice water'. The Decadent style is summed up by how he
smokes: 'He got the cigarette wearily into his mouth and drew on it
with the infinite languor of a decadent aristocrat mouldering in a
ruined chateau.' Marlowe, impatient, gives as free rein to his nasty
comments as with Spink: 'I forgot to bring my prayer-book. . . .
This is the first time I knew God worked on commission.' Spink is
horrified; Ballou, however, hears authority in the tone, dismisses
his 'darlings', and gets up to discuss the blackmail Marlowe has
come about. Gradually Marlowe recognises that Ballou is tired,
not dissipated. His manner is urbane, melancholic, realistic. He
has 'a deep pleasant effortless laugh', and his conversation is laced
with *aperçus* from his profession: 'The fear of today always
overrides the fear of tomorrow', 'If suspense and menace didn't

defeat reason, there would be very little drama', etc. (94). While holding forth, Ballou walks 'up and down inside the house with a Piccadilly stroll and a monkey stick in his hand'. Marlowe grunts, 'It could only happen in Hollywood'; but he finds 'all six feet two' of the other 'a very fine hunk of man'. The feeling is mutual. On leave-taking, Ballou signals his attraction indirectly: 'One of these days ... I'm going to make the mistake which a man in my business dreads above all others. ... I'm going to find myself doing business with a man I can trust and I'm going to be just too goddamn smart to trust him' (98).

If the course of Marlowe's adventures is a search for 'hidden truth', discovery of that truth increasingly requires confrontation with a version of God. The process is typical of this genre of novel, as of the romances from which it derives. Spade must confront Gutman before he can achieve his Holy Grail; Parzival must confront Amfortas with the question, 'What ails thee, Uncle?' Parsifal in Wagner's version of the romance must also confront the anti-God figure of Klingsor in order to win back the Holy Spear, symbol of manhood necessary to restore strength to the Grail Order and, mythically, restore fertility to the waste land of the fisher king, of whom Amfortas is a version. Gutman for Spade is also an anti-God figure, and in the titanic figures Marlowe must meet there is a similar merging of evil with good. In the post-Nietzschean moral climate of the twentieth century what distinguishes God above all is His power, and that power can be as mischievous and inimical to mankind as the machinations of an indifferent capitalist. Who are these God-figures then for Marlowe? Versions of the weakened fisher king appear in General Sternwood and Lewin Grayle. The final three novels offer characterisations of supreme power in Julius Oppenheimer, Harlan Potter and Henry Clarendon IV. The first is the silliest. As Marlowe passes on his way to the studio, he sees Oppenheimer sitting by a fountain watching his three boxer dogs urinate on the bench at his feet. The fact that the dogs always pee in the same order fascinates the great man: 'Question of seniority, it seems' (99). They even do so in his office, Oppenheimer reveals, which upsets his secretaries – 'What's the matter with women nowadays?' A mail-girl passes 'making music with her hips' for the great man. 'You know what's the matter with this business? ... Too much sex. ... Gets to be like flypaper.'

Oppenheimer offers Marlowe a cigar; when Marlowe indicates that he already has a cigarette, the great man tosses the cigar into the fountain. 'Wasted fifty cents . . . save fifty cents in this business and all you have is five dollars' worth of bookkeeping. . . . Fifteen hundred theatres is all you need. . . . The motion picture business is the only business in the world in which you can make all the mistakes there are and still make money' (100).

The God of *The Little Sister* is revealed to be a senile sentimentalist. 'The eyes of your dog', Oppenheimer babbles as an underling ushers him off, 'the most unforgettable thing in the world' (101). The function of this meeting with the Almighty seems to have been to show that the mortal hero, the detective, is the true crown of creation: more attractive, sensible, and even perhaps effective than the invisible mover. Chandler is on the side of humankind. So much is the message of Marlowe's more extensive encounter with Potter in *The Long Goodbye*. Marlowe is taken to this God-figure by his daughter, Linda Loring. The setting is a house Potter bought for her in the exclusive suburb Idle Valley: 'Damnedest-looking house I ever saw . . . wedding-cake decorations . . . outside spiral staircase . . . tower-room. . . . Whoever built that place was trying hard to drag the Atlantic seaboard over the Rockies . . . trying hard, but he hadn't made it.'[87] A French count named La Tourelle built it. A miniature of the Château de Blois, it was a gift for his wife, Ramona Desborough, star of silent films. Neither she nor La Tourelle ever lived in the house, however: she left him and he killed himself.[88] Confiding that she has always hated the house, Linda leads Marlowe through the entry-halls into a dimly lit reception-room where the great man is waiting. Like Sheridan Ballou, he is tall and majestic: 'six feet five and built to scale' (340). His fastidious grandeur suggests an ethos more WASP-pure, however: 'He wore a grey tweed suit. . . . He looked at me like an entomologist looking at a beetle. . . . He didn't look as if he was having any fun. . . . "Don't smoke please. I am subject to asthma." . . . His voice seemed to come from a long way off. He drank his tea as if he hated it.' Potter's mission is to discourage Marlowe from pursuing investigation of the murder of his 'bad' daughter (Linda is his 'good' daughter). Marlowe, however, like the Luciferian rebel from Godly tyranny that the romantic hero must be, expresses his commitment to individual judgement: 'Maybe you had better let me have my own notions, Mr Potter. They're not important, naturally, but they're all I have'

(341). The false modesty masks a gut-level disquiet with the order Potter represents: 'A man doesn't make your kind of money in any way that I can understand' (342).

Frowning, listening to his own thoughts rather than what Marlowe inserts, Potter delivers a sermon which sums up the misanthropic world-view of the conservative ultra-rich Californian, whom Chandler had come to know at close hand since moving to exclusive La Jolla:

> Be careful, young man. I don't like irony. . . . We live in what is called a democracy, rule by the majority of the people. A fine ideal if it could be made to work. The people elect, but the party machines nominate, and the party machines to be effective must spend a good deal of money. Somebody has to give it to them, and that somebody, whether it be an individual, a financial group, a trade union or what have you, expects consideration in return. What I and people of my kind expect is to be allowed to live our lives in decent privacy. I own newspapers, but I don't like them. I regard them as a constant menace to whatever privacy we have left. . . . There's peculiar thing about money. . . . In large quantities it tends to have a life of its own. . . . The power of money becomes very difficult to control. Man has always been a venal animal. The growth of populations, the huge cost of wars, the incessant pressure of confiscatory taxation – all these things make him more and more venal. The average man is tired and scared, and a tired, scared man can't afford ideals. He has to buy food for his family. In our time we have seen a shocking decline in both public and private morals. You can't expect quality from people whose lives are a subjection to a lack of quality. . . . We make the finest packages in the world, Mr Marlowe. The stuff inside is mostly junk. (343–4)

Marlowe's response: 'I was sitting there with my mouth open, wondering what made the guy tick. He hated everything.' Marlowe says as much, though not in so many words. Suddenly Potter, no doubt starved for frank conversation, flashes 'a big rugged smile with a reasonable amount of friendliness in it' and counsels, 'Don't be a hero, young man. There's no percentage in it. . . . One of these days I might be able to throw some business your way. . . . And don't go away thinking that I buy politicians or law enforcement officers. I don't have to' (345).

Potter's cynicism reflects the axiom Chandler came to express, that in the twentieth century man is ruled by pressures not principles;[89] and to some degree Potter may represent the voice of Chandler grown rich, celebrated, suburban and secure. His disquiet with democracy and the power of money, however, show Chandler still uncomfortable with the 'system' he had berated in *Farewell*; and a tinge of 1930s radicalism lingers in Marlowe's attitude. Animus against the very rich persisted in Chandler right down to his last unfinished outing, about another haven for southern Californian wealth, Palm ('Poodle') Springs. But, beyond Chandler himself and the rich he had met in La Jolla, Potter embodies other faces of the Anglo-Saxon elite. The Ramona Desborough story suggests the creator of San Simeon and lover of Marion Davies, thus links to the eccentric and nearly invisible rich Californian of north as well as south who hovers behind novels of London and Steinbeck. He is a more urbane, individualistic version of the men of the Philomath Club in San Francisco who try to bribe Ernest Everhard out of his radical activities and, when he refuses, warn him that they will crush him under their 'iron heel'. More generally he links, as do Hearst and the Philomaths, to the steel-hard grey-faced WASPs of the Eastern Establishment who attempt to swindle Burning Daylight, and who rule the world in the *Weltanschaung* of radicals such as B. Traven. He is of the flock whose black sheep would be the perverted yet still powerful Winston Hawes; a Californian version of the Yankee 'samurai' of *Mutiny of the Elsinore*; a preview of the Los Angeles businessmen, inheritors of Harrison Gray Otis's strain of elitism, who make up Ronald Reagan's kitchen cabinet. Most intriguing, Potter suggests a figure whom, considering his profession and Anglophilia, Chandler was well placed to be impressed, intimidated and irritated by: T. S. Eliot. Potter shares physical and stylistic traits with the poet (also with Stephen Spender, equally tall and majestic, through whom Chandler might have met Eliot on one of his recent trips to London), and his world-view has several Eliotic touches: detachment from life, elitism, a Baudelairean sense that human nature is venal. 'He explained civilization to me', Marlowe quips to Linda Loring on leaving the great man's presence; 'He's going to let it go on for a little while.' This sounds like a probable Chandler response to Eliot's position of God-paring-His-fingernails in, say, *The Waste Land* or *After Strange Gods*. The tip-off that Chandler may have the poet in mind comes in Marlowe's exchange with

Potter's black chauffeur after the latter has delivered him from Idle Valley: 'I offered him a buck and he wouldn't take it. I offered to buy him the poems of T. S. Eliot. He said he had already read them' (351).

The Eliot resonance attaches to the last great of Chandler's career: to belong to that Grail order which had eluded him as a youth, literary London. The story of Chandler's last years is of travelling to London with visions of being received as a hero of the 'Hemingway–Rockefeller–Bogart' ilk, then recoiling in alcoholic paranoia of being excluded by some 'Derrick–Peter–Nigel' old-boy conspiracy.[90] La Jolla, boring and philistine as he found it, was Chandler's true final home. His last completed work, *Playback* (1958), provides a stinging, satirical picture of this prototypical Californian suburb for the rich. In the midst of it, in one of the hotels housing dowagers who come to the Pacific to die, Marlowe encounters his last God-figure, retired aristocrat Henry Clarendon IV. Clarendon's views on omnipotence and the divine joke come closer to the truth Chandler was after than most others, and they serve as a fine epitaph to this remarkable writer's career:

Do you believe in God, young man? . . . But you should. . . . It is a great comfort. We all come to it in the end because we have to die and become dust. Perhaps for the individual that is all, perhaps not. There are grave difficulties about the after-life. I don't think I should really enjoy a heaven in which I shared lodgings with a Congo pygmy or a Chinese coolie or a Levantine rug peddlar or even a Hollywood producer. I'm a snob, I suppose, and the remark is in bad taste. Nor can I imagine a heaven presided over by a benevolent character in a long white beard locally known as God. These are foolish conceptions of very immature minds. But you may not question a man's religious beliefs however idiotic they may be. Of course I have no right to assume that I shall go to heaven. Sounds rather dull, as a matter of fact. On the other hand how can I imagine a hell in which a baby that died before baptism occupies the same degraded position as a hired killer or a Nazi death camp commandant or a member of the Politburo? How strange it is that a man's finest aspirations, dirty little animal that he is, his finest actions also, his great and unselfish heroism, his constant daily courage in a harsh world – how strange that these things should be so much finer than his fate on earth. That has to be somehow made reasonable. Don't tell me that honour is merely a chemical reaction or that a man who deliberately gives his life for another is merely following a behaviour pattern. Is God happy that life is cruel and that only the fittest survive? The fittest for what? Oh no, far from it. If God were omnipotent and omniscient in any literal sense, he wouldn't have bothered to make the universe at all. There is no success where there is no possibility of failure, no art without the resistance of the medium. Is it blasphemy to suggest that God has his bad days when nothing goes right, and that God's days are very, very long? [91]

5 The Sixties and After

Chandler died in 1959, Hammett in 1961, Steinbeck in 1968, Cain in 1977. All but Hammett were active till the end; and, though there was slackening of power in their later works, all retained considerable influence. Chandler and Steinbeck in particular bear relation to the movements of the late 1950s, 1960s and 1970s. Steinbeck's *Travels with Charley* (1960) was itself derivative of the movement of a younger generation back to the populist road he had travelled in the 1930s. Jack Kerouac was the seminal figure in this movement, his *roman à clef*, *On the Road* (1957), its Bible. As Frederick Feied points out in his monograph *No Pie in the Sky*, Kerouac was last in a line of American practitioners of a genre that had its origins in Whitman but first major prose enunciation in London's *The Road* (1907).[1] The California lodestone had been influential in this genre's development. Twain's *Roughing It* was an early road book. Harte's 'My Friend, the Tramp' was the first sympathetic literary depiction of its type of hero. Henry George provided one of the first analyses of this new type in *Progress and Poverty* (1880):

> The 'tramp' comes with the locomotive, and almshouses and prisons are as surely the marks of 'material progress' as are costly dwellings, rich warehouses, and magnificent churches. Upon streets lighted with gas and patrolled by uniformed policemen, beggars wait for the passer-by, and in the shadow of college, and library, and museum, are gathered the more hideous Huns and fierce Vandals of whom Macaulay prophesied.[2]

In the Middle Ages and after, Feied argues, the *clericus vagus, picaro* and 'sturdy beggar' had been happy wanderers whose chief antagonist was a supervening existential force – a kind of angry Yahweh. In the industrial era this force came increasingly to be identified with capitalism. Norris was among the first to dramatise the connection, in *The Octopus*. London made it a major theme;

185

Steinbeck used it to propel his collective 'tramp' book, *Grapes*. Implicitly the connection stands behind Kerouac's work. But Kerouac, Feied points out, also harks back to more general existential concerns: 'Kerouac's migrant may be a young man from the middle class who sees life on the road as a form of rebellion against conformity and middle class mores.'[3]

Lower middle-class and suburban in background, Kerouac spent much of his youth like the other Jack, as an urban proletarian.[4] Like London, he went to sea. Like London, he proved indifferent to university yet set out after knowledge 'with a club'.[5] Like London, he produced an immense body of highly autobiographical writing before dying at an early age. Kerouac may have read Marx at Columbia in the 1940s, but he never supported himself with the prop of socialism that London claimed to have saved him from Martin Eden's abyss. A more applicable historical analysis for him came from Oswald Spengler. The West was in decline; America, having taken the baton of culture, would lead the race through twilight into darkness. 'We foresaw that America was going to take some awful fall', Allen Ginsberg recalls of the period in which Beat epistemology was generated; 'some massive nervous breakdown'.[6] Kerouac and the poets around him made it their business to study themselves as symptoms of the breakdown and, by studying, to evolve a new set of values for America and the West. The course of their quest took them from New York to California, with side trips to Europe and Mexico and Morocco – all places where they imagined a more spiritual orientation might be found. These journeys are the subjects of their writing. As they travelled, they carried huge rucksacks of literary self-consciousness with them. Blake was a favoured forbear: 'The road of excess leads to the palace of wisdom.'[7] Other models for Kerouac included Goethe, Joyce, Thomas Wolfe ('the American Faust'),[8] London ('The Nietzschean beast raked over his dreams, made him literally hear "the call of the wild", taught him of the free ones, the hobos, the bums, left him with a vision of freedom and the open road'[9]) and Hammett, whose 'world was like theirs, a place of black and white and gray, anything but "clean, orderly, and sane". His greatest character, Sam Spade, was an "existential knight" . . . . Spade had little respect for society's rules, but he worked with a sense of honor . . . sliced through the fraud, the phoniness, the corruption, the lies, to the bonehard facts.'[10]

The bonehard facts were a virtue: realism. Something intensely mystical, however, was the goal. In approaching this goal, a denser, more layered, inward and psychological style was needed. Kerouac imitated the conversation of his great male comrade and hero of *On the Road*, Neal Cassady. Cassady's mode, Ginsberg remembers, was 'eager, excited, high fraternal talk . . . a sort of American-Denver talk, but with Proustian detail'.[11] Kerouac's realisation of the style came in *Visions of Cody* (1959), which he typed in an attic on Russian Hill where he lived with Cassady and his wife, Carolyn. San Francisco, later San Jose, and finally the La Honda forest home of Ken Kesey and the Merry Pranksters is where the road led Cassady. Kerouac diverged to become a 'lonesome traveller', writing chronicles of Beat life exactly as he lived it. His evocation of northern Californian poet-ecologist Gary Snyder in *The Dharma Bums* (1958) is one of the best of these. Another is *Big Sur* (1962), which includes portraits of Lawrence Ferlinghetti, Michael McClure, Lew Welch and Philip Whalen. These fellow 'Six Gallery' poets shared Kerouac's Cassady-inspired enthusiasm for 'spontaneity'. 'We were opposed', Ginsberg explains, 'to the rigidification of mind in poetry, say in the '40s when we came on the scene – which was totally a question of scratching and rewriting and rewriting and rewriting; we were after no more fear of embarassment at the possibility of simply even forgetting to leave a record behind, but just simply giving forth inspiration to the air.'[12] From the French of *fin-de-siècle*, Mallarmé as well as Proust, they inherited the aspiration to imitate in words the spirit of music. Where the French had looked to Wagner, they looked jazz. 'When we confronted literary problems, which are art problems, the example of the jazz musician was never very far from our idea of how these things might be solved', recalls John Clellon Holmes; 'This is why Jack continually compared his writing to the problem of spontaneous creation, which is what jazz musicians do. It did not seem a cheap analogy; it seemed a most apt analogy.'[13]

The great inspiration for Kerouac, though, remained Cassady. Even after he had ceased to practice his friend's hell-bent neo-Nietzschean roadism, Kerouac proclaimed his adulation: 'Mighty genius of the mind Cody whom I announce as the greatest writer the world will ever know if he ever gets down to writing.'[14] But Cassady was the fulfilment of a more Rimbaud-like *fin-de-siècle* ideal: 'Becoming a writer holds no interest for him because life is so holy for him there is no need to do anything but live it.' Cassady's intense 'living living living' was in fact a refutation of the high

value the Beats put on literature. Allied with an eclectic spiritua-
lism (Cassady's own 'faith' became the teachings of Edgar Cayce)[15]
this gained precedence over the lonely ideal of writing in the San
Francisco matrix, and Kerouac began to feel alienated: 'All that
fancy rigamarole about spiritual matters I wonder if it isn't just a
big secret hustler outfit tho' I also realise that I've noticed it before
in San Francisco a kind of ephemeral hysteria that hides in the
air over the rooftops among certain circles there leading to suicide
and maim.'[16] *Big Sur* he thought of as 'a symbolic obituary' of the
Beat movement.[17] He could not flow along into the nascent,
burgeoning Hippy movement. *Big Sur* offers one explanation why
in his lack of complete attachment to its venue: '[I'm] always an
ephemeral "visitor" to the Coast never really involved with
anyone's lives there because I'm always ready to fly back across the
country.'[18] Retreating to the East, Kerouac took to the bottle. His
constant companion was his Catholic, conservative, anti-Semitic
mother. When Cassady arrived in New York driving the Merry
Pranksters in their psychedelic bus, he invited Kerouac to a party.
'Nearly everyone but he had taken LSD that night, and the
environment – floodlights, endless robot screeching tapes, complex mirrors that distorted reality, an American flag as a couch
cover – made no sense to him.'[19] Drunk, he accused the revellers of
being Communists and went home early to his lower-middle-class
suburb. There five years later, parked in front of the TV and
bottle in hand, he burst an artery and haemorrhaged to death.

'He had an inspiration,' Ginsberg comments with characteristic
charity, 'which is really necessary, which is to include the redneck
hard-hat view.'[20] Reading back, one recognises that Kerouac
always felt reservations about the bizarrerie he gave himself to.
Nudity among Ferlinghetti, McClure and friends annoyed him.[21]
Homosexuals were 'faggots' and 'fairies': he missed the Gay 'heart-
throb sexuality' Ginsberg celebrates, 'the tenderness'.[22] Hard
drugs did not appeal to him as to his friend William Burroughs;
marijuana was always more Cassady's thing. Perhaps owing to the
early death of his beloved older brother,[23] he felt a kind of arrested
adolescent buddyism which propelled him into intense, hero-
worshipping attachments with people whose 'trips' he did not at
base care for. A sense of environmental concern came with association to Snyder and passed when that association faded. Buddhism
was originally borrowed from Ginsberg, nor did it survive the *Big
Sur* disillusionment: 'All those philosophies and sutras . . . become

empty words, I realise I've been playing like a happy child with words words words in a big serious tragedy.'[24] Kerouac's literary self-consciousness itself was dependent on the enthusiam of those around him; and, when the crowd thinned, his production grew forced and irresolute. 'The soulful moving thing was Kerouac's heart,' Ginsberg concludes; 'the Bodhisattvic compassion aspect was the big influence.'[25] More than his experiments in Proustian narration, metaphysical explorations, or chronicles of eccentric life-styles, this is what Kerouac bequeathed to the Sixties. His point of view differed radically from that of the Steinbeck–Chandler generation in its openness and naïveté. Kerouac could not simply view; he had to become one with what he was viewing, whether another person, the road, or the sea at Big Sur. Compulsive over-identification resulted in an existential pessimism that makes Philip Marlowe seem positively chirpy. But Kerouac showed the merit in *not* setting oneself apart, like Marlowe; constructing often-defensive analyses, like Steinbeck; or simply gratifying personal lusts, like Cain. His message was to 'get in the skin' of all life and, by doing so, perhaps reform existence. Seeing himself as product of a system whose old values were rotting to bits, Kerouac imagined this the one possible road to salvation.

'The Beat Generation *believes* that there will be some justification for all the horror of life', Kerouac wrote.[26] His biographer continues,

> Beatific in the tradition of St Francis, the Beats were 'sweating for affirmation' in a search for gnosticism, absolute belief in a 'Divinity of Rapture'. Jack concluded, 'I believe God is Ecstasy in His Natural Immanence.' True humanity was only possible when one was nakedly honest and free to rave unashamed. The mystical and rhapsodic 'Beatific' tradition was an ancient as the Alchemical Brotherhood of medieval times, and was related to the nineteenth-century's Diggers, Romantic poets, and American Transcendentalists.

It was related too, as Feied points out, to the Wobblies, the International Workers of the World, active early in the century in the Northwest.[27] This was one of the factors that made San Francisco an appropriate venue for the explosion:

It was the end of the land, and for many reasons it was different.
. . . The beauty of the setting and the Mediterranean *dolce far
niente*. . . . Too, San Francisco had not experienced the
Stalinist/Capitalist New York political split of the Cold War,
because from World War II on it had an active Anarchist Circle
that welcomed draft resistors from the Waldport, Oregon
camp. . . . Perhaps the atmosphere dated all the way back to the
1840s, when the city was settled, as Kenneth Rexroth liked to
point out, not by Protestant farmers and merchants . . . but by
lunatic miners, whores, pirates, Latinos, and Asians. . . . It was
freer.[28]

It was also not Los Angeles, a city symbolic of a creeping materialistic future, whose spread the Beats perceived and loathed. 'San
Jose like a great monstrous Los Angeles beginning to grow south of
Frisco.'[29] Los Angeles culture meant the commercial panderings of
Hollywood. Beatific love was impossible there. Kerouac sums it up
in describing a starlet his agents set him up with: 'She turns out to
be a big bore trying to read me her poetry and wont talk love
because in Hollywood man love is for sale.'[30] In *Visions of Cody*
Joan Crawford comes to North Beach to shoot a film on location: 'a
clanking mechanical abomination of technique rather than inspiration, a machine that could produce only fraud,' Kerouac
curses; 'You muster up a falsehood for money.'[31]

So it was in San Francisco that the 'counter-culture' happened:
in Ferlinghetti's bookshop in North Beach, in McClure's Victorian
in the Haight, in rickety clapboard houses in Berkeley and Mill
Valley inhabited by Ginsberg and Snyder, in Perry Lane behind
Stanford, where Kesey conducted 'alternative' courses, having
dropped out of the creative writing programme at the university.[32]
As Kerouac's prominence faded, Kesey's grew. Moving from Perry
Lane to the redwoods atop the coastal mountains, he presided over
the communal scene Tom Wolfe describes in *The Electric Kool-
aid Acid Test* (1968).[33]

Suddenly people were stripped before one another and behold;
as we looked on, we all made a great discovery; we were beautiful. Naked and helpless and sensitive as a snake after skinning,
but far more human than that shinning nightmare that had
stood creaking in previous parade rest. . . . We were alive and
life was us. We joined hands and danced barefoot amongst the
rubble. We had been cleansed, liberated! We would never don

the old armors again. But we reckoned without the guilt of this country.[34]

They reckoned as well without the vengeance of Dionysus. Cassady, nicknamed 'Speed Limit', revered as 'the holy primitive, the holy beast, the Denver kid', was snared and writhing the persona Kerouac had created for him.[35] Over forty now, he became a Pentheus racing among the youths after the Stranger God. The Proustian 'American-Denver talk' hit them as sound more than sense: 'Neal was a teacher of perception, an expert on subjects that haven't been identified yet', opined Jerry Garcia, lead guitarist of the Grateful Dead; but 'people tuned him out when he tried to get thoughtful'.[36] To mature observers such as his estranged wife, Cassady's energy now seemed 'the product of a deep self-hatred'.[37] To Kesey and those committed to the new heterodoxy it had to be interpreted otherwise: 'Neal's path was the yoga of a man driven to the cliff edge by the grassfire of an entire nation's burning material madness. Rather than be consumed by this he jumped, choosing to sort things out in the fast flying but smog free moments of a life with no retreat.'[38]

The 1960s, Kesey says in 'The Day After Superman Died', was an era for 'counting'.[39] Cassady caught pneumonia while in Mexico: he was walking the railway north, trying to count the ties all the way to the border. This end underlines the pathetic neo-Decadence of the Beat quest. 'The only people for me', Kerouac had written, 'are the mad ones, the ones who are mad to live, mad to talk, mad to be saved, desirous of everything at the same time, the ones who never yawn or say a commonplace thing, but burn, burn, burn.'[40] For his great friend as for him the 'hard, gem-like flame' burned out. For Ginsberg a way to survive was found in the gentler megalomania of being a cultural messiah. For Gary Snyder there was preaching his neo-primitive, reclusive faith in the earth. For Ferlinghetti there was City Lights; for McClure the complete licence of Beast language, Fuck odes, and 'We all go blotto!' Lew Welch, however, retired to the mountains of remote northern California and shot himself; and Kesey, recognising how the Dionysian dance swirled on to a dervish of death, left the San Francisco area after a final acid test for his backwoods origin. 'The frantic obsession with motion, which so characterised the Pranksters [gave] way to a distinct and rather conventional straight sense of place.'[41] The place was Oregon. It had been the setting of his best-selling novels *One Flew over the Cuckoo's Nest* (1961) and *Sometimes a Great Notion* (1963). These books show that Kesey had always been suspicious of California. 'Do take me, big boy', a California millworking girl begs the Oregon Indian narrator in a flashback in *Cuckoo*; 'Outa this here mill, outa this town, outa this life. Take me to some ol' duck blind someplace.'[42] Back to the land is a leitmotiv in Kesey as in London, only the Valley of the Moon is no longer far back enough. From the Oregonian's perspective all California has become infected with the diseases of modern civilisation: smog, bureaucracy, Eastern-style social life, decadence, yearning for apocalypse. It is the disturbing place Kerouac began to see it as in *Big Sur*. Yet Kesey, like Kerouac, had thrown himself into the disturbance and conceived his best work there; and, curiously, he has not written anything of consequence since departing seventeen years ago.

Why has a writer of such seemingly boundless energy gone mum? Motion, media and music are factors. The motion was the frantic *On the Road*-ism of the bus in which Cassady drove the clan across country. The media were the audio-visual paraphernalia that taped and filmed everything the group did in the naïve expectation, derived from Kerouac's reportage of Beat minutiae, that all would prove of interest. Rebelling against the Hollywood culture 'programmed' into receptive young minds by TV, Kesey and his kind thought they could substitute their own 'movie', the *avant-garde* novelty of which would be assured by LSD fantasies. But film, like writing, requires some shred of discursive narration, and this requires some sense of the order that only established values can provide. Having thrown out these values, the movement could only come close to projecting its stoned-out, *tabula rasa* alternative through the least discursive art-form, music. During the mid-Sixties, Kesey spent more time experimenting with feedback and blowing kazoos than writing novels. Ginsberg simultaneously was moving from written poetry through mantra to chants-with-music. McClure was given an autoharp by Bob Dylan and dedicated *The Blossom* to Jim Morrison, lead singer of the Doors, who wanted to play lead in his 'movie', *The Adept*. The Grateful Dead, performing at Kesey's acid tests, developed a new style by combining the Cassady–Kerouac road message with electronified jazz and later old country standards such as 'Goin Down the Road Feelin' Bad', which the Okies had sung on their way to the 'promised land'. Garcia inherited Kesey's woman, Mountain

Girl, when the writer moved back to Oregon. This might be an emblem for him in the later Sixties the literary Beat gave way to the musical Hippy. 'The Sixties produced no literature to speak of', Clellon Holmes opines; 'most of the literary effort went into song lyrics'.[43] Jazz-inspired Beat words attended the simplified, formalised jazz of 'acid rock'. Bob Dylan was a part of this new mass-media process, as was the 'San Francisco Sound' built around Garcia, Janis Joplin and Jefferson Airplane.[44]

Kesey's silence has also to do with the character of his writing. *Cuckoo's Nest* is an economical book, superbly direct, imaginatively narrated, well fitted out with a cast of lunatics. While writing this book, Kesey was working nights at the Menlo Park Veterans' Hospital on a ward where patients were being treated for psychic disorders with drugs. During the day he attended creative writing-classes at Stanford. In one place mental behaviour was being scrutinised, in the other all verbal utterance. It is not surprising that the all-Oregon wrestler should have chosen as his theme Prometheus breaking through bureaucratic restraints to manly freedom. But *Cuckoo* suggests that Kesey thrived on the very repression he has his hero opposing; and *Sometimes a Great Notion* raises the possibility that such repression was necessary for him to write well. Malcolm Cowley, who taught Kesey at Stanford, praises him for not falling victim to 'the fatal notion of some Beat writers, that the first hasty account of a vision was a sacred text not to be tampered with'.[45] But *Sometimes*, created as Kesey was breaking loose from a Veterans' Administration job and writing-class, is full of such visions. Fitted into the plot of weak intellectual brother versus strong woodsman brother, these have psychological relevance; but there is too much of them. The Proustian excess which Kerouac had avoided by chopping his books off at 100,000 words creeps into *Sometimes*, marring it perhaps even for its creator. 'Keeping up a frantic free-association which he hoped would, by some miracle, save the day in spite of his monumental absence' is how he makes Hank Stamper, woodsman brother, describe his verbal behaviour.[46] 'The thing about being removed,' he puts in the mouth of Lee Stamper, intellectual brother, 'thanks to modern technique, is, while it may afford objectivity and perspective – with all events tunnelling back from this point like images in opposing mirrors, yet each image changed – it presents a tricky problem of tense.'[47]

A problem of tense is apparent throughout the book's 300,000 words. So too is a problem of narration. There is the overall third-person, and there are Hank's and Lee's first-persons. Within the latter there are interpolated voices from early youth and other moments in time. Strewn through all are further voices and narratives belonging to lesser characters, natural forces (the river), even dogs. Some of the confusion this multiplicity creates is cleared up by modulation of typefaces and use of parentheses. A sense of being buffetted toward a whirlpool by unseen currents is held in check by comprehensible, often amusing dialogue. But this too has its excesses, and again the text notes as much: 'a charge of dialogue so overdone in the colloquial vein that it was difficult to remember this was a real person speaking real lines, not a character from an Erskine Caldwell novel'.[48] Kesey's ambivalence shows through at such places. His Californian sophistication made him suspicious of the enormous partisanship for rural Oregon his novel was proposing; his creative writing-school self-consciousness lingered on to make him wonder if this wild woodsy undertaking wasn't in fact a bit woolly – neither so entertaining nor so purposeful as he had expected. Like Steinbeck in *East of Eden*, Kesey had set out to write the saga of his family and province. Such a saga no doubt would have a certain interest. But, like Steinbeck, Kesey was over-proud of his origins and became expansive; and to justify his long wind he had to offer portentous suggestions that the situation of family and place was really a metaphor for something crucial that had happened in America at large. Here Kesey over-reaches as much as Steinbeck did; the creaking device of the family album is evidence (this may have been a misappropriation of ideas from Wallace Stegner, who also taught in Stanford's Creative Writing Program when Kesey was there).[49] As Steinbeck would have done better to have stuck to shorter, more dramatic forms like *In Dubious Battle*, so would have Kesey. His recent experiment in a still more solipsistic form of interior monologue, *Seven Prayers For Grandma Whittier* (1977), blazes an errant trail for the writers-of-the-future.[50]

Kesey has pursued a Proustian line of development where he grew famous because of a presentation rather more in the vein of Chandler. Proustianism he should have left with Kerouac, who took it as far as it could go for the time and was better suited to its sensuality, having more psychological complexity to unravel. As a recently published poem admits, Kesey is an actor, a mimic, a puppet-master more than a lonesome visionary.[51] He is a true novelist where Kerouac was a 'Great Rememberer',[52] and it is a shame that he has isolated himself from any conurbation with enough variety of lunatic humanity for him to exercise gifts shared with Dickens and Balzac. The cult of the strong man may be at the root of this. A great novelist will learn to put higher value on observation than subjective projection. But Hank Stamper's 'NEVER GIVE AN INCH' philosophy remains precious to his creator;[53] indeed, it turns *Sometimes* into a polemic against the necessity for collective action that London posed against Nietzscheanism and Steinbeck dramatised in *Grapes*. It may seem ironic that this writer who played a seminal role in the communalism of the Sixties should preach a doctrine of the romantic loner; but Kesey in fact is a rejecter of life. The racism apparent in Chief Brom's description of the orderlies in *Cuckoo* is not substantially refuted by Lee's correspondence with his black room-mate in *Sometimes*, or old Henry's colourful outbursts: 'We ain't some bunch o' niggers or Jews or *ordinary* people; we're *Stampers!*'[54] The caricature of the domesticating female in Nurse Ratched, which outraged feminists,[55] is not wholly eclipsed by the portrait of Hank's 'wildwood flower': Viv, after all, plays a crucial role in the demise of Stampers. Both Kesey's novels confirm the attitude discernible in his public persona that other people are petty and venal, if essentially good-hearted. Both books reserve full affirmation for the strong man, the hero, the amoral figure who can play his own God. This kind of figure will draw the malleable around him, becoming their leader. Kesey's glorification of such a process in art and life is at base in the charge of fascism that is sometimes levelled against him. It is the point at which his ethos connects with that of another graduate of the Haight–Ashbury matrix, Charlie Manson.

Manson is an extra-literary phenomenon of significance to California writing at this juncture. In him impulses to 'liberation' and neo-Nietzscheanism ran amok. In background a Mugridge-like Underman, his sense of social injustice remained unleavened by any but the most self-seeking principle of collective responsibility. Manson's hatred of cops is an exaggeration of tendencies we have seen in most of the writers discussed here; his contempt for materialism and the hypocrisy of the Establishment recalls motifs from *The Iron Heel*, *Grapes* and B. Traven; his risking of damnation links him to the psychopaths of Cain – like Phyllis Nirdlinger, he and his 'Family' imagined that they were performing acts of terrible beauty by delivering earthbound souls into death.[56] It seems apt that Manson committed his crimes in Los Angeles, whose literary tradition was dominated by the corruption concerns of Chandler. The cult of Love which reigned in the San Francisco of the Sixties became debased in the LA of 1969. Especially in Hollywood, there was a 'mystical flirtation with the idea of "sin"'.[57] Joan Didion recalls 'this sense that it was possible to go "too far"' (41). Sex and drugs were not so much sacraments of a new gnosticism as doors to perception of a diabolical new amorality. 'Roman Polanski and I were godparents to the same child', Didion recalls (48). Old Hollywood was being ploughed under. 'Anticipation of imminent but not exactly immediate destruction lent the neighborhood its particular character' (16). Decadence was abroad in many guises. The apartments off Sunset Strip and mansions in Bel Air were more than ever inhabited by transients from Europe and New York, jet-setting 'beautiful people' to whom the city was a clearing-house for money-making fantasies, the state a 'hotel' whose natives received little more consideration than hall-maids or desk-clerks. Didion recalls the paranoia that gripped this Hollywood after the Manson murder of Polanski's wife and friends. It is the spectacle of a coterie of *haves* barricading themselves against *have-nots*. 'In its tropism toward survival Hollywood sometimes presents the appearance of the last extant stable society' (155), Didion remarks, emphasising the *ancien régime* aspect. 'We don't go for strangers in Hollywood', she quotes from the Hollywood-brat narrator of Scott Fitzgerald's *Last Tycoon* (157).

Didion is the most exasperating of writers. She says odious things in an attractive manner. Her mode is to present herself as an instrument to record the shocks, psychic as well as seismic, of her time and place. She writes in the bitty, chopped-up style that a mass public has become used to through television and magazines. A native of Sacramento, she left California in her twenties after a youth described in her first, Steinbeckian, novel, *Run River* (1963). She lived in New York and worked for *Vogue*. In the later Sixties she and her husband, John Gregory Dunne, author of *True Confessions* (1977), migrated to Hollywood. Originally peripheral, they have become celebrated members of the film–media community. Didion's point of view combines the Episcopalian, bourgeois values of her native background with a New York–Hollywood orthodoxy not unlike that which Steinbeck came to espouse. A sentence early in the title essay of her latest book, *The White Album* (1979), tags her: 'I appeared, on the face of it, a competent enough member of some community or another, a signer of Air Travel cards, a citizen' (11–12). It is not surprising that this voice found its audience in the 1970s, the 'selfish', materialistic decade of reaction against the collectivist, spiritualistic 1960s. Though a contemporary of Kesey's and sharer in the existential pessimism of Kerouac, Didion has never been comfortable with Beat to Hip points of view. Like Cassady's widow or Kerouac's East Coast friend Clellon Holmes, she feels that 'there was also destructiveness and wastage in ... this kind of experience'.[58] The title essay of *Slouching toward Bethlehem* (1968) shows her as a detached observer of Haight–Ashbury as well as participant; an appalled reactor rather than enthusiast. Didion's undertaking has been to prove the Beat formula that the culture was going through a massive nervous breakdown. Her epigraph to *Slouching toward Bethlehem* includes Yeats's phrase 'the centre cannot hold'. Her doctor's diagnosis that she is suffering from a slow, withering strain of multiple sclerosis seems to her at the end of 'The White Album' to provide an apt metaphor for what has been happening around her since the late 1960s.

Didion refuses a structure for her social analysis. Traditional radicalism would provide one way to explain a world she claims not to be able to comprehend or order properly; the Spenglerian model Kerouac found applicable might provide another. Didion also refuses to take seriously the spiritual disciplines that have attempted to fill the vacuum: Beat Buddhism; Scientology; Christianity, whether in Bishop Pike or Jesus-freak form; the doctrines of Edgar Cayce, which she refers to as 'poignant' at the end of her Pike essay (58). It would seem that writing, as for another laconic Episcopalian journalist-turned-'writer', Hemingway, provides the salvation for her; yet at the end of 'The White Album' she argues against writing as a system of faith by telling how one of the murderers of Ramon Navarro won first prize in a PEN contest, 'discovered' writing, and proclaimed it as the way to 'reflect on experience and see what it means' (48). Didion counters, 'Writing has not yet helped me see what it means.' Since all faiths may attract crackpots, she eschews all faiths. In the end this eschewal becomes a dogma itself. By implication it also becomes an apology for the status quo. The world is a mass of random fragments, the argument goes. Attempts to arrange the fragments are, in this media-age, motivated by desire for publicity as much as by sincere faith. This Didion demonstrates in her treatment of the Black Panthers. Their Marxist attacks on the Establishment are 'a wall of rhetoric' designed to keep them from 'talking about themselves' (30). They are 'autodidacts', she says, 'for whom all things specific and personal present themselves as minefields to be avoided even at the cost of coherence, for whom safety lies in generalisation'. For Didion safety lies in detailing the trivia of bourgeois life, however 'aimless'.[59] A list of the contents of her travelling-bag is presented as as revealing of the time and place as any larger social phenomena. Didion is a media-person. The only data valid to her are those which can be exposed in a few catchy paragraphs or well edited frames of film. Her writing illuminates the incompatibility of deeply explored ideas or thoroughgoing presentation with the media as they exist.

Didion is part of the fruition of London's prediction that the 'iron heel' would produce an era of artists who renouce sympathy with the abyss and cultivate aesthetic brilliance. Her prose is marvellously clear and calculated. While not as entertaining as Chandler's (this is no longer the era of the wisecrack, T. J. Binyon points out in his informative essay on Chandler's successors[60]), it is nearly as compulsive; and it continues the tendency noted in Chandler of putting style over content. Performance becomes an end in itself. The fact that she has published only five slim volumes in fifteen years indicates Didion's bias: economical art over sprawling life. Not for her the prodigious productivity of London, Sinclair or Kerouac, any more than their tireless pursuit of ideals. Disbelieving in a findable truth, Didion is marked by a fatalism similar to Hemingway's; and one must wonder, especially considering the prominence of suicide in her novels (major characters kill themselves in her first two), whether she is not going to find it impossible to take her *macho* forbear's route out of existence one day. In *Run River* she suggests that there may have been some order to hold onto in the Sacramento of the Victorian Governor's Mansion, before housing-tracts and Nancy Reagan's 'Taj Mahal'.[61] In *Play It As It Lays* (1971) she shows a Los Angeles lacking memory of any holdable order in the past or hope for one in the future. In *Book of Common Prayer* (1977) she continues in this desperate, bottom-line vein. It may be significant, however, that the heroine of Didion's most recent imaginative work meets her death when beginning to engage in relief work for victims of oppression and revolution in Latin America. Inadequate as this half-hearted resurrection of middle-class Episcopalian charity may seem, it does show the writer – her persona, at least – slouching toward some moral commitment. The heroine's death implies a despair that such commitment will provide salvation. Nevertheless, there is a note of redemption wholly lacking in the alternative of a death while mired in the petty decadences of idle-rich Yankee imperialist 'life-style'.

If Didion truly believes in the bleak picture she paints, and this thesis that 'the centre cannot hold', then there are least two remedies she might do well to consider. First, as she is apparently a believer in the value of tradition, she might return to the roots of literary thought in her native land and attempt to cultivate from them some set of beliefs to help, if not the cultural centre to hold, at least her own ideologically-blasted psychological centre. Second, if she does not at base welcome changes in the status quo to bring on greater social justice and reason (and much in her work makes one suspect that, in fact, she does not), she might attempt to renovate her world-view so that it opens out rather than closes in; so that, like Kerouac confronting new phenomena that alarm him in *Big Sur* or Kesey confronting the hoodlum hippies that invade his farm in 'The Day After Superman Died', she forces herself to try to understand to *other* and *outer*, and by understanding begin to rebuild trust and faith in existence generally. If some such development is truly not possible in her culture post-Manson, then there can be little hope that successive writers will not beat an ever faster retreat into the ivory towers of style and self-contemplation. This process was implicit in Chandler, who posited a world that was substantially crime-ridden and unliveable-in. It was halted, even reversed, by the efflorescence of the Sixties; and, if we regard Chandler as part of a counter force to the openings-out of London and the early Steinbeck, we might see Didion as such to those of her generation. Perhaps some pattern of the sort may be at work among California writers altogether; an opening outward into psychological exploration and ideological enthusiasm, followed by a scuttling inward to attend to style, superficials, images of decay and fatality. If so, it may be that this has to do with location as well as generation: that northern California retains from London's day, if not further back, a sense of possibility that southern California has not inherited. Cultural stereo-types beyond literature have maintained this; and, if a culture is a matter of what beliefs radiate into and out of a capital city, then perhaps the idea of considering a body of California writers as one is in error.

California writing, like California culture, is a tale of two cities. The San Francisco matrix extends to Oregon in the north – Richard Brautigan, whose fantasies comment amusingly on many issues discussed here[62] – and down the Peninsula to the south – Wallace Stegner, who has grappled more soul-searchingly than Didion with his disquiet over the new values of the Sixties in books such as *All the Little Live Things* (1967).[63] The Los Angeles orbit swirls south toward the Mexican Indian philosophies Carlos Castenada has evoked and draws in wanderers such as the west Texan Larry McMurtry, Kesey's old confrère at Stanford Creative Writing School,[64] who has written one of the most original Hollywood novels of recent years, *Somebody's Darling* (1978). Los Angeles, via Hollywood, the centre of the music industry as well as film and television, is coming to take the dominant position in a culture that began in the north; but no longer can that culture be seen in isolation from the media-shrunken world. 'Hotel California', title of a recent rock hit, seems an apt designation for this land now, certainly as it is seen through literature. Transience is more than ever a way of life; and the transient eye-view of the place, in part owing to the continued location of the important publishers in New York, has taken over. This encourages the eccentricity latent in the culture; it encourages the conservatism and xenophobia of the natives; it discourages impulses to community and social justice. California writers have always been concerned with individual excellence, self-transcendence, heroism, and God. With the great writers discussed here these things were allied to or held in tension with commitment to the Underman, the land, art, civilisation and the heart. If the tendency to mythologise the place as a 'hotel' where all and sundry may come to exercise their fantasies without greater responsibility is allowed to remain unchecked – is simply taken as inherent or passively lamented in the Didion manner – then the projection of apocalypse – the *Day of the Locust* fantasy[65] – may increasingly become fact. If, on the other hand, California can stop admiring its eccentricity in media-reflection long enough to recall the ideals of social justice that have contributed to its attractiveness, it may at last come of age as the decent society of the imaginative, the beautiful, and the adventurous that at its best it has promised to be.

Notes

NOTES TO CHAPTER ONE: INTRODUCTION

1. Lawrence Ferlinghetti, *Literary San Francisco* (New York and San Francisco: Harper & Row/City Lights, 1980).
2. See *Mark Twain's San Francisco*, ed. Bernard Taper (New York: McGraw-Hill, 1963).
3. On Harte's career see Richard O'Connor, *Bret Harte: A Biography* (Boston, Mass.: Little, Brown, 1966).
4. On Bierce and his period see Carey McWilliams, *Ambrose Bierce* (New York: Boni, 1929).
5. See Leslie Fiedler, *The Return of the Vanishing American* (London: Paladin, 1972).
6. Lew Welch, 'The Song that Mt Tamalpias Sings', in *The San Francisco Poets*, ed. David Meltzer (New York: Ballantine, 1971).
7. Edmund Wilson, *The Boys in the Back Room* (San Francisco: Colt Press, 1941).
8. For these paragraphs I am indebted to Warren French's *Frank Norris* (New York: Twayne, 1962).
9. See ibid., ch. 4: 'The Gilded Cage'. Hayakawa's *Language and Thought in Action* is quoted on p. 72.
10. See ibid., ch. 5: 'Victorian Valkyries'.
11. Frank Norris, *The Octopus: A Story of California* (New York: Doubleday, 1901). Further references in text.
12. Quoted and trans. by F. W. Watt in *John Steinbeck* (New York: Grove Press, 1962) p. 42.
13. John Steinbeck, *The Grapes of Wrath*, critical ed. Peter Lisca (Harmondsworth: Penguin, 1977) p. 445.
14. See F. I. Carpenter's 'The Metaphysical Joads' in *College English*, Jan 1941; repr. in *A Casebook on 'The Grapes of Wrath'*, ed. Alice MacNiell Donohue (New York: Crowell, 1968).
15. See *Farewell, My Lovely*, in *The Raymond Chandler Omnibus* (London: Hamish Hamilton, 1953) p. 171.
16. John Steinbeck, *Of Mice and Men* (London: Heinemann, 1937) pp. 50-1.
17. Joan Didion, *Slouching toward Bethlehem* (London: Deutsch, 1969). 'John Wayne: a Love Song' appears on pp. 29-42.
18. Joan Didion, *The White Album* (London: Weidenfeld & Nicolson, 1979) pp. 21-5.
19. Steinbeck, *Mice*, pp. 47, 117-18, etc.

20. See *Steinbeck: A Life in Letters*, ed. Elaine Steinbeck and Robert Walsten (Harmondsworth: Penguin, 1976) p. 154.
21. Norris, *Octopus*, pp. 82–5.

NOTES TO CHAPTER TWO: JACK LONDON

1. *Letters from Jack London*, ed. King Hendricks and Irving Shepherd (London: MacGibbon & Kee, 1966) p. 308 (quoting from his own 'What Life Means to Me').
2. Jack London *The Sea Wolf* (London: Macmillan, 1904) p. 13. Further references in text.
3. Jack London, *The People of the Abyss* (London: Macmillan, 1903) pp. 157–62 ('The Sea Wife'). Further references in text.
4. Andrew Sinclair, *Jack* (London: Weidenfeld & Nicolson, 1978) pp. 88, 89.
5. Philip Foner, *Jack London: American Rebel* (Berlin: Seven Seas Press, 1974) pp. 48–52, 67.
6. See Sinclair, *Jack*, p. 244. Also Richard O'Connor, *Jack London* (Boston, Mass.: Little, Brown, 1965) p. 6. Quotes Krupskaya on Lenin's love for London's stories, which he had read to him on his death-bed.
7. The Journeyman paperback edition (1977) shows an iron-heeled boot stomping on a poster of Allende.
8. Jack London, *The Iron Heel* (London: Everett, 1908) p. 89. Further references in text.
9. Earle Labor, *Jack London* (New York: Twayne, 1974) p. 102.
10. Sinclair, *Jack*, p. 120, referring to the story 'Planchette': 'His description of himself through the girl's words might be called vanity, except that it was true.'
11. See *Letters*, pp. 235–44. There was also an argument about the advisability of publishing *The Road*.
12. Ibid., p. 367.
13. Ibid., p. 467.
14. Sinclair, *Jack*, p. 253.
15. Ibid., pp. 194, 196.
16. Joan London, *Jack London and His Times* (Seattle and London: University of Washington Press, 1939, 1968) p. 362.
17. Sinclair, *Jack*, p. 110.
18. Jack London, *The Star Rover* (London: Macmillan, 1963) p. 101. Further references in text.
19. *Letters*, pp. 463–4.
20. Ibid., p. 407.
21. O'Connor, *Jack London*, pp. 4, 222–8, and elsewhere.
22. Sinclair, *Jack*. See the chapter 'The Illusion of the Snark', pp. 144–57.
23. Ibid., p. 221.
24. O'Connor, *Jack London*, p. 369.
25. Jack London, *The Mutiny of the Elsinore* (London: Mills & Boon, 1915) p. 394. Further references in text.
26. Sinclair, *Jack*, p. 109.
27. Sam Baskett argues this in 'London's Heart of Darkness' in *Jack London:*

Essays in Criticism (Santa Barbara: Peregrine Smith, 1978).
28. Jack London, *A Daughter of the Snows* (London: Ibister 1904) p. 111. Further references in text.
29. Jack London, *Adventure* (London: Macmillan, 1911) ch. 1. Further references in text.
30. London, *Daughter*, p. 137.
31. Jack London, *The Valley of the Moon* (London: Mills & Boon, 1913) p. 21. Further references in text.
32. O'Connor (*Jack London*, p. 333) quotes George Sterling to this effect: 'One [Jack London] is a mixer, a go-getter. The other is heart-hungry for an ivory tower where he can be an artist.' O'Connor identifies London's ivory tower as the 'Beauty Ranch'.
33. Sinclair, *Jack*, p. 153.
34. *Letters*, p. 351.
35. Jack London, *Burning Daylight* (London: Macmillan, 1910) pt 2, ch. 5. Further references in text.
36. *The Complete Works of Friedrich Nietzsche*, ed. Oscar Levy (London: T. N. Foulis, 1909–13) vol. VI, *Human, All-too-Human*, I, p. 384.
37. Ibid., vol. X: *The Joyful Wisdom*, p. 60.
38. Van Weyden and Maud Brewster engage in a discussion of the theories of the rationalist academic who became president of Stanford University during their escape from the *Ghost* and struggle to survive on Endeavor Island near the end of *The Sea Wolf*.
39. Sinclair argues that homoeroticism and repressions related to it constituted an important motive force in London's life and work. See *Jack*, p. 69, on London's relationship with George Sterling; p. 97, on his attempt to project elements of his desire for 'the great Man-Comrade' into Charmian; p. 104 and elsewhere, on his cult of the perfect male body. This point of view seems more appropriate to the time and place from which Sinclair was writing, the later 1970s in America, than to London's epoch and climes.
40. Jack London, *The Little Lady of the Big House* (London: Mills & Boon, 1916) chs 1–6. Further references in text.
41. As O'Connor contends – *Jack London*, p. 365.
42. *Letters*, p. 374.
43. Ibid., p. 476.
44. Ibid., p. 452.
45. Martin Green in his *Dreams of Adventure, Deeds of Empire* (London: Routledge & Kegan Paul, 1980) discusses the opposition between the two strands of our literary tradition in English. London, like Kipling and Twain and others whom Green discusses at length, belongs clearly to the adventure-*machismo* genre in popular works such as *The Sea Wolf* and *Call of the Wild*. But throughout London's career there is a tendency toward the genteel. This triumphs over Nietzscheanism in *The Sea Wolf*, for instance. It only becomes a pervasive force in the anomalous *Little Lady*, however.
46. Edmund Wilson, *Axël's Castle* (New York: Charles Scribner's Sons, 1931) p. 177.
47. Ezra Pound, *Canto XIII*, lines 56, 58.
48. *Letters*, p. 374.
49. Sinclair, *Jack*, p. 49.

50. Ibid., p. 207.
51. See Foner, *Jack London*, p. 83.
52. O'Connor, *Jack London*, p. 370, writes of London's desire to separate from his wife in this period.
53. Clarice Stasz, for one, in her 'Androgyny in the Novels' in *Jack London: Essays in Criticism*, otherwise a fine study on London and women.
54. O'Connor, *Jack London*, p. 366: 'Sterling criticized the book so sharply it almost ruptured their friendship.'
55. *Letters*, p. 419.
56. Jack London Square in Oakland, site of lobster restaurants and fashionable shops, is one prominent commercial enterprise flourishing under his name. The proximity of this tourist trap to one of the worst ghettos in California is an irony that would not have been lost on the author of *The People of the Abyss*.

NOTES TO CHAPTER THREE: JOHN STEINBECK

1. Steinbeck, *Grapes*, ed. Peter Lisca, p. 47. Further references in text.
2. Wilson, 'John Steinbeck', in *The Boys in the Back Room*.
3. See ibid.; also Warren French, *John Steinbeck* (New York: Twayne, 1961) ch. entitled 'The Education of the Heart'.
4. Steinbeck's most famous title, suggested by Ed Ricketts, comes from Robert Burns. See Thomas Kiernan, *The Intricate Music: A Biography of John Steinbeck* (Boston, Mass.: Little, Brown, 1979) p. 108.
5. French, *John Steinbeck*, pp. 98-9.
6. The phrase is H. K. Crockett's in 'The Bible and *The Grapes of Wrath*', *College English*, Nov 1956; repr. in *Casebook on 'Grapes'*, ed. Donohue, p. 112.
7. In 'The Tragedy of El Dorado', *Kenyon Review*, Autumn 1939; repr. in *Casebook on 'Grapes'*, p. 77.
8. As Carpenter points out in 'The Philosophical Joads', ibid. pp. 82-9.
9. Charles Dougherty, 'The Christ Figure in *The Grapes of Wrath*', *College English*, Dec 1962; repr. in *Casebook on 'Grapes'*, p. 117.
10. Thomas Dunn, 'The Pauline Apostleship of Tom Joad', *College English*, Dec 1962, and '*The Grapes of Wrath*', ibid., Apr 1963; repr. in *Casebook on Grapes'*, pp. 118, 123.
11. Ibid., p. 111.
12. See French, *John Steinbeck*, pp. 101, 103-4.
13. Ibid., p. 112.
14. *Casebook on 'Grapes'*, p. 89.
15. See Maxwell Geismar, 'John Steinbeck: of Wrath or Joy', *Writers in Crisis: The American Novel (1925-40)* (Boston, Mass.: Houghton Mifflin, 1942) p. 265.
16. Watt, *John Steinbeck*, p. 56.
17. Jackson, reviewer for the San Francisco *Chronicle* and personal friend of Steinbeck's, is quoted by Leo Gurko in *The Angry Decade* (New York: Dodd, Mead, 1947). Excerpts in *Casebook on 'Grapes'*.

18. In Harry T. Moore, *The Novels of John Steinbeck* (New York: Kennikat, 1968) p. 61 (first published 1939).
19. See ibid., p. 42.
20. Wilson, *The Boys in the Back Room*, p. 46.
21. Quoted and trans. Watt, *John Steinbeck*, p. 58.
22. Malcolm Cowley, 'A Farewell to the 1930s' in *Think Back on Us . . . A Contemporary Chronicle of the 1930s*, ed. Henry Dan Piper (Carbondale, Ill.: Southern Illinois University Press, 1967); repr. in *Casebook on 'Grapes'*.
23. John Steinbeck, *In Dubious Battle* (London: Heinemann, 1936) pp. 1–9. Further references in text.
24. French, *John Steinbeck*, p. 67.
25. *Casebook on 'Grapes'*, p. 137.
26. Joseph Fontenrose, *John Steinbeck: An Introduction and Interpretation* (New York: Holt, Rinehart & Winston, 1963) p. 49.
27. French, *John Steinbeck*, ch. entitled 'Parsifal's Last Stand'.
28. Ibid., p. 70.
29. Watt, *John Steinbeck*, p. 56.
30. Quennell's review in *New Statesman and Nation* is cited in French, *John Steinbeck*, p. 23.
31. See Samuel Sillen, 'Censoring *The Grapes of Wrath*', and F. J. Taylor, 'California's *Grapes of Wrath*', *Forum*, vol. CII (Nov 1939) pp. 232–8; repr. in *Casebook on 'Grapes'*, pp. 4–19.
32. *Steinbeck: A Life in Letters*, ed. Steinbeck and Walsten, p. 98. Further references in text.
33. McCarthy's review in *The Nation* is quoted ibid., p. 122. See also Wilson, *Boys in the Back Room*, p. 46.
34. Ibid., pp. 42–8.
35. Quoted by Lewis Gannett in 'John Steinbeck's Way of Writing', in *Steinbeck and His Critics*, ed. E. W. Tedlock and C. V. Wicker (Albuquerque: University of New Mexico Press, 1957) pp. 32–3.
36. See Norman Valjean, *John Steinbeck: The Errant Knight* (San Francisco: Chronicle Books, 1975) p. 169. Also Kiernan, *Intricate Music*, p. 211.
37. French, *John Steinbeck*, p. 20.
38. In the Junius Maltby episode in *Pastures of Heaven* (London: Philip Allan, 1933) pp. 112–49.
39. See Valjean, *John Steinbeck*, p. 41.
40. Ibid., p. 8.
41. Wilson, *Boys in the Back Room*, p. 42.
42. See Steinbeck's introduction to *The Short Novels of John Steinbeck* (New York: Viking, 1947).
43. Kiernan, *Intricate Music*, p. 222.
44. *Steinbeck: A Life in Letters*, p. 30.
45. French, *John Steinbeck*, p. 87.
46. *Grapes*, ch. 19: 'We ain't foreign. Seven generations back American.'
47. John Steinbeck, *Tortilla Flat* (London: Heinemann, 1935) p. 53. Further references in text.
48. Moore calls Steinbeck a master of *Stimmung*, more so than any writer since D. H. Lawrence (*Novels of Steinbeck*, p. 157).

49. Fontenrose, *John Steinbeck*, p. 41.
50. See Kiernan, *Intricate Music*, p. 240.
51. See Valjean, *John Steinbeck*, p. 170.
52. See *Steinbeck: A Life in Letters*, p. 265.
53. Kiernan, *Intricate Music*, p. 274.
54. John Steinbeck, *Cannery Row* (London: Heinemann, 1945) p. 64. Further references in text.
55. Fontenrose, *John Steinbeck*, p. 108.
56. French, *John Steinbeck*, ch. entitled 'The Intricate Music of Cannery Row'.
57. Ibid., p. 135.
58. Edmund Wilson, 'John Steinbeck's Newest Novel and James Joyce's First', *New Yorker*, 6 Jan 1945.
59. *Casebook on 'Grapes'*, p. 139.
60. Ibid., p. 142.
61. *Steinbeck: A Life in Letters*, pp. 280–1.
62. Kiernan, *Intricate Music*, p. 279.
63. Ibid., p. 286.
64. Quoted in Valjean, *John Steinbeck*, p. 181. Following quotes from *Steinbeck: A Life in Letters*.
65. Valjean, *John Steinbeck*, p. 182.
66. Peter Lisca, *The Wide World of John Steinbeck* (New Brunswick, NJ: Rutgers University Press, 1958) p. 284.
67. Ibid., p. 292.
68. Watt, *John Steinbeck*, pp. 100–1.
69. French, *John Steinbeck*, p. 158.
70. An interview quoted by Lisca in *Wide World*, p. 276.
71. James M. Cain, *Three of a Kind* (New York: Knopf, 1942) p. v.
72. John Steinbeck, *Sweet Thursday* (New York: Viking, 1954) p. 36. Further references in text.
73. Fontenrose, *John Steinbeck*, p. 129.
74. Claude-Edmond Magny, 'John Steinbeck, or the Limits of the Impersonal Novel', trans. Francoise Gourier, in *Steinbeck and His Critics*, p. 216.
75. The term is E. B. Bergum's. See 'The Sensibility of John Steinbeck', ibid., p. 104.
76. Whether Steinbeck was familiar with Wagner is unclear. His liking for classical music, however, is well documented. He listened to Dvorak's 'New World' Symphony over and over while writing *Cup of Gold*. Another early novel, which he suppressed, was also created out of a musical inspiration – *Dissonant Symphony*. His taste for the Baroque, Bach and Monteverdi, and for such modernists as Ravel, is reflected in Doc's musical preferences in *Cannery Row* and *Sweet Thursday*. Steinbeck undoubtedly fed his musical appetite from the phonograph rather than the concert-hall; the radio too – country music sounds subliminally behind *Grapes of Wrath*.
77. See Moore, *Novels of Steinbeck*, p. 14.
78. John Steinbeck, *Cup of Gold* (New York: Robert McBride, 1929) p. 148. Further references in text.
79. The term is Moore's (*Novels of Steinbeck*, p. 16).
80. Regarding problems with women, Steinbeck wrote in 1950 to his Scandi-

navian friend Bo Beskow, 'I wonder whether your flypaper soul has caught and held a buzzing guilt. Inspect this closely and see whether you do not love the whip. I know my own tendency that way' (*Steinbeck: A Life in Letters*, p. 418).

81. Peter Lisca comments on the prevalence of the male bond in Steinbeck: 'It is very seldom that boy meets girl; instead, man meets man' (*Wide World*, p. 206). Morgan and Coeur de Gris, Mac and Jim, Danny and Pilon, George and Lennie, Tom Joad and Jim Casy, Doc and Mac and the boys, Juan Chicoy and Pimples, Adam Trask and Sam Hamilton are all versions of this male brotherhood. Steinbeck displays to some degree the tendency, remarked by D. H. Lawrence in *Studies in Classic American Literature*, for the hero to escape the domesticating influence of the female and regain the primitive in a form of *Blut-brüderschaft*.

82. Most commentators make this point. Steinbeck's later career seems to constitute a 'split up' before the forces of civilisation; a 'sell out', to use French's term, to the dominant system of the 1950s, American liberalism, with its nerve-centre in New York.

83. See Kiernan, introduction to *Intricate Music*, esp. p. x.

84. The phalanx theory had passed. Steinbeck's new faith was expressed in a letter to John O'Hara in 1949: 'I think I believe one thing powerfully – that the only creative thing our species has is the individual, lonely mind' (*Steinbeck: A Life in Letters*, p. 359).

85. The story began as a lyrical exposition of the career of Steinbeck's maternal family in the Salinas Valley. Then, as Lisca says, 'the Trasks intruded' and, by the time he realised it was their story, 'the two families were inextricably tangled'. He 'reduced the story of his own family to its vestigial elements,' Lisca goes on, 'and struck out all the special passages written to his sons'. Still, much of the Hamilton story remains, probably too much. As Lisca concludes, it is the book's 'essential failure' (*Wide World*, p. 263). Much of the Hamilton story is first-person, 'moral essays in the manner of Thackeray'; this is in conflict with the greater part of the novel, which cannot be told by 'I', as it deals with events that Steinbeck could neither have witnessed nor heard about. These in fact are the true fiction. 'The Hamiltons', says Joseph Fontenrose, 'can be dropped out without affecting the Trask story at all' (*John Steinbeck*, p. 119). Watt and French regard the generalised pastoral evocations to be 'impressive' and 'appealing', but I think it can be argued that the book would have been better had Steinbeck stripped away these, as well as the Hamiltons, and left a direct narrative on the Trasks. One quarter of the book might thus have been cut. Steinbeck's editors advised something of the kind, but Steinbeck had woven a cocoon of great-writerism around himself in order to produce a monumental work and dismissed the advice loftily. It must have said something to him, however, that his friend Elia Kazan later made the film *East of Eden* by using only Steinbeck's fourth and last section, the most direct and succinctly written – by the latter stages of composition he had worked out the authorial confusions that mar much of the novel.

86. Note in this connection that Steinbeck was writing the book expressly for his little sons, who were still living with their mother, Gwyn, whom

Steinbeck had come to regard as having betrayed him with something like the gratuitous viciousness with which Cathy betrays Adam Trask, himself the father of two infant sons.

87. John Steinbeck, *East of Eden* (New York: Viking, 1952) p. 72. Further references in text. Note the language of this sentence. It is indicative of what Lisca calls the 'failure of language' in the book as a whole: '[Sam Hamilton's] blarney may be excused as coming from an old Irishman, but it seems to be a contagious language. . . . Even the author speaks a kind of blarney . . . figurative language . . . pseudo-poetry' (*Wide World*, p. 270).

88. Steinbeck editorialises lavishly on this subject. Watt finds the 'almost Shavian description of the coming of the highest forms of "culture" [the church and the whorehouse] to the Far West' as one of the best passages in the book (*John Steinbeck*, p. 94). There seems, however, to be a prurient nostalgia mixed in with the lofty wit which would not have appealed to the more puritan Shaw: 'At the present time the institution of the whorehouse seems to a certain extent to be dying out. Scholars have various reasons to give. Some say that the decay of morality among girls has dealt the whorehouse its death-blow. Others, perhaps more idealistic, maintain that police supervision on an increased scale is driving the houses out of existence. In the late days of the last century and the early part of this one, the whorehouse was an accepted if not openly discussed institution. It was said that its existence protected decent women. An unmarried man could go to one of these houses and evacuate the sexual energy which was making him uneasy and at the same time maintain the popular attitudes about the purity and loveliness of women. It was a mystery, but then there are many mysterious things in our social thinking' (*East of Eden*, pp. 90–1).

89. This analogy is drawn by French in his chapter 'Patchwork Leviathan'.

90. Steinbeck's use of the Cain and Abel myth is not as deft and subtle as his use of the Arthurian myth in *Tortilla* or the Everyman framework in *Wayward Bus*. The naming of Trasks by 'A' or 'C' according to where they stand in the good–evil dialectic is a transparent device which contributes to the book's overwrought Manicheanism. The Hebrew word *timshol*, with which Steinbeck attempts to resolve the split, is misspelled, as Fontenrose points out (*John Steinbeck*, p. 123), and misused to mean 'may' or 'mayest' when in fact it means 'may *rule*'. 'Many a sermon', Fontenrose generously concludes, 'has drawn a fine meaning from a faulty translation of a corrupt text.' French is more damning: 'The meaning of the Cain and Abel story, centring around the interpretation of the Hebrew word *timshel* . . . might be more appropriately discussed in an essay than a novel' (*John Steinbeck*, p. 156). In general, the academic tendency that was shortly to move Steinbeck to a prolonged study of the medieval origins of *Le Morte d'Arthur* is increasingly apparent in *East of Eden*, first in the persona of Sam Hamilton, later in that of the garrulous and somewhat improbable Lee, Adam's Chinese servant.

91. French, *John Steinbeck*, p. 156.

92. The bugaboo 'respectables' of the interchapters of *Cannery Row* become focused in Mr and Mrs Pritchard of *Wayward Bus*. The Pritchards are

repressed and hypocritical, the husband a Babbit and the wife a sort of school marmish old maid. American as the Rotary Club or Harry Truman, Mr Pritchard is a particular butt of Steinbeck's satire. This kind of Establishment organisation-man, essentially an Easterner, offended the writer's boisterous Western–Lawrentian prejudice of what a man should be. But Pritchard is what Steinbeck in his last phase, as Easterner, Nobel laureate, and apologist for the Vietnam War, would in fact in part become.

93. Steinbeck's animus against petty capitalism, demonstrated by the picture of the used-car dealers in *Grapes*, has vanished by *East of Eden*: Adam's scheme is treated sympathetically, and even Will Hamilton's used car dealings are accepted. An intermediate stage in this progress of Steinbeck's might be seen in the picture of Ernest Horton in *Wayward Bus*: his predatory capitalist intentions are humanised by a love of gadgetry and sense of humour, and his position seems that of a struggling Underman in comparison to that of Pritchard. Steinbeck himself had demonstrated a Horton-like streak of quirky capitalism in the early 1930s: he, Carol, Dook Sheffield and his wife tried to market a substance, Negocol, for the making of death-masks under the commercial name of 'Faster Master Plaster Casters' (see Valjean, *John Steinbeck*, pp. 125–7). The project was typical of the blithe pranksterish mood of that period of Steinbeck's career and abandoned as readily as it was taken up.

94. Didion, 'Some Dreamers of the Golden Dream', *Slouching toward Bethlehem*, pp. 3–28.

95. Praisers of the book include Watt: 'Within its severely limited scope, *The Wayward Bus* is a *tour de force*. Its psychological and social realism is built up with a density of texture which can only be hinted at. . . . The symbolic interpreter in the end [is] tantalized but still athirst' (*John Steinbeck*, p. 91). Also Carlos Baker, whose *New York Times* review, 'Mr Steinbeck's Cross Section', is quoted in Lisca, *Wide World*, p. 16: 'Richness of texture . . . solidity of structure . . . even more solid unity than that which distinguished *In Dubious Battle* . . . as subtle and neat a horizontal structure as Steinbeck has ever evolved.' *Wayward Bus* has been seen as too satiric to be 'non-teleological' and too 'non-teleological' to be morally conclusive; as a novel, however, I should have to agree with those who see it as a fine balance of form and content, simple while ambitious, in some ways perfect. Critics such as French who resent the picture of a 'sweetheart' world-view that would dominate the 1950s can hardly deny its accuracy and prescience. 'The decade was a manic burst of inventive, occasionally screwball materialism, a wild exploitation of pastels and plastics, superhighways and suburban tracts', a recent issue of *Time* magazine (never partial to Steinbeck) has explained (see Lance Morrow, 'Dreaming of the Eisenhower Years', *Time*, 28 July 1980, pp. 22–3). 'The entire culture seemed to have teenage glands.'

96. John Steinbeck, *The Wayward Bus* (New York: Viking, 1947) pp. 98–119. Further references in text.

97. Watt, *John Steinbeck*, p. 91. He adds, however, 'Steinbeck seems to have forgotten that Chicoy's bus is only a four-cylinder one.' Over-hasty revision.

98. Lisca, *Wide World*, p. 236.
99. Walcutt's *American Literary Naturalism* is quoted in French, *John Steinbeck*, p. 147.
100. The hero of 'Flight' is the fine example. The protagonists of *The Pearl* and *The Forgotten Village*, however, also have to flee in order to escape dead-end existences.
101. Steinbeck's first publisher, Robert McBride, found *Pastures of Heaven* his finest work; as percipient a critic as Geismar shares this opinion. The early collection of related stories lacks, however, in the words of Moore, 'the bold strength of Steinbeck's later prose and [has] not yet picked up his rhythms' (*Novels of Steinbecks*, p. 22). Those who might take his best-known work, *Mice*, as his most accomplished, fail to recognise the 'trickery' and 'contrivance' that both Moore and Edmund Wilson point out – *Mice* shows Steinbeck's tendency to load his argument at its worst; and the final scene in which Curly and Carlson fail to appreciate the sympathy Slim shows for George is but one of many examples of how the author attempts to manipulate the readers' responses. In *Grapes* such manipulation appears less contrived: Steinbeck seems powerless to restrain his own inspiration and, in compensation for being bullied into a point of view, the reader is given a kind of prose music the author never achieved elsewhere. French's argument for *Cannery Row* as Steinbeck's most artful outing is only partially convincing. Steinbeck's own youthful preference for his much-laboured *To a God Unknown* presages the poor judgement that would lead him to regard *East of Eden* as the book for which all the others had been 'practice'. *To a God* is fatally marred by what Moore, quoting Hemingway, calls 'erectile writing' (*Novels of Steinbeck*, p. 27). *East of Eden* at best should be considered, in the words of R. W. B. Lewis (quoted in Watt, *John Steinbeck*, p. 112), 'a suggestive, a representative, and a completely honourable failure'.

NOTES TO CHAPTER FOUR: THE TOUGH GUYS

1. Ross MacDonald, 'Homage to Dashiell Hammett', in *Mystery Writers of America – 1964* (annual) (New York: Harper & Row, 1964) p. 8.
2. Peter Wolfe, *Beams Falling: The Art of Dashiell Hammett* (Bowling Green, Ohio: Bowling Green University Press, 1980) p. 122. This is the most valuable study of Hammett and his work to date.
3. Ibid., p. 127.
4. Ibid., p. 8 and elsewhere.
5. In 'The Simple Art of Murder', *The Second Raymond Chandler Omnibus* (London: Hamish Hamilton, 1962) p. 12.
6. *The Dashiell Hammett Omnibus* (London: Cassell, 1952) p. 425. Further references in text.
7. See Lillian Hellman's introduction to Dashiell Hammett, *The Big Knockover and Other Stories* (Harmondsworth: Penguin, 1969) p. 18.
8. Martin Green, *Children of the Sun: Narrative of 'Decadence' in English after 1918* (London: Constable, 1977).
9. Wolfe, *Beams Falling*, pp. 114–15.

10. Ibid., p. 40.
11. Ibid., p. 30.
12. Ibid., pp. 115–16.
13. Ibid., pp. 119, 120.
14. Ibid., pp. 121–2.
15. See ibid., pp. 1–12.
16. Hammett, *Big Knockover*, p. 14.
17. *Hammett Omnibus*, p. 308.
18. Wolfe, *Beams Falling*, pp. 6–9.
19. Ibid., p. 5.
20. Hammett, *Big Knockover*, p. 8.
21. Ibid., p. 11.
22. Ibid., p. 21.
23. An excellent little study is William Bloodworth's *Upton Sinclair* (Boston, Mass.: Twayne, 1977). I am indebted to it for this section.
24. *The Autobiography of Upton Sinclair* (New York: Harcourt, Brace & World, 1962) p. 35.
25. Upton Sinclair, 'Unity and Infinity in Art', *Metaphysical Magazine* (New York) Jan 1899.
26. Upton Sinclair, *The Overman* (New York: Doubleday, 1907) pp. 71–4, various places.
27. See Upton Sinclair, *Love's Pilgrimage* (New York: Mitchell Kennerley, 1911) pp. 202–4.
28. Upton Sinclair, 'On Bourgeois Literature', *Collier's Magazine* (New York) 8 Oct 1904, pp. 22–5.
29. The phrase is from J.B. Gilbert, *Writers and Partisans* (New York: Wiley, 1968) p. 10.
30. In Floyd Dell, *Upton Sinclair: A Study in Social Protest* (New York: G. H. Doran. 1927) p. 178.
31. *Hammett Omnibus*, pp. 470–3.
32. For this section I am indebted to Will Wyatt's *The Man Who Was B. Traven* (London: Cape, 1980).
33. As translated ibid., p. 302.
34. Ibid., p. 197.
35. Ibid., p. 123.
36. It seems significant that Huston cast his father in this role.
37. B. Traven, *The Treasure of the Sierra Madre* (London: Chatto & Windus, 1934) p. 97. Further references in text.
38. James N. Cain, *Serenade* (New York: Alfred A. Knopf, 1937) pp. 175–6. Further references in text.
39. See Frank McShane, *The Life of Raymond Chandler* (London: Cape, 1976) p. 101, quoting a letter to Alfred Knopf.
40. Cain, *Three of a Kind*, p. 288.
41. Ibid., p. 288.
42. Ibid., p. 207.
43. Wilson, *Boys in the Back Room*, pp. 11–14.
44. For this section I am indebted to Donald Madden's *James M. Cain* (New York: Twayne, 1970) pp. 24–42.
45. Cain, *Three of a Kind*, pp. v–vi, vii, ix–x.

46. Madden, *Cain*, p. 141.
47. Ibid.
48. Ibid., p. 125.
49. James N. Cain, *The Postman Always Rings Twice* (London: Cape, 1934) p. 47.
50. Ibid., p. 21.
51. Madden, *Cain*, p. 170.
52. Wilson, *Boys in the Back Room*, p. 14.
53. Cain, *Three of a Kind*, pp. xi–xii.
54. James N. Cain, *Mildred Pierce* (London: Robert Hale, 1943) p. 9. Further references in text.
55. This point is intimated by several of the contributors to Miriam Gross's rather 'literary London' selection of essays, *The World of Raymond Chandler* (London: Weidenfeld & Nicolson, 1977).
56. In 'Omnes Me Impune Lacessunt', ibid., p. 42.
57. In 'His Own Last Goodbye', ibid., pp. 127–58.
58. Ibid., p. 131.
59. McShane, *The Life of Raymond Chandler*.
60. In her introduction to *World of Chandler*, p. 3.
61. McShane, *Life of Chandler*, pp. 125–6.
62. Edmund Wilson, 'Who Cares Who Killed Roger Ackroyd?', *New Yorker*, 20 Jan 1945.
63. Chandler shared with Jack London the opinion that style was the most valuable investment a writer could make with his time. He also shared with London the opinion that he was not a good constructor of plot. See McShane, *Life of Chandler*, pp. 137, 144; also *Letters from Jack London*, pp. 61, 108.
64. According to Natasha Spender (*World of Chandler*, p. 154).
65. In 'On the Fourth Floor of Paramount', ibid., p. 48.
66. McShane makes this comparison (*Life of Chandler*, p. 67).
67. *World of Chandler*, p. 117.
68. 'The Simple Art of Murder', in *Second Chandler Omnibus*, pp. 14–15.
69. Pound's statement may be found in *Blast!*, journal of the Vorticist Movement, ed. with Wyndham Lewis, I (1914) pp. 153–4. One of Mailer's characteristic statements on metaphor may be found in *Cannibals and Christians* (New York: Dial Press, 1966) pp. 310–11: 'That is, in fact, the unendurable demand of the middle of this century, to restore the metaphor and thus displace the scientist from his centre.'
70. *World of Chandler*, p. 119.
71. *The High Window*, in *Chandler Omnibus*, p. 334. Further references in text.
72. W. H. Auden's phrase in 'The Guilty Vicarage', *Harper's Magazine*, May 1948.
73. *The Lady in the Lake*, in *Chandler Omnibus*, p. 584.
74. *Farewell, My Lovely*, ibid., pp. 280–1. Further references in text.
75. London, *The Iron Heel*, p. 62.
76. Wilson, in *New Yorker*, 20 Jan 1945. See also McShane, *Life of Chandler*, p. 134.
77. Ibid., p. 149.

78. *World of Chandler*, p. 50.
79. See McShane, *Life of Chandler*, pp. 151, 153, etc.
80. Ibid., p. 154.
81. *Letters from Jack London*, p. 117.
82. As Russell Davies points out in *World of Chandler*, p. 39.
83. *The Little Sister*, in *Second Chandler Omnibus*, throughout ch. 12 and elsewhere. Further references in text.
84. Raymond Chandler, 'Writers in Hollywood', *Atlantic Monthly*, Nov 1945.
85. *World of Chandler*, p. 37.
86. See McShane, *Life of Chandler*, p. 139.
87. *The Long Goodbye*, in *Second Chandler Omnibus*, pp. 338–9. Further references in text.
88. Note the *fin-de-siècle* motifs here, as in Sheridan Ballou and Hammett's God-figures.
89. Quoted by Michael Gilbert, *World of Chandler*, p. 110.
90. Ibid., p. 153.
91. *Second Chandler Omnibus*, pp. 516–17.

NOTES TO CHAPTER FIVE: THE SIXTIES AND AFTER

1. Frederick Feied, *No Pie in the Sky: The Hobo as American Cultural Hero in the Works of Jack London, John Dos Passos, and Jack Kerouac* (New York: Citadel, 1964) ch. 1.
2. Quoted ibid., p. 7.
3. Ibid., p. 19.
4. For Kerouac's biography see Dennis McNally's *Desolate Angel: Jack Kerouac, the Beat Generation, and America* (New York: Random House, 1979).
5. *John Barleycorn* offers up this image in a number of places.
6. 'An Interview with Allen Ginsberg', *The Beat Journey*, ed. by Arthur and Kit Knight (California State College, Penn.: the unspeakable visions of the individual, 1978) pp. 9, 12.
7. McNally identifies this as an overall Beat philosophy (*Desolate Angel*, p. 111). Kerouac misquotes it in *Big Sur*: 'the pathway to wisdom lies through excess'; and answers it disillusionedly, 'Wisdom is just another way to make people sick' – *Big Sur* (London: Panther, 1980) p. 97. Blake was the particular favourite of Ginsberg, who from time to time claimed to have been visited by the poet in visions.
8. The phrase is McNally's (*Desolate Angel*, p. 41). Thomas Wolfe was also an influence on Ken Kesey, whose character Lee Stamper sets out to 'prove wrong' Wolfe's thesis that 'you can't go home again'. See *Sometimes a Great Notion* (London: Methuen, 1976) p. 77.
9. *Desolate Angel*, p. 40.
10. Ibid., p. 77. Kerouac collaborated with William Burroughs on a detective tale after Hammett.
11. *Beat Journey*, pp. 35, 38.
12. Ibid., p. 21.

13. 'An Interview with John Clellon Holmes', ibid., p. 163.
14. Keronac, *Big Sur*, p. 118.
15. See McNally, *Desolate Angel*, pp. 180-1. McNally, describes Cayce as 'a mystic American healer who identified people's past lives by entering into a trance, and his preachings were an extended version of modern Christianity which incorporated belief in reincarnation, clairvoyance, Atlantis, and especially karma'.
16. Kerouac, *Big Sur*, p. 127.
17. In conversation. See McNally *Desolate Angel*, p. 297.
18. Kerouac, *Big Sur*, p. 150.
19. McNally, *Desolate Angel*, p. 315.
20. *Beat Journey*, p. 44.
21. Kerouac, *Big Sur*, p. 92: 'It's very typical of me and Cody that we wont undress in this situation (we were both raised Catholics?)'
22. *Beat Journey*, p. 29. Kerouac never consummated his love for Cassady in sexual terms. Though prodigiously heterosexual in self-estimation, Cassady had the occasional homosexual affair, with Ginsberg notably.
23. McNally argues this as a leitmotiv of Kerouac's career (*Desolate Angel*, p. 6, 90, and elsewhere). *Visions of Gerard*, about the dead brother, was one of Kerouac's later published works.
24. Kerouac, *Big Sur*, p. 157. Kerouac was suffering acute alcoholism at this period.
25. *Beat Journey*, pp. 24, 43.
26. In *Pageant* magazine. See McNally, *Desolate Angel*, p. 247.
27. The relationship of Wobbly and road philosophies is a particular subject of Feied's chapter on Dos Passos. Feied sees the Wobbly influence entering Kerouac's work most prominently in the portrait of Gary Snyder: 'Dean Moriarty of *On the Road* is an unconscious caricature of Nietzsche's Superman, and Japhy Ryder of *The Dharma Bums* is the natural descendent of the Vanishing Wobbly' (*No Pie in the Sky*, p. 60). It is worth remembering here, perhaps, that B. Traven was thought by many to be a fugitive Wobbly, or even group of Wobblies. The unexpected environmentalism of Howard in *Treasure of Sierra Madre* is Wobbly in spirit. *The Wobbly*, of course, is one of Traven's titles.
28. McNally, *Desolate Angel*, p. 201.
29. Kerouac, *Big Sur*, p. 57.
30. Ibid., p. 25.
31. Excerpts published (New York: New Directions, 1960). See p. 118. See also McNally, *Desolate Angel*, p. 146.
32. Malcolm Cowley tells of Kesey's period as 'the man whom other young rebels tried to imitate, almost like Hemingway at Montparnasse'. See 'Ken Kesey at Stanford' in *Kesey*, ed. Michael Strelow and the staff of the *Northwest Review* (Eugene, Oregon: Northwest Review Books, 1977) p. 3.
33. Kesey has called Wolfe's picture '96% accurate' (ibid., p. v).
34. Quoted in McNally, *Desolate Angel*, p. 314.
35. Wolfe's opinion, reported ibid., p. 314.
36. In an interview, quoted ibid., p. 314.
37. Carolyn Cassady's book *The Third Word*, shows the self-destructive streak in her husband from at least the *Big Sur* period, after his release from a two-

year stay in San Quentin for marijuana possession: 'As usual, Neal astounded everyone with his speed and efficiency. . . . But when he came home so physically exhausted, I fear he was using this manual labour to work out much of his bitterness as well as a penitent flagellation of himself' (*Beat Journey*, p. 73).

38. Quoted from *The Realist*, May–June 1971, p. 51, in McNally, *Desolate Angel*, pp. 314–15.

39. This essay, which may be Kesey's best piece of writing since *Sometimes*, appeared in *Esquire*, Oct 1979.

40. Jack Kerouac, *On the Road* (New York: Viking, 1957) p. 9.

41. The observation of John Clark Pratt in 'On Editing Kesey: Confessions of a Straight Man', in *Kesey*, p. 16.

42. Ken Kesey, *One Flew over the Cuckoo's Nest* (London: Methuen, 1962) pp. 36–8.

43. *Beat Journey*, p. 158.

44. Ginsberg argues strongly for Dylan as a Beat inheritor (ibid., pp. 18, 44, etc.). McNally mentions Steely Dan, Soft Machine, the Rolling Stones, Boz Scaggs, and David Bowie as other inheritors (*Desolate Angel*, p. 315). 'Jack Kerouac', he quotes from a prominent Sixties music-critic, 'was rock and roll.'

45. *Kesey*, p. 3.

46. Kesey, *Sometimes*, p. 178.

47. Ibid., p. 81.

48. Ibid., p. 181.

49. Viv introduces the album when trying to explain Stamper resistance to a strike against the lumber companies (ibid., p. 21). Kesey uses the album as a launching-pad for his history of a century of Stamper migrations across America. Like Steinbeck, he threads the Cain motif into this: 'born cursed', 'curse of the Wanderer', 'curse of the tramp', etc. (ibid., p. 24). His ironic history raises narrative difficulties which he attempts to defuse beforehand by haranguing the reader: 'GET A NEW VIEWPOINT. Look . . . Reality is greater than the sum of its parts, also a damn sight holier' (ibid., p. 22). This sounds like the redwoods guru's echo of some instruction blue-pencilled at creative-writing school. Stegner had been a proponent of putting the Western American experience into an historical context since the 1930s. His most celebrated use of the family-album device comes in *Angle of Repose* (1971), called his 'most fully integrated, most complex, most compelling and satisfying work'. His liberal faith in cultural continuity seems largely incompatible with Kesey's Sixties belief in the apocalyptic importance of the Now.

50. Parts of this have been published in Kesey's own *Spit in the Ocean* magazine (1976) and in *Kesey* (p. 61, etc.).

51. Ibid., p. 190: 'Hsst. Over here. In the wings . . . .'

52. This phrase was originally Clellon Holmes's. Ginsberg appropriated it for his memoir 'Visions of the Great Rememberer' (*Beat Journey*, p. 149).

53. The opposition of this philosophy and 'Blessed are the meek' is set out as the theme of the novel (Kesey, *Sometimes*, p. 39).

54. Ibid., p. 87. Old Henry at many places reminds one of Granpa Joad in Steinbeck's *Grapes*, and his faith is the Joad faith in the 'fambly': 'We're a

family first, and that's most important.' Kesey may have been aware of this resonance as he wrote: the first time Lee sees Viv she is singing 'The Battle-Hymn of the Republic' (ibid., p. 92).

55. Pratt discusses the varied female reactions to *Cuckoo* in *Kesey*, p. 12.
56. The most accurate account of the Manson phenomenon is prosecutor Vincent Bugliosi's *Helter Skelter*. This is marred by over-simplification and misrepresentation of Nietzsche among others in the realm of ideas on which Manson is alleged to have drawn. An informed account of the genealogy of Manson's deformed Hippy philosophy would no doubt show a relation to lines of thought we have traced in California writers.
57. Didion, *White Album*, p. 41. Further references in text.
58. The phrase is Clellon Holmes's (*Beat Journey*, p. 148).
59. She speaks of 'the aimlessness of the bourgeoisie' (*White Album*, p. 41).
60. 'A Lasting Influence?', in *World of Chandler*. Binyon gives an assessment of the quality of Ross MacDonald and chronicles the recent descent of the Chandler mode into slapstick parody.
61. Governor Jerry Brown used this phrase to describe the $1,400,000 ranch-house the Reagans built by the American River with taxpayers' money. Brown refused to live in it. See 'Many Mansions' in the 'California Republic' section of *The White Album*.
62. Of particular interest may be *A Confederate General at Big Sur* (1964), which gives a more whimsical account of the type of scene Kerouac had chronicled in his Big Sur book of two years before, complete with motifs of buddyism and impotence and with the surrealistic framework of a Civil War novel like the one Kerouac talked about writing but never did; *In Watermelon Sugar* (1968), the quintessential Hippy novel, describing the intra-movement struggle between flower children, who believe in Peace 'n Love, and Hell's Angels/ex-con types, whose amoralism would lead on to the blood-lust of Manson and self-destruction; *Dreaming of Babylon* (1977), whose subtitle *A Private Eye Novel, 1942* suggests the Hammett–Chandler parody framework – an incompetent and penniless San Franciscan dreamer plays at being Sam Spade; his progress, like much of Brautigan's work, gets muddled by twee and trivial fantasising, designed to appeal to a marijuana-puffing readership.
63. A thorough study of Stegner has been carried out by F. G. and M. G. Robinson (*Wallace Stegner*, Boston, Mass.: Twayne, 1977). *All the Little Live Things*, set in Stegner's home of Los Altos Hills, is a serious treatment of the effect of the Beat–Hippy 'revolution' on the social fabric at large, and surely the best novel about the 'Generation Gap' from the point of view of the Steinbeckian generation passing. Stegner's recent novel *The Spectator Bird* (1977) resurrects the narrator and some of the issues of *Live Things* (also of the long story 'Field Guide to Western Birds', 1956) and shows the author at his humanist best. Stegner is one of those rare writers to have found his strongest and most characteristic (certainly most Californian) voice in later middle age.
64. McMurtry has turned out to be the most durable writer of this generation and world-view. Cowley recalls him at Stanford as a 'bespectacled cowboy' who had read all of English literature, a good deal of French, and had written a dissertation on the Earl of Rochester (*Kesey*, p. 3). McMurtry has

included his period in North Beach and around Kesey at Perry Lane in *All My Friends Are Going to Be Strangers* (1972), a formalised road-book whose narrator shares with Kerouac the persona of the lonesome traveller with soulful heart.

65. West's fantasy is clearly the projection of a baffled, uncomfortable outsider in Hollywood. Didion argues (*White Album*, p. 153) that Scott Fitzgerald is the only outsider of a previous generation to have captured the spirit of place as it feels from the inside.

Index